PRESIDENTS AND THEIR PARTIES

*Copublished with the Eagleton Institute of Politics,
Rutgers University*

PRESIDENTS AND THEIR PARTIES

Leadership or Neglect?

Edited by

Robert Harmel

American Political Parties and Elections

General editor:
Gerald M. Pomper

PRAEGER SPECIAL STUDIES • PRAEGER SCIENTIFIC

Library of Congress Cataloging in Publication Data

Main entry under title:
Presidents and their parties.

(American political parties and elections)
Includes bibliographies and index.
1. Presidents—United States—History—Addresses,
essays, lectures. 2. Political parties—United States—
History—Addresses, essays, lectures. I. Harmel, Robert,
1950-   . II. Series.
JK518.P749   1983   353.03'23   83-14003
ISBN 0-03-062012-0 (alk. paper)

Published in 1984 by Praeger Publishers
CBS Educational and Professional Publishing
a Division of CBS Inc.
521 Fifth Avenue, New York, NY 10175 U.S.A.

© 1984 Praeger Publishers

456789 052 987654321

Printed in the United States of America
on acid-free paper

PREFACE

*T*his is a book about the relationships of American presidents with their national political parties. As the title implies, the book does not simply assume and describe presidential party *leadership*, but rather delves into a complex relationship that also involves quantities of presidential neglect and domination of the parties. Though a rich and interesting history is recounted in these pages, each chapter goes well beyond mere historical recollection to assess the underlying political nature of president-party relations.

The authors of this book are recognized experts in the areas that they have chosen to explore for this collective effort, and it has indeed been my pleasure to work with such an interesting and interested group of dedicated scholars. Although each chapter maintains its own integrity and can easily stand alone, each of the authors has been exemplary in his willingness to modify an original draft so as to better complement the rest of the book. I would venture to guess that few editors have enjoyed greater cooperation or a higher level of professionalism from their coauthors. Hence, my largest debt of thanks must go to Hal Bass, Roger Brown, George Edwards, Jeff Fishel, Ralph Goldman, Sid Milkis, and Howard Reiter.

Others are also deserving of recognition for genuine and important contributions to this book. I would like to thank Gerald Pomper and Betsy Brown for their early and sustained interest in the book on Praeger's behalf, and Dotty Breitbart for all of her support as editor during the final phases of the project. Theresa Cipcic, Shari Curtis, Jeff Grymkoski, John Kay, Carol Mackland, Marilyn Richardson, and Pete Richardson helped "field test" portion of the manuscript in their capacities as students of Political Science 610 during the fall of 1982. Edward Portis, John Robertson, and Keith Hamm, all colleagues at Texas A&M, provided encouragement and wise counsel concerning various aspects of the book. The Lyndon Baines Johnson Foundation provided some financial support for my own research, and the Lyndon Baines Johnson Library was very helpful in providing essential support services. Sylvia Sylvester and Kathleen Harder supported the project as graduate research assistants, and Judy Hogg, Terry Schiefen, and Wendy Devitt provided typing assistance at Texas A&M. The editors of the Presidency Research Group Newsletter

(George Edwards) and VOX POP (Kenneth Janda) very graciously permitted me to use their newsletters as vehicles for soliciting potential contributors to this book.

Finally, I would like to dedicate my own efforts on this project to three people to whom I owe a long-standing intellectual debt: to the memory of Pearl Mortensen, who first planted an interest in presidents and parties; to Richard Bates, who nurtured that interest in its infancy; and to James Rhodes, who helped guide it to maturity.

Robert Harmel

CONTENTS

LIST OF TABLES

PART I

BACKGROUND FOR PRESIDENT-PARTY RELATIONS

1

THE ROOTS OF PRESIDENT-PARTY RELATIONS: INTELLECTUAL, CONCEPTUAL, AND CONTEXTUAL

Robert Harmel

From a national standpoint, a party in power belongs to the president. It is his to do with as he sees fit—to use it, abuse it, or ignore it altogether.

George E. Reedy
The Twilight of the Presidency

*A*lthough the Constitution is silent with regard to political parties, it has been taken for granted since parties first arrived on the American scene that the president should serve as the primary spokesman for his national party, should be recognized as the major symbol of that party in government, should assume the role of national party "leader." Virtually all presidents since Thomas Jefferson have—for better or worse—played the role to some extent. Throughout the period, president-party relations have been marked with strains, antagonisms, and outright rifts. Presidents have led, but they have also used, abused, and ignored their parties.

In recent years, the American parties have experienced a well-documented period of decline in popular support (for example, see Burnham 1970; Ladd 1978; Crotty and Jacobson 1980). Concurrently, presidents have grappled with some of the most pressing problems of the twentieth century. Yet the parties have been of limited help to their presidents, and vice versa. The time is right, it would seem, for a thorough appraisal of the president-party relationship in the United States. It is the purpose of this book to place recent president-party relations in both historical and political context, in the hope of furthering our understanding of the causes, the nature, and the consequences of this complex relationship. Later chapters are devoted to specific dimensions of the relationship. This first chapter is devoted to a consideration of its "roots."

INTELLECTUAL AND HISTORICAL ROOTS

The idea that presidents can or should lead the party in the United States has a long history, both in practice and in philosophy. Presidents since Thomas Jefferson have done it, and political scientists since Woodrow Wilson have thought about it.

Wilson is normally recognized as the first — and probably the most important — intellectual source of the idea that it is not only natural for presidents to act as party leaders but desirable as well. Wilson was the first American political scientist to argue for the establishment of responsible party government, where the people would exercise control over government by choosing and replacing the parties that are responsible for the government's actions. Although he first argued that this should be accomplished in the United States by moving to cabinet government, thereby placing (and perhaps at that time, simply recognizing) greater responsibility for leadership in the hands of Congress, Wilson later abandoned that argument in favor of what he had come to see as greater promise in presidential leadership. Presidential leadership should extend, though, to both government *and party*. Ranney (1954, p. 41) ably summarized the thinking behind Wilson's second formulation:

> The president, he argued, was the only national officer elected by all the people and representing all the people. He was therefore the one national officer in whose activities the people were really interested, and who might therefore be legitimately and effectively held responsible by the people for how the whole government was carried on.
>
> The president also had the potentiality of becoming the great national leader of his party. After all, Wilson said the stakes of power embodied in the presidency were so great for American parties that the president could not help being leader of his party if he wished. . . .
>
> The president was also a potentially powerful party leader, whose office was the one great goal for both parties. And, most important of all, said Wilson, the presidency united both government and party leaders *in the same person.* Thus the whole nature of the presidency made for exactly the kind of identification of the party leader with the official governmental leader that would constitute the foundation of responsible party government.

In Wilson's own oft-quoted words:

> He cannot escape being the leader of his party except by incapacity and lack of personal force, because he is at once the choice of the party and of the nation. . . . He can dominate his party by being spokesman for the real sentiment and purpose of the country, by giving direction to

opinion, but giving the country at once information and the statements of policy which will enable it to form its judgments alike of parties and of men" (1908, pp. 67-68).

Certainly not all have agreed with Wilson's argument for the *desirability* of strong presidential party leadership, some (for example, Ranney 1954) for practical reasons and others (for example, Robinson 1974; Reedy 1970; Croly 1914) on philosophical grounds (and chiefly because presidents *can* dominate their parties, not always to the benefit of the party or the nation). But few would argue today with the basic premise that presidents loom the largest of all elected officeholders, and that they are best qualified (or at least best placed) to lead their parties. The strongest evidence is provided when a party does not hold the presidency and finds that its major "spokesman" is plural and splintered — and most importantly, that no one is listening.

The most recent presidential candidate remains the titular head of his party until the next nomination takes place, but as leader of the losing cause he can normally maintain little influence or attention. Former presidents could do it, but without office or the prospects of holding one they have little leverage. So the tendency is to turn to "leaders" of the party in Congress. Since there is no single congressional party leader, however, the party's spokesperson often speaks with many different voices and many different points of view. While there is seldom a shortage of congressional repre-sentatives — and especially representatives who see themselves as potential presidential candidates — willing to lead, it is not so easy to identify the willing followers. Perhaps the greatest obstacle for the would-be party leader who is not in the presidency, though, is the one identified by former President Jimmy Carter when asked to explain the Democrats' impotency against Reagan administration programs:

> The crucial element that's missing is a leader in the White House. The president can command attention from the press and therefore from the public. But it's almost impossible for a Democratic leader, no matter how able or enlightened, to capture that attention. Kennedy can't do it. Tip O'Neill can't do it. Bob Byrd can't do it. John Glenn and the others. The chairman of the party can't do it. Who *can* be the spokesman for the party? Fritz Mondale can't do it. Jerry Brown. . . (Rader 1981, p. 8).

When it comes to gaining the attention of the public — or the government for that matter — any nonpresident is a poor substitute for the occupant of the White House.

In practice, presidents are the best situated to lead their parties, and—for better or worse—party leadership has been subsumed under the presidency. Among the practitioners of the office, the thoughts and strategies of Jefferson, Jackson, Van Buren, and Franklin Roosevelt have often been cited as critical in the development of the role. They were not alone, however, as Goldman develops fully in Chapter 2 of this book. Virtually all presidents since Jefferson have been willing to play the role to some degree, and all modern presidents have been *expected* to do so.

Today it is simply taken for granted that presidents will don their parties' porkpies as just one of the many presidential hats that they will wear while in office. Rossiter (1974, p. 37) includes party leadership among his seven roles of the president as "focus of leadership" in the United States, and Robinson (1974, p. 1) has suggested that "it is a staple of 'the textbook presidency' that party leadership is one of the president's basic roles" and that this role as party leader includes three major aspects: "for the party in general, he stands as a symbol and prime spokesman; for the Electoral Party, he is the source of direction and purpose; and for the Governing Party, he develops programs, supervises their passage and staffs the bureaucracy"—"according to the traditional presentation." Parker and Kearny (1981, p. 82) argue that "the president is much more entangled with his political party and assumes much more of a party leadership role than the Founding Fathers would have wished." Cronin (1980b, p. 178) suggests that according to today's "textbook model," the president should "promote party platforms, reward party loyalists, punish party mavericks, run proudly with the party ticket, and heed the interests and advice of party leaders."

So far we have established three things about the role of party leadership by American presidents: some scholars want it; all Americans expect it; and most presidents have done it—at least to some extent. What we have not established yet, however, is what it is!

CONCEPTS

There are nearly as many definitions of leadership as there are scholars who have written about it. Any attempt to impose upon the discipline a single definition at this point would be futile if not foolish. Nor would it be particularly useful even if it could be accomplished, since debate would undoubtedly shift then to the meanings of the terms used in the definition. So it is hardly my purpose here to develop a definition of party leadership that would satisfy everyone—or even all of the contributors to this book—but rather to suggest how careful conceptualization can help reveal potentially useful distinctions among different forms of presidential involvement with the party.

The chapters that follow report many examples of presidents and parties influencing, depending upon, and using one another. Some involve presidents merely showing themselves to be partisan: making partisan statements, attending partisan functions, managing partisan machinery, thinking partisan thoughts. Some involve presidents using—indeed, dominating—their parties for personal gain, often to the parties' detriment. Others involve the use of presidential influence (or alternatively, parties' influence on the presidents) to obtain benefits for both president and party. Although all of these forms of the president-party relationship are clearly related activities, they are not part and parcel of one another, and they do not always accomplish the same purposes.

An argument can legitimately be made that party "leadership" is directly involved in only some of these activities, that leadership is only one subset of presidential involvement with the party. Indeed, others have already suggested that it is possible and valid to distinguish between leadership and partisanship, between leadership and management, and between leadership and domination—all of which are distinctions that have relevance to president-party relations.

Most definitions of party leadership incorporate the notion of leaders purposefully influencing others to take particular actions. For example, my own preference among the myriad of available definitions is that of James MacGregor Burns (1978, p. 18) who suggests that "leadership over human beings is exercised when persons with certain motives and purposes mobilize, in competition or conflict with others, institutional, political, psychological, and other resources so as to arouse, engage, and satisfy the motives of [both leaders and followers]." Merely thinking in partisan terms may in some instances influence or arouse others, but much partisanship is neither purposeful nor particularly active. Brown and Welborn (1982, p. 304) have made a careful distinction between party leadership and partisanship: two related but separable dimensions of the president-party relationship.

> The first is *party leadership*. . . It refers, of course, to the encouragement and development of party organization and to the active solicitation of public support for a party's objectives and candidates. The second dimension is *partisanship*, or a president's attitudinal dispositions toward his party in the affective and symbolic sense.

After analyzing the records of the five presidents serving between 1960 and 1980, they conclude that while there is a relationship between the two dimensions, it is not necessarily the case that strong partisanship leads to strong party leadership. Richard Nixon is cited as an example of lack of congruence: "For most of his career and part of his presidency he demonstrated strong partisanship, but as president he stood somewhat at a distance from the affairs of the Republican Party" (p. 305). For presidents as for other Americans, thinking of and even describing oneself as a "strong" Democrat or Republican does not necessarily yield a commensurate level of activity on the party's behalf, such that partisanship cannot be considered a completely sufficient condition (or indicator) for leadership.

Neither can all presidential *activity* on behalf of the party be considered "leadership." If leadership involves pursuit of motives beyond simply organizational maintenance, then "positions" have been or must be taken by the leaders. This places party leadership in the category Katz (1973, p. 205) calls "political leadership," which is concerned with affecting "decisions about policies and about resource allocation" and which excludes the mere "application of existing rules by bureaucrats." The latter activity may be important for the organization, but it is not "political leadership." Odegard (1956, p. 77) seems to have been making the same distinction when he argued:

> Most presidents unfortunately have been content either to ignore the intraparty battles of their own party by refusing to take sides or to compromise them on terms that kept the party at dead center on the theory that "if we cannot all move together, we'll not move at all." In other words, most presidents have not been conspicuously successful as party leaders, being content at best to be party managers, and at worst party hacks.

Addressing national committee meetings, attending fund-raising dinners, and endorsing party "membership" drives are expectations of all modern presidents, and only sometimes are they used to extend beyond party management to actual party leadership.

Neither is party leadership the same thing as complete domination of the party by the president for his or her own benefit. The latter situation would be an example of what Burns calls the "power" relationship, but it would not qualify as leadership. For Burns (1970, p. 18) (and for me),

> power over other persons . . . is exercised when potential power wielders, motivated to achieve certain goals of their own, marshal in

their power base resources (economic, military, institutional, or skill) that enable them to influence behavior of respondents by activating motives of respondents relevant to those resources and goals. This is done in order to realize the purposes of the *power wielders, whether or not these are also the goals of the respondents.*

Leadership is just one form of the power relationship, where the goals of the respondents—in this case the party—*are* taken into account. When a president dominates a party for his own selfish benefit, that may be power, but it is not party leadership. That the relationship of president and party in the United States may sometimes border on that other type of power (that is, domination) is suggested in this statement of Cronin's (1980b, p. 176): "In practice, successful presidents usually control their national committees and, often, their national conventions as well.... Modern presidents hire and fire national party staff almost at will. Several of our recent presidents have ignored their national party committees. Some have treated them with contempt." Observation of such practices undoubtedly contributed to Burns's (1978, p. 326) more general assessment that "the influence of the party-leaders-in-government in most [Western parliamentary democracies] is dwarfed in comparison with the *domination* of government leaders over party organization in the United States" (emphasis added) and Reedy's (1970, p. 118) that the national party is the president's "to do with as he sees fit—to use it, abuse it, or ignore it altogether." Of the alternative forms of president-party relations, leadership is clearly to be preferred from the parties' standpoint. But the exchange required for leadership makes it in some ways the most difficult and the most problematic alternative for the president, who may at times find it simpler to dominate the party or profitable to ignore it altogether.

Party leadership is a *relationship* where the leader leads and does not simply dominate the party. The activity that the leader mobilizes is purposeful activity, and at least some of the purposes are shared by president and party alike. According to Burns, such "purposes" or "motives" are one of two requirements for leadership, the other being resources. Leaders need a reason to lead, and followers must see some benefit in following. Leaders and led must have something of value ("resources") to offer one another in order to make the relationship worthwhile. It is this notion of "motive" and "resource" requirements that makes Burns's conception of leadership especially relevant to a study of presidential party leadership in the United States, because the special American brand of government and politics has resulted in limited quantities of both motives and resources, and therein lies the key to understanding the unique and often strained relationship that exists between American presidents and their parties.

CONTEXT OF PRESIDENT-PARTY RELATIONS

Koenig (1981, p. 124) has stated that "the party role was plastered onto the presidential office after the main structure was built." That insight goes far toward explaining the history of presidents' relationships with their parties. The role is one that was "plastered on," and in fact it has never fit in very well with the prevailing pattern of structures and relationships that make up the rest of American government and politics. If anything, presidential leadership of parties is even less natural today than it was in the past.

When the founding fathers drafted their Constitution they did not provide for political parties; to the contrary, many of them openly feared the formation of "divisive factions" and their expected effects in early American society (for example, see George Washington's Farewell Address). Hence the Constitution is silent concerning any relationship that might exist between president and party.

As American party politics has developed, the extraconstitutional role that has arisen for the president as party leader has necessarily been shaped—and indeed severely limited—by institutions of government that are enshrined in the Constitution. Federalism in combination with other decentralizing forces in American politics has resulted in a system of state and local parties that often sees little need and has little desire to follow dictates of the national party (see Harmel and Janda, 1982, Chapter 5), let alone its titular leader. Koenig (1981, p. 125) has described the situation:

> The local and state party organizations are beyond his control and are subject, at most, to his influence. The major parties function as viable national organizations only quadrennially, when their state and local parts more or less unite to win the presidency and its stakes of power. Thereafter the parts conduct themselves with jealously preserved autonomy. The state and local organizations command a solid corps of workers and followers, assert their own discipline, control the selection of senatorial and congressional candidates, and possess financial resources of their own.

Parker and Kearny's (1981, p. 83) assesssment of the decentralized nature of the American parties led them to conclude that the "national parties are extremely weak support systems for presidents attempting to lead in the modern era."*

The role of president as a national party leader has been even more profoundly shaped by the constitutional provision for separation of powers. The separation strips presidents of tools of discipline that are available to prime ministers in parliamentary systems, leaving them with for fewer official resources with which to engender congressional party loyalty for their programs. Odegard (1956, p. 66) has described Britain's parlimentary system as one in which "party discipline and unity are inescapable requirements. Without such unity, the government falls; with it, the Prime Minister and his government are in complete command, not only of the executive branch but of the legislature too." He then described America's presidential system as one where the premium is placed "not on party unity but on diversity, not on discipline but on independence—independence not only of the president but also the party organization of which the president is the formal leader" (p. 68). This system where members of Congress stand or fall not together, but alone, and where their nomination and election can be little influenced by the national party, is hardly conducive to presidential direction.

Separation of powers has meant that presidents have never had much direct impact on the nomination of their parties' candidates for

---

*It is the purpose of this book to describe and analyze presidential relations with the *national* party—both at party headquarters and in Congress—but we would be remiss not to at least mention presidential involvement with state and local party organizations and leaders as well. The bifurcation of the national and state levels of party organization has resulted in a situation where the president serves as leader of the national party and governors are, to some extent, the president's counterparts at the state level (Muchmore and Beyle 1980). State and local parties have been largely independent of the national party organization, and as such their ties to the president as party leader and spokesman have been even more tenuous.

Although there was a time when presidents may have been dependent on coalitions of state and local organizations for renomination (Epstein 1978), for campaign organizations (Seligman 1978, p. 300), and on individual organizations for assistance in nudging reluctant congressmen to support their programs (Seligman, p. 298), decline in state party control over national convention delegate selection (Epstein 1978, pp. 179 and 192), presidential control over patronage (Brinkley 1956, p. 67), and state and local organizational control over their congressmen through campaign help have seriously reduced the strength of the ties that at one time did bind, if only loosely, the predident to state and local parties. It should also be noted that presidents have never had much impact on the selection of local and state party leaders (Cronin 1980b, p. 183), further reducing even the indirect influence that presidents might otherwise enjoy.

Congress, and now reforms have taken away other resources that presidents could potentially use to support appeals for party loyalty. Patronage appointments, for example, could at one time be used to reward party faithful, but civil service reform, "senatorial courtesy," and the practice of making nonpartisan appointments to some offices not covered by merit rules have severely reduced the scope and effectiveness of patronage as a presidential resource (Odegard 1956, p. 70). Even at campaign time, the parties provide congressmen with scarcely little that presidents could threaten to withdraw. It is commonplace for candidates to run their own campaigns, largely devoid of party influence, often promoting their personalities through expensive media campaigns that are far more substantially funded by interest groups than by parties (Hodgson 1980, p. 179; Odegard 1956, p. 68; Harmel and Janda 1982, p. 125-26). As Cronin (1980b, p. 185) has noted, various congressional reforms have reduced reliance on the parties even more by giving congressmen

> more and more resources (trips home, larger staffs, more research facilities, more home office staffs in their districts, and so forth) to help themselves win reelection. These kinds of developments have enhanced reelection changes for most members while, at the same time, making them less dependent on the White House and less fearful of any penalty for ignoring presidential party appeals.

Indeed, the party provides the president with few relevant resources with which to entice his copartisans in Congress to follow him as a party leader.

If his party has little motive to follow, the president himself may find little reason to lead. There are costs involved in party leadership — political costs as well as the obvious commitments of time, effort, and personal prestige. The very stability of legislative support that could make the investment worthwhile can hardly be assumed today. To the contrary, as Koenig (1981, p. 125) argues, "the unreliability of his party, the likelihood that numbers of its congressional members may oppose him, must lead any president to ponder privately just what good his party really is to him." The new relationship of president and Congress seems to be one largely of ad hoc coalition building, where party may be no more important (and possibly is even less so) than a myriad of other tools that the president may engage to win his legislative battles (see Hodgson 1980 p. 166).

As for the party organization outside of Congress, here too the incentives that might once have motivated presidents actively to lead the parties have either faded or disappeared altogether. As presidential nominating bodies, the national parties have never played much of a role, leaving that decision to the caucuses and later to national conventions that tended to be dominated by party leaders. "Accordingly, a successful presidential candidate had to build a coalition of party leaders at those levels," argues Epstein (1978, p. 192), while today, "instead of relying mainly on such intermediaries, successful candidates build their own organizations and go directly to voters through the mass media, direct mailing, and primaries."

If the nomination can be won without appeal to the party organization, it is not much exaggeration to say that nearly the same is possible for the general election campaign. The party organization that "ran" the presidential campaign is an historical artifact. The party's fund-raising role has been all but supplanted by public campaign finance, and its educational and "spirit-building" functions (including the rallies that still bring tears to the eyes of nostalgic old-timers) have been replaced by direct-to-the-people television appeals and slick Madison Avenue advertising campaigns that are produced and funded not by the party but by the presidential candidates' own staffs of political advisors and campaign experts. As Broder (1972, p. 3) has summarized the consequences of these developments, presidential candidates today "count on their 'personal image' more than their partisan affiliation to win them votes and worry more about their television appearance than the solidity of their ties to the organization."

The nonparty presidential campaign has come about not only because it is possible today, but also because it seems *desirable* in many ways. Cronin (1980b, p. 189) argues that one reason for the greater reliance on media than party organization, for example, "is that the media route is easier." Public campaign finance is preferable to the alternative (which is still available if the candidate refuses all public funding), in that the candidate is freed from much of the necessity to grovel for "fat cat" contributions and, as importantly, is relieved of the fear of being seen engaging in such undignified behavior.

Perhaps the most important stimulus to the nonparty campaign, though, is the fact that that the public seems to prefer it. In short, it seems to "fit" today's independently oriented electorate. This is not to suggest that this lure to nonpartisanship is totally new; the tradition of antipartyism in America began before the Constitution was written and has continued without significant interruption (see Gelb and Palley 1975, Chapter 1; Ranney 1975, esp. Chapter 2; Dennis 1978). Neustadt (1976, p. 262) has written of the "yearning in our national electorate for political leaders 'above politics' " and Johnson administration insider George Reedy (1970, p. 119) has noted that "many citizens are repelled by a political party [and] they want their presidents to be untouched by the muck of partisanship." This has been true in the past, and it is even more pronounced in a period of marked decline of the parties in the electorate. The number of voters who label themselves as "Independents" and/or vote "split tickets" has increased dramatically since the 1950s (Ladd and Hadley 1978; Tarrance and DeVries 1972), significantly reducing the numbers of voters who might respond to partisan appeals. The likely reactions of presidential candidates are very understandable. "In an era of weaker party identification and rising independents, it is inevitable that presidents will strive to be impartial officeholders" (Cronin 1980b, p. 180). As Reedy (1970, p. 119) has argued, "presidents are probably correct in their judgment on the efficacy of nonpartisan election machinery. It is an excellent source of otherwise unobtainable votes, and men campaigning for office tend to hold such sources in very high regard."

What we have described thus far is a context that is hardly conducive to strong presidential party leadership. Leadership is a relationship that involves the pursuit of mutually beneficial motives, and yet neither the president nor his potential party followers (including especially state and local party organizations and members of Congress) would seem to have a great deal to gain from investing heavily in such a relationship today. The situation is one where the "leader" has few resources with which to lead, and hence the potential followers can be offered little incentive to follow. In addition, the presidents themselves have very little incentive to lead their parties, since their election and subsequent powers are little tied to party-related resources.

Even in this context, however, there are still *some* relevant resources and motives, and the story of party leadership today involves how and why presidents make use of those limited resources to provide benefits for themselves, for their parties, and for their programs. Part of the story relates to the personalities and persuasive skills of individual presidents. In his classic work on the presidency, Neustadt (1960) carefully distinguished between formal powers of the presidency and the president's own personal powers of persuasion. The distinction has obvious applicability here. With few "formal" resources at his command as party leader, the president who wishes to lead on party terms must rely heavily on personal skills. As Koenig (1981, p. 134) has argued, "the president's success in party affairs is a mixture of many things: his own personality, his public popularity, his skill at maneuvering, his intuitive sense. It is a game played not with rules but with a master's instinct for the shifting sources of power." It is a game played not with rules and not with many tangible resources. That is why presidents who wish to play the game must be creative in the use of the limited resources that they have.

To variant degrees, all modern presidents—including the most recent ones—have chosen to play at least some of the time. In their study of the party relationships of the five presidents from Kennedy through Carter, Brown and Welborn (1982, p. 303) found that those presidents

> in instance after instance have used their position as nominal party head to attempt fence mending among warring party factions, both on the national and state levels; have invested time and the prestige of their office for party fund-raising purposes and in the election campaigns of fellow partisans; and have, with varying degrees of success, sought a measure of party cohesion in Congress.

The presidents have still been interested in doing these things, Brown and Welborn (p. 314) suggest, because (1) though weakened as a cue, party affiliation remains "the single most important variable in explanations of voter behavior," (2) candidates whose partisanship appears "strong and real" would have the edge in otherwise equal nomination fights, and (3) the parties' admittedly weakened ability to accumulate "substantial generic support" for presidential programs is even more important when the particularistic pulls of other forces" have contributed to the factionalization of American politics and ultimately diminished presidential effectiveness. Though each of these is an important reason for expecting some continued presidential involvement in party affairs, it is the third that could prove to be the most significant in the long run. Recent presidents have already learned that legislating by coalition is more difficult and more risky when there is not a substantial segment of party faithful who can be counted on to respond to a partisan appeal.

FORMAT OF THIS VOLUME

It is our purpose in this book to begin a thorough exploration of the nature, the consequences, and the prospects for change of the relationship of presidents to their parties. In following chapters will be demonstrated the true complexity of president-party relations, which today are based on an interplay of tradition, events and necessities of the moment, presidents' backgrounds and personal political skills, and the governmental, political, and social context within which presidents and their parties coexist. Each chapter draws upon both historical and more recent presidential experiences in an attempt to assess how, why (or why not), and to what extent presidents have made use of resources available to them to lead their parties.

In Chapter 2, Ralph Goldman provides an historical perspective on president/party relations, beginning with the establishment of the role in what he calls the "Madison Cycle."

Part II of the book deals with the president's relationship to components of the national party organization. In Chapter 3, Harold Bass considers the relationship of the president to the national committee — and especially the national chairman of the party — vis-a-vis White House political operations. Chapter 4, which consists of excerpts from a 1982 television interview with then-departing Republican National Committee Chairman Richard Richards, presents a chairman's perspective on some of the same topics treated in Bass's work. Howard Reiter, in Chapter 5, deals with the president's relationship to the party's quadrennial national convention: Does he lead it or dominate it, and to whose benefit?

In Part III, Chapters 6 and 7, deal with the president as creator and dispenser of party "rewards" for congressional candidates. Roger Brown emphasizes the "positive" campaigning and fund raising that presidents may engage in during midterm elections, and Sidney Milkis discusses the possibility — and likely consequences — of presidential "purge" campaigns.

Part IV includes two chapters that consider aspects of the president's relations with the party-in-government, and the consequences of those relations. George Edwards' Chapter 8 analyzes the president's relationship with his party in Congress, and in Chapter 9 Jeff Fishel assesses presidential efforts, once in office, to fulfill party campaign promises.

Finally, in Chapter 10 I attempt in a concluding overview to assess the record of recent presidents as party leaders, to suggest some likely consequences of that record, and to consider the prospects for altering the relationship in the future.

REFERENCES

Binkley, Wilfred E. 1956. "The President as Chief Legislator." *Annals of the American Academy of Political and Social Science* 307 (September): 92-105.

Broder, David. 1972. *The Party's Over: The Failure of Politics in America.* New York: Harper and Row.

Brown, Roger G., and David M. Welborn. 1982. "Presidents and their Parties: Performance and Prospects." *Presidential Studies Quarterly* 12 (Summer): 302-16.

Burnham, Walter Dean. 1970. *Critical Elections and the Mainsprings of American Politics.* New York: W. W. Norton.

Burns, James MacGregor. 1978. *Leadership.* New York: Harper and Row.

Croly, Herbert. 1914. *Progressive Democracy.* New York: Macmillan.

Cronin, Thomas E. 1980a. "A Resurgent Congress and the Imperial Presidency." *Political Science Quarterly* 95 (Summer): 209-37.

_____. 1980b. "The Presidency and the Parties." In *Party Renewal in America,* ed. Gerald M. Pomper, pp. 176-93. New York: Praeger.

Crotty, William J., and Gary C. Jacobson. 1980. *American Parties in Decline.* Boston: Little, Brown.

Dennis, Jack. 1978. "Trends in Public Support for the American Party System." In *Parties and Elections in an Anti-Party Age,* ed. Jeff Fishel. Bloomington: Indiana University Press.

Epstein, Leon. 1978. "Political Science and Presidential Nominations." *Political Science Quarterly* 93 (Summer): 177-95.

Gelb, Joyce, and Marian Lief Palley. 1975. *Tradition and Change in American Party Politics.* New York: Thomas Y. Crowell.

Harmel, Robert, and Kenneth, Janda. 1982. *Parties and Their Environments: Limits to Reform?* New York: Longman.

Hodgson, Godfrey. 1980. *All Things to All Men: The False Promise of the Modern American Presidency.* New York: Simon and Schuster.

Katz, Daniel. 1973. "Patterns of Leadership." In *Handbook of Political Psychology,* ed. Jeanne N. Knutson, San Francisco: Jossey-Bass.

Koenig, Louis W. 1981. *The Chief Executive.* New York: Harcourt Brace Jovanovich.

Ladd, C. Everett, Jr. 1978. *Where Have All the Voters Gone?* New York: W. W. Norton.

_____, and Charles D. Hadley. 1978. *Transformation of the American Party System,* 2d ed. New York: W. W. Norton.

Muchmore, Lynn, and Thad L. Beyle. 1980. "The Governor as Party Leader." *State Government,* Summer, pp. 121-24.

Neustadt, Richard E. 1960, 1976. *Presidential Power: The Politics of Leadership,* 1st ed. 1960. New York: John Wiley.

Odegard, Peter H. 1956. "Presidential Leadership and Party Responsibility." *Annals of the American Academy of Political and Social Science.* 307 (September): 66-81.

Parker, Joseph, and Edward N. Kearny. 1981. "The President and Political Parties." In *Dimensions of the Modern Presidency*, ed. Edward N. Kearny. St. Louis: Forum Press.

Rader, Dotson. 1981. "Living with Defeat." *Parade*, July 19, pp. 6-9.

Ranney, Austin. 1954. *The Doctrine of Responsible Party Government*. Urbana: University of Illinois Press.

————. 1975. *Curing the Mischiefs of Faction: Party Reform in America.* Berkeley: University of California Press.

Reedy, George E. 1970. *The Twilight of the Presidency*. New York: New American Library.

Robinson, Donald A. 1974. "Presidents and Party Leadership: An Analysis of Relations between Presidents, Presidential Candidates, and their Parties' National Committee Headquarters since 1952." Paper delivered at the Annual Meeting of the American Political Science Association, Chicago, September.

Rossiter, Clinton. 1974. "The Presidency: Focus of Leadership." In *Perspectives on the Presidency*, ed. Stanley Bach and George Sulzner, pp. 35-40. Lexington, Mass.: D. C. Heath.

Seligman, Lester. 1978. "The Presidential Office and the President as Party Leader (with a Postscript on the Kennedy-Nixon Era)." In *Parties and Elections in an Anti-Party Age*, ed. Jeff Fishel, pp. 295-302. Blomington: Indiana University Press.

Tarrance, Lance, and Walter DeVries. 1972. *The Ticket-Splitter: A New Force in American Politics*. Grand Rapids: Willian B. Eerdmans.

Wilson, Woodrow. 1908. *Constitutional Government in the United States*. New York: Columbia University Press.

2

THE AMERICAN PRESIDENT AS PARTY LEADER: A SYNOPTIC HISTORY

Ralph M. Goldman

*P*resident Woodrow Wilson said it well and he has been quoted scores of times. "[The President, once elected,] cannot escape being the leader of his party except by incapacity and lack of personal force, because he is at once the choice of the party and of the nation. He is ... the only party nominee for whom the whole nation votes" (Wilson 1908). From Washington to Reagan none has escaped. Despite the fact that the presidency and the political parties were novel political institutions in 1789, from the beginning each president has related to the party in his own way, usually with significant consequences for the politics and institutional development of the nation. Today, the consequences reach from neighborhood politics to international relations.

This party role is hardly delineated by a clear script. The opportunities and motivations for different interpretations of party leadership have, for a number of reasons, been substantial. The president is not an officer of his party; there are no formal rules or expectations regarding his party status. The broadly representative character of his public office, as servant of *all* the American people, often requires that he "rise above" partisanship. His role as party leader is only one of a number of public roles: chief executive, chief legislator, commander-in-chief, head of state, supreme judge, world leader, and so on. The exercise of party leadership tends to be seasonal, for example, during election campaigns, as well as functional, for example, declaring which votes in Congress shall be "party issues."

Some presidents have personally thrived on partisan styles while others have shunned or decried them, and some presidents, for example, Washington, did not even have organized parties to lead. What, then, have been the *patterns* of presidential behavior in the party leadership role?

FACTIONAL BEHAVIOR AS A TEST OF PARTISANSHIP

How might one evaluate the attitudes and activities of presidents in their party leadership role? Several approaches are possible. One could solicit ratings on "party leadership" in a survey of scholars and experts on the presidency. However, such surveys tend to become popularity contests, and more general impressions of a president might bias the assessment of his party leadership.[1] Another approach would be based on self-assessments by the presidents as revealed in their speeches, correspondence, memoirs, and other statements. The difficulty with this approach is that not many presidents have been systematically articulate on the subject of the party role, the few notable exceptions being Jefferson, Madison, Van Buren, and Wilson. (For example, on Jefferson's writings, mainly in correspondence, See Bowers 1925; Madison 1787 and 1792; on Madison, see Fornoff 1926; Wilson 1908.) A third approach would be to identify some particular attribute as a test of partisanship. For example, this author chose factional behavior as a test in a previous study (Goldman 1969, pp. 384-410). Finally, a fourth procedure would involve more elaborately operationalizing the concept of American presidential party leadership. Such a definition would include several analytical questions testing the attributes of each case. A primitive version of this procedure will be undertaken in this chapter.

First, it is useful to review the simple typology based on factional behavior that was used in the earlier study (Goldman 1969). The classifications of titular leaders were: Nonpartisan, Subpartisan, Transpartisan, and Partisan. The categories were defined with modest rigor, giving attention to factional considerations. The *Nonpartisans* were those titular leaders, usually with little prior party involvement, who assumed a posture "above" party and faction, that is, an explicit detachment. The *Subpartisans* either behaved or were perceived as factional leaders before, during, and sometimes after incumbency in the presidency. This factional identification frequently haunted their efforts to bring the party together. The *Transpartisans* were those whose party identification was weak or ambiguous to the extent of actually encouraging the formation of another party or themselves moving to another party. Finally, the *Partisans* were those who were explicit, articulate, even proud of their party identity, relatively active in the party's management, and willing to solicit popular support for it.

This typology was originally applied to titular leaders—in the presidency and out—from the formation of the first national nominating convention in 1832 through 1968. The listing in Table 2.1 adds (in capital letters) the pre-1832 and post-1968 presidents. The assignment of individuals to the four categories was accomplished by this writer alone and was based on findings in his earlier studies (Goldman 1951 and 1966), and with the modest intention of providing a convenient outline of presidents' factional performance as an aspect of the role of party leader.

TABLE 2.1: Factional Types of Presidential Partisanship (year of first inauguration indicated in parentheses)

Nonpartisan	*Subpartisan*	*Transpartisan*	*Partisan*
WASHINGTON (1789)	J. ADAMS (1797)	Tyler (1841)	JEFFERSON (1801)
J. Q. ADAMS (1825)	Pierce (1853)	Fillmore (1850)	MADISON (1801)
W. H. Harrison (1841)	Buchanan (1857)	Lincoln (1865)	MONROE (1817)
Taylor (1849)	Hayes (1877)	A. Johnson (1865)	Jackson (1829)
Grant (1869)	Arthur (1881)	Cleveland (1893)	Van Buren (1837)
Eisenhower (1953)	Taft (1909)	T. Roosevelt (1901)	Polk (1845)
	Harding (1921)		Lincoln (1861)
	CARTER (1977)		Garfield (1881)
			Cleveland (1885)
			B. Harrison (1889)
			McKinley (1897)
			Wilson (1913)
			Coolidge (1923)
			Hoover (1929)
			F. D. Roosevelt (1933)
			Truman (1945)
			Kennedy (1961)
			L. B. Johnson (1963)
			Nixon (1969)
			FORD (1974)
			REAGAN (1981)

Despite the shortcomings of this typology (some of which will be noted below), several acceptable generalizations can be inferred from table 2.1. The majority of presidents have been Partisan, with 21 cases as compared to only 6 or 8 in other categories. Presidential partisanship is largely a post-Reconstruction phenomenon, and this complements our knowledge that the national parties settled into a relatively stable two-party system only after the 1880s. Five of the six Nonpartisans were generals who were objects of popular rather than partisan affection, and hence were most comfortable in what they saw as more lofty positions "above" party.

A fourth generalization suggests that the Transpartisans operated at times of great instability in the party system, experiencing much shifting of coalitions among party factions. For example, Tyler was a Democrat who became a Whig president. Fillmore was a Whig whose party disappeared under him. In 1865 Lincoln put Andrew Johnson on his ticket as part of a deal with War Democrats. In 1896, Cleveland, alienated from the Silver Democrats, supported a separate Gold Democratic ticket. Theodore Roosevelt marched with many of his fellow-partisans into the Progressive Party.

A fifth generalization is that most Partisans have been Democrats while most Nonpartisans and Transpartisans have been of Federalist, Whig, or Republican lineage. This fits the oft-made observation that the Democrats have been more dependent upon party organization as their key to victory and have also been the majority party for most of American experience. For its part, the minority party has had to minimize partisanship in order to attract unhappy Democrats, independents, and nonpartisans. Presidential behavior has generally reflected these different party needs.

ELABORATING THE TEST OF PARTISAN ROLE BEHAVIOR

The factional-behavior criterion used above is admittedly a narrow one and does not always reveal a clear picture of presidential partisanship. For instance, in some cases it fails to account for changes in behavior — for example, Washington's tendency toward partisanship as parties emerged at the end of his second term. In other cases it overlooks rampant partisanship surrounding and condoned by the president — for example, Grant's Stalwart Republican colleagues. Other criticisms will readily occur to the reader. Hence, there are good reasons to continue the search for a better operationalization of "party leader" as this role pertains to presidents.

Other chapters in this volume suggest in some detail behavior that may be part of a definition of party leadership. It suffices here to identify some of these characteristics. If an index of "Degree of Presidential Partisanship" were designed, it should undoubtedly include qualitative ratings on at least the following seven attributes: self-assessment, nomination circumstances, vice-presidential preference, cabinet choices, national headquarters relations, congressional relations, and image of program priorities. It is not the purpose of this study to provide such an index, though we can at least consider questions pertinent to each of the seven attributes.

Self-Assessment

With respect to party identity, how does the president refer to himself? The president's own assessment, regardless of how accurate, must be admitted as *prima facie* evidence of his acceptance of an explicit partisan role. Men like Van Buren, McKinley, and Franklin Roosevelt were comfortable with their party labels and regularly referred to themselves as Democrat or Republican. In contrast, Lincoln, a skillful party operator, ackowledged his party's minority status by avoiding such references and even changing party labels when necessary. Content analysis of presidential speeches, memoirs, and correspondence is an obvious technique for measuring self-assessments.

Nomination Circumstances

The interparty and factional circumstances under which a presidential nomination is made have been the subject of numerous studies (Bain and Parris 1973; Pomper 1966; David, Goldman, and Bain 1960). The circumstances vary in a number of ways that influence the partisan behavior of the nominee. For instance, at the interparty level the presidential electorate may be lopsidedly in favor of one of the parties or closely balanced between the parties. Franklin Roosevelt, particularly during reelection campaigns while the New Deal coalition was at full strength, could joyously display his partisanship, with campaign songs ("Happy Days Are Here Again") to match. When the popular former Democratic national chairman, James A. Farley, challenged "in the interest of party and country" Roosevelt's nomination bid for an unprecedented third term, Roosevelt's own overwhelming popularity destroyed the credibility of the challenge. Eisenhower had a different situation. His opponent for the Republican nomination was Senator Robert Taft, "Mr. Republican." The electorate was evenly divided, with the surprise 1948 Truman defeat of Dewey still fresh in mind. Democrats controlled both houses of Congress but

"Ike" was personally more popular than his party, by at least 5 or 6 percentage points in the polls. Disaffected Southern Democrats were needed to carry the Electoral College. Eisenhower had little choice but to rise and remain "above party."

At the level of intraparty factions, similar patterns of factional balance—overwhelming dominance or even division—tend to produce similar results: outspoken partisanship or playing down party role. For example, after years of organizational effort, the conservative wing of the Republican Party gained enough support by 1980 to defeat Gerald Ford, a former president seeking the nomination, and to nominate and unprecedentedly elect his opponent, Ronald Reagan. Reagan comfortably displays his conservatism and his Republicanism. In contrast, after nominating conventions with strong and evenly divided factions, the nominee, seeking to rise above faction, may continue rising above party as well. Two such cases, Pierce and Buchanan, were "Northern nominees with Southern principles" who would fail any test of strong party identity.

Nomination circumstances are, of course, complex and difficult to operationalize. Yet the party balance in the presidential electorate and the factional balance of a party at the nominating convention are manifest and measurable. Both measures would be relevant to the partisan conduct of the nominee who becomes president.

Vice-Presidential Preference

This factor is both important and changing in its relevance to party leadership. In the early decades of the Republic, the vice-presidency was clearly a partisan stepping stone to the highest office. This was first encountered in the successions to the presidency of Vice-Presidents Adams and Jefferson. The Jacksonians tried to revive the sequence by establishing the Democratic National Convention in 1832 in order to assure Van Buren's nomination for vice-president. The vice-presidential nomination was also sometimes used to balance the national ticket by giving second place to a party "regular": Aaron Burr, Chester Arthur, John Nance Garner, Calvin Coolidge, Richard Nixon, and others. Presidential nominees who agreed to this recognition of the "regulars" could more safely play down their own partisanship without losing the essential support of the party organization.

The Twenty-second Amendment, limiting the number of presidential terms to two, created a set of conditions that may have increasing importance for the party roles of presidents and vice-presidents, particularly in their second terms. As a lame-duck, the president may become obligated to support his vice-president for the succession in order to maintain his own otherwise declining political influence. At the same time the vice-president may become increasingly obligated to carry party fund-raising, campaign, and other duties on behalf of the outgoing president and to gather political IOUs for himself. Nixon did this as Eisenhower's vice-president and Humphrey as Johnson's. With the presidency as battered by crises as it has been during the last three decades, the expected pattern is not yet fixed. Two tendencies that do seem clear are the presidential nominee's tendency to choose a factionally compatible running mate and to incorporate the vice-president more fully into White House operations.

Cabinet Choices

When he constitutes his cabinet, a president often reveals his constituency obligations and his programmatic plans. Political balance, variously defined, has been a key principle in composing most presidential cabinets. Washington kept those great adversaries, Hamilton and Jefferson, in his official family as long as possible in the interest of national unity. Factional balance and loyalty to party became a major test for prospective appointess during the Jacksonian Era, reaching exaggerated emphasis under Polk, many of whose cabinet officers overshadowed him in party roles. By the end of the nineteenth century, expertise and competency in the substantive concerns of cabinet departments gained major consideration.

At the same time recognition of party was relegated to the postmaster-general seat and perhaps one or two other posts, for example, William Jennings Bryan as secretary of state under Wilson. How a president took party into account when making cabinet appointments not only varied with individual presidents but also with the conditions of the times. For more than a century postmasterships were a prime patronage resource for the winning party. Civil service statutes and the conversion of the Post Office into a profit-making enterprise dried up that resource. As the senior cabinet post, the office of secretary of state was cherished by senior party leaders, for example, Monroe under Madison, Calhoun under Jackson, Bryan under Wilson, Cordell Hull under Franklin Roosevelt, and others. It may be difficult but not impossible to rate presidents as partisans in the making of cabinet choices; the record of these decisions is readily available.

National Headquarters Relations

The national committee and national party chairmen were created in 1848 by the Democrats and in 1856 by the Republicans, originally serving as campaign organizations, more recently as permanent party bureaucracies. They offer one of the most explicit occasions for a president to demonstrate his attitude toward his party role. He may wish the national party chairman also to be manager of his presidential election campaign, or he may appoint a campaign manager outside the party organization. The president may nourish the development of a well-managed, strong headquarters organization, but certainly not all have done so. He may consult national party executives, or he may choose to ignore them, during the making of his presidential programs. He may clear presidential appointments with the national chairman, but he is not obliged to do so. The president may provide liaison among White House, Congress, and party headquarters operations, or he may neglect linkages to the party. Above all, though, the president shows his attitude toward party in the kind of national chairman he prefers, and in the way he goes about having his preference selected.

McKinley and Franklin Roosevelt selected strong political managers — Mark Hanna and James A. Farley, respectively — as national chairmen; the national headquarters flourished organizationally and politically, reinforcing the president's party role. Others — Wilson, Lyndon Johnson, and Carter, for example — neglected their national committees and thereby undermined one of their party resources. To a large degree the current weakness of the parties may be attributed to the view that some presidents have of their own party headquarters as merely another among many claimants — media, single-issue groups, congressional factions, and so on — for presidential attention and resources.

Congressional Relations

Party is traditionally considered an essential institutional bridge among the governmental branches in a system of divided powers. A president may maintain that bridge by coordinating the work of his own staff with that of the party leaders in both houses of Congress. He may be generous or penurious during his negotiations for support of his policies and strategies. No other party leader has the range of initiatives available to the president if he chooses to exercise congressional relations as a positive factor in the performance of his party role.

The president may do a number of things to whip his congressional copartisans into line. In his State of the Union and

Budget messages he may fashion the agenda of issues on which his party colleagues may have to campaign at the next election. His use of the veto may become a test of party or factional wills. He may declare which issue before Congress constitutes a "party matter," thereby putting colleagues on notice that they are either with or against him on this particular vote.

Here again the president's party role is overt and well-known, but there has yet to be developed an index that summarizes the components that make up the partisan side of his activities as chief legislator.

Image of Program Priorities

Running the government of a heterogeneous political community is a complex enterprise. Presidential and party programs deal with scores of public policy areas. Each president, consciously or not, acquires a programmatic image that adheres to him and his party role at election time and in the history books. The image may rest upon an ideological label—liberal, conservative, and so on—or a small set of salient issues such as tariff, welfare, inflation, and so on. For example, an early impetus to party politics came from the divisions over Hamilton's financial program. Jackson is well remembered for his partisan assault on the national bank and his rejection of South Carolina's states' rights claims, Lincoln for freeing the slaves and coping with the Civil War, and so forth. Some of the more activist presidents have adopted program labels—Square Deal, New Deal, Fair Deal—that have become deeply identified with their party's history, a lasting programmatic image reinforcing their partisanship.

Without a program label or some single overriding issue such as "Hoover's Depression," a president's party leadership may be difficult to track. Since we are dealing with his program's *image*, much of the evidence must be derived from what others see: the press, the opposition, the historian. Sometimes a president's best efforts to provide a program label, for example Carter's New Spirit, may fall by the wayside if overlooked or rejected by others. This is another element in the president's party role that could probably respond to content analysis. Such an analysis would need to notice whether the image and its label originate with the president, the press, the opposition, or the historians and whether they also attach to his party.

These seven elements are principal sources of evidence about the party behavior of presidents.[2] If numerical scales were developed for these elements, each president would probably score differently for each element and produce a seven-score index different from the other presidents. Such an index would undoubtedly be a better measure than any single-factor criterion such as factional behavior, and given the importance of the president's party role, the measurement would be well worth the effort. However, in this brief survey our purpose is not to compute batting averages but rather to report historical highlights.

PRESIDENTIAL PARTISANSHIP CYCLES

While studies of the partisanship and party leadership of individual presidents can be very informative in themselves, it is also important to view each administration in the larger frame of time, so as to recognize patterns, and possibly even long-term trends. To those ends, the discussion that follows is based on this author's intuitive classification of five (and now possibly six) "cycles" of presidential partisanship in American history (see Table 2.2).

TABLE 2.2: Cycles of Presidential Partisanship

Madison	*Van Buren*	*Chandler*	*Barnum-Hanna*	*Farley*
Washington	Jackson	Lincoln	Cleveland	F.D. Roosevelt
J. Adams	Van Buren	A. Johnson	B. Harrison	Truman
Jefferson	W.H. Harrison	Grant	Cleveland	Eisenhower
Madison	Tyler	Hayes	McKinley	Kennedy
Monroe	Polk	Garfield	T. Roosevelt	L.B. Johnson
J.Q. Adams	Taylor	Arthur	Taft	Nixon
	Fillmore		Wilson	Ford
	Pierce		Harding	Carter
	Buchanan		Coolidge	
			Hoover	

In each cycle there is at least one leader, not always the president, who gives special thrust to party organization and the president's role in it. In each cycle there is a kind of backlash to party mobilization, sometimes from the president himself. As envisioned here, though, these are not periodic cycles with inherent rhythms of their own. It does appear that each cycle has experienced changing style and locus of presidential partisanship, and this may offer some hint of the *future* of the party role of presidents.

Although Jefferson's name was the best known in party development during the first era of the Republic, Madison's was the most consequential when it came to party organization. Madison initiated the Democratic-Republican caucus in the House of Representatives, following the British parliamentary party model. This caucus eventually nominated and, in effect, elected presidents. Ironically, John Quincy Adams's election in 1824 was the result of a caucus deal even though Adams railed against political parties before, during, and after his incumbency.

Van Buren, the "Little Magician," broadened the president's party leadership beyond Congress into the electorate. The presidential era is Jacksonian but party development was the contribution of Van Buren. Four popular generals were president during the Van Buren Cycle, responding to the voters' need for heroes. The party national convention and national committee were created. Urban political machines gained importance. The disintegration of parties under the last four presidents of the cycle was a major contributing cause of the Civil War.

Zachariah Chandler, senator from Michigan, is not a well-known figure in American party history but he was probably the most influential national party manager of this cycle. He was a key figure in mobilizing the Radical Republicans to harass Lincoln, oust Andrew Johnson, impose a Republican machine on the South during Reconstruction, and surround Grant with a cabal of senatorial bosses. Presidential patronage reached such notoriety as to provoke a civil service reform movement. In this cycle much of the president's party leadership involved bringing together coalitions of state party machines and bosses.

William H. Barnum (Democrat, not related to P. T. Barnum of circus fame) and Marcus A. Hanna (Republican) converted their respective national committees into powerful fund-raising and campaign organizations. The national chairmanship also became a frequently contested post, often a prize fought over by the president's personal entourage on the one hand and some coalition of state and local bosses on the other. During this cycle, the president's party role became increasingly overt, as Woodrow Wilson noted in his famous text (Wilson 1908).

James A. Farley brought in the contemporary era of permanent national headquarters and professionalism in party management. National headquarters have become a major tool of presidential party leadership for those who know how to use them (Roosevelt, Truman, Kennedy, and Nixon). This cycle also experienced advances in mass media technology—radio, television, national newspapers, and so on—that brought the presidency into every citizen's home on a daily basis. Despite the expanding organizational development of the national parties, a decline in party attachment among the voters also has been occurring, a tendency reflected in the inclination of some presidents themselves to neglect their own party attachment.

As noted earlier, the Reagan victory in 1980 was in large measure the achievement of a well-organized conservative wing of the Republican Party. This included the management of Republican national headquarters; a network of conservative substructures (fund-raising firms, campaign agencies, political action committees, and so on) has provided national headquarters with resources, technology, and organization. Is it impression or fact that this is the beginning of a new cycle in presidential party leadership? Before addressing that question, we must first consider the major features of each of the historical cycles.

The Madison Cycle
(1789 to 1828)

National unity was the principal objective of Washington's election and leadership. In deportment Washington endeavored to be a Whig King, above the party battle.[3] Organizationally, there were no national parties when he took office, only local political clubs, including democratic societies and veterans' groups such as the Tammany Society of New York City. Washington was explicit about achieving nonpartisanship in his cabinet, to be accomplished by making it broadly representative. Both Hamilton and Jefferson were members. However, when Washington gave tacit endorsement to Hamilton's economic policies (national assumption of state debts, creation of a national bank, promotion of domestic manufacturing), he was supporting an essentially Federalist Party program.

As Democratic-Republican grass-roots opposition to Washington's administration's politics grew, electing anti-Federalists to Congress and possibly provoking the Pennsylvania Whiskey Insurrection, the president descended from statesmanship to partisanship in his message to the Third Congress (November 19, 1794) wherein he condemned the activities of "certain self-created societies" (local Democratic-Republican clubs). The Federalists in the House failed by a single vote to pass a resolution supporting the president's statement. Retirement ended Washington's public nonpartisanship. When the war between France and England led to passage of the Federalists' Alien and Sedition laws in 1798, Washington, writing from Mount Vernon of his support of the laws, referred angrily to the

Democratic-Republicans as "the opposition" (Freeman 1957, Vol. VII, pp. 539-42; Dauer 1953, Appendix III, Chart IV for party vote on the Alien and Sedition bills).

Although John Adams tried to maintain the image of a nonpartisan president in the Washington model, his efforts were doomed from the start. Even before he succeeded to the presidency, he and Hamilton became rivals within the Federalist Party. Hamilton was labeled a "High Federalist" and Adams tagged as a "Half Federalist," implying a less pure quality. Adams continued the cabinet of Washington's second term but by 1800 ended all pretense of nonpartisanship by appointing men loyal to himself. Adams thus became the first president to discard the principle of balance and impose his personal rather than party or national preferences in the composition of his cabinet. His party leadership was also affected by the Electoral College's selection system that made Jefferson, leader of the opposition, his vice-president. This was later modified by the Twelfth Amendment. Further complicating matters was the widespread unwillingness of Federalist politicians to acknowledge that they were a political party; in fact, antipartyism became an explicit Federalist principle.

Adams was well acquainted with the development of political parties, having read the works of Bolingbroke five or more times (Morse 1923, p. 46). "All nations under all governments must have parties; the great secret is to control them. There are but two ways, either by a monarchy and standing army, or by a balance in the constitution." Adams preferred the latter, that is, separation of the branches of government (Adams 1850-56, pp. 587-88). He accepted parties as a necessary evil: "There is nothing I dread so much as the division of the Republic into two great parties, each under its leader.... This in my humble apprehension is to be feared as the greatest political evil under our Constitution" (Adams, October 1792, as the second presidential election was in progress, cited in West 1918, p. 343). When charges were made during congressional debate that Adams had become the head of a political party, Representative Samuel Sewall, Adams's colleague from Massachusetts, jumped to the president's defense, denied the charges, and agreed that an opposition had a right to exist but ought not try to degrade the *executive branch* in this way (Annals 1798, January 26, 1798, Vol. II, p. 942). For his part, Adams considered the threat of resignation, in the parliamentary fashion, as his strongest instrument of party discipline. "If the federalists go to playing pranks, I will resign the office, and let [Vice-President] Jefferson lead them to peace, wealth and Power if he will" (Adams 1841, Vol. II, pp. 247-48, 252, March 9, 17, 1797).

Jefferson was the real Whig, in the sense that he understood the role of an opposition party as it had evolved in the English system. He and Madison worked closely in matters of party management; Jefferson was the older and more public figure. Of the two, Jefferson tended to be the philosopher of dissent and Madison the theoretician of party as a form of social organization. Jefferson directly associated the principle of periodic revolution with the development of political parties and representative democracy. However, he thought disunion and violence were by no means essential for his conception of revolution.

> In every free and deliberating society, there must, from the nature of man, be opposite parties, and violent dissensions and discords; one of these, for the most part, must prevail over the other for a longer or shorter time. Perhaps this party division is necessary to induce each to watch and relate to the people the proceedings of the other.... Seeing that we must have somebody to quarrel with, [why not keep the familiar kinds of division rather than create strange new ones?] (Lipscomb 1905, Vol. X, p. 45, Letter to John Taylor, June 1, 1978).

In short, the ascendancy of one party over the other should be considered a temporary circumstance over which the Union ought not necessarily be destroyed. Given the American republic's devotion to majority rule and respect for the right of dissent, Jefferson believed that the United States had no counterpart in history.

By 1792, in anticipation of the second American presidential election, Jefferson tried to resign from Washington's divided cabinet. He remained, giving the appearances of unity until after the election, and resigned instead in 1793 in order to give free rein to the opposition to Hamilton's programs. His partisanship is well expressed in a letter written from Monticello to those more active in party affairs during 1795, the year before he was elected vice-president:

> Were parties merely divided by a greediness for office as in England, to take part with either would be unworthy of a reasonable or moral man, but where the principle of difference is as substantial and as strongly pronounced as between the republicans and Monocrats of our country, I hold it as honorable to take a firm and decided part and as immoral to pursue a middle line... (Cunningham 1957, pp. 75-76, Letter to William B. Giles, December 31, 1795).

This, of course, was an elegant way to say: "If you ain't with us, you're agin' us."

As vice-president in the presiding seat of the Senate, Jefferson was active in selecting the issues that would test party loyalties, for example, the Alien and Sedition laws. As president, though, he lowered his partisan profile in the interest of national unity and in deference to Congress in an era of legislative supremacy, particularly since the House of Representatives had directly elected him in the Electoral College crisis of 1800 and the Democratic-Republican caucus would renominate him by a near-unanimous vote in 1804. Jefferson's legislative program, including the controversial Louisiana Purchase, was submitted and managed by his well-organized party colleagues in Congress as the president himself refrained from exercising visible pressure. None, however, doubted for a moment who was the party's boss, and Jefferson was able to see his old colleague, Madison, succeed him in office.

Madison's credentials as a self-conscious leader and theoretician of party were long-standing (Madison 1792a; Madison 1792b; Fornoff 1926). His authorship of Federalist Paper Number 10, wherein he sets forth his theory of faction (read: party, organized interest group) as an essential component of a democratic society, was grounded in his experience in the rough-and-tumble of Virginia politics where he earned the enmity of Boss Patrick Henry. Elected to the House of Representatives in the First Congress, Madison soon became the "parliamentary" leader of the loyal opposition, that is, the Democratic-Republicans, also known as "Madisonians."

By 1792 the Democratic-Republicans were numerous and well-organized enough to dominate the legislative branch, introduce the concept of party loyalty, and through its nominating process control the choice of president for three decades. Madison was pleased with Jefferson's resignation from the cabinet in 1793: "Better a complete separation and open opposition than a further pretense at an unworkable coalition of the two parties" (*Letters and Other Writings of Madison*, 1867, Vol. II, p. 17, Letter to Jefferson, May 25, 1794). Jefferson in response expressed the hope that Madison would soon be elevated to "a more efficacious post," that is, the presidency or vice-presidency, and that his own retirement be respected (Lipscomb 1905, Vol. IX, pp. 293-97, Jefferson to Madison, December 28, 1794; Ford, 1904-05, Vol. VII, pp. 9-10, Jefferson to Madison, April 27, 1795). Of course, it was not, though Madison was finally nominated and elected president in 1808.

In the presidency, Madison and Monroe continued the tradition of low-profile, nonpartisan leadership to the extent that they could. It was not easy. Interparty competition had dwindled into an "Era of Good Feeling," a euphemism for a one-party, multifaction politics following upon the decline of the Federalist Party. Nearly every politician referred to himself as a Jeffersonian Republican. Intraparty competition was on the increase in the form of regional factions led by a new generation. New York replaced Virginia in 1812 as the most populous state, and Van Buren's "Albany Regency" began to challenge the Virginia Dynasty's "Richmond Junto" for national preeminence. The frontier had expanded through Ohio, Indiana, Tennessee, Kentucky, and Mississippi, bringing in enough new Western representatives to elect Henry Clay of Kentucky to the Speakership. The party of Jefferson became a billowing tent for a diverse collection of ambitious young leaders. Only in New England were there remnants of the Federalist past, for a time resuscitated by "Mr. Madison's War" of 1812, which caused substantial economic distress in the Northeast.

As Madison endeavored in 1816 to pass the torch to Monroe, the junior member of the Virginia Dynasty, there were challenges in the congressional caucus. By 1820 there were few good feelings in the party, the congressional nominating caucus was not convened, and Monroe had his renomination by default. The voter turnout was proportionally the lowest to date for several reasons: disinterest in the national ticket among party leaders; disaffection among farmers and workers as a consequence of the Panic of 1819; the reluctance of newly franchised voters to go to the polls.

Ironically, Monroe's final term, as the last of a dynasty of party builders, was marked by total disintegration of party cohesion in Congress and the absence of party organization in the new presidential electorate. The latter problem awaited the arrival of a popular hero, Andrew Jackson, to galvanize the new voters, especially on the frontiers, into action on election day. The former, a problem of congressional disunity, led to the election in the House of Representatives (Jackson failed to achieve an absolute majority in the Electoral College in 1824) of an outspoken antiparty politician, John Quincy Adams.

For want of meaningful party designations, politicians, particularly in Congress, began to refer to themselves as "Adams men" and "Jackson men." The Adams "party" was never well organized but did manage to set up a central corresponding committee in Washington in time for the 1828 election (Weston 1938, pp. 99-103, 113-14, 155, 159). Penny newspapers had come into vogue during this period and what coordination and voice the Adams men did have seemed to come through two newspapers: the *National Intelligencer* and the *National Journal*. Adams personally disavowed the party and assumed he was being pejorative when he referred to Senator Van Buren as the head of Jackson's "privy council" and as his "great electioneering manager." Adams left dealings with Congress in large measure to Secretary of State Henry Clay, the former Speaker, who had a good working relationship with Daniel Webster, leader of a small group of representatives and senators who still considered themselves Federalists.

Clay and Webster were constantly irritated by Adams's refusal to use patronage as the cement of party organization (Carroll 1925, p. 20). Both men were keenly attentive to party organization but found themselves allied to a president who conceived of public office as a trust to be won and held by merit alone. In his Inaugural Address Adams warned against being "palsied by the will of constituents." He derided nominating activities, the distinctive and essential function of parties. He wrote of

> the great impropriety of private interviews between members of Congress and the President in relation to nominations for office; the tendency for misinterpretation in all statements infected with the venom of party; the extreme difficulty, even for men in the highest stations, to preserve entire propriety of conduct in delicate situations; and the malignant aspect which a want of candor and explicitness gives to incidents trivial or insignificant of themselves (Adams 1876, Vol. VI, p. 296).

As ironic as the demise of the parties under Monroe was the closing of the Madison Cycle by a president who abhorred parties. This irony was precisely expressed by Thurlow Weed, a New York party leader: "Mr. Adams, during his administration, failed to cherish, strengthen, or even recognize the party to which he owed his election; nor as far as I am informed, with the great power he possessed did he make a single influential friend" (Weed and Barnes 1884, Vol. I, p. 180).

The party behavior of the six presidents in the Madison Cycle is particularly worth noting since their behavior reflected philosophies, attitudes, and practices that set precedents and styles for all presidents thereafter. The dilemmas of public nonpartisanship and covert party management, executive management in a time of legislative supremacy, democratic unity and dissent, and coalitions of class against class became manifest during this period. As the cycle ended, a new dimension was being added to presidential party leadership, namely, the development of a significant presidential party-in-the-electorate. The need to win popular votes became a new requirement that revolutionized the presidency and the party role of those who aspired to it. General Jackson and his managers understood the trend perfectly.

The Van Buren Cycle
(1829 to 1860)

The second cycle covered a period marked by newly franchised voters, presidents who were popular military heroes, new units of national party organization, intensified regionalism in party politics, astute but now forgotten party managers, and a second breakdown of the party system. In 1824 there were 1.9 million potential voters in a population of 10.9 million; only 356,000 cast ballots. The Jackson candidacy brought 1,115,000 to the polls in 1828, an increase of 225 percent. Of those eligible, 21 percent voted in 1824; this jumped to 57 percent in 1828. By 1860 the turnout percentage rose to 71 percent of a potential presidential electorate of 6.6 million.

Originally designed as an instrument of presidential selection by an elite, the Electoral College, for all practical purposes, became a procedure of mass choice, and the growing millions in the electorate had to be mobilized by love of a hero and by good organization. The heroes of this cycle: Jackson, Harrison, Taylor, and, in a nostalgic way, Pierce. The great organizers: Martin Van Buren, Thurlow Weed, and Robert A. Walker. Van Buren, as the senior builder of the Jacksonian electorate and party, became president. Weed was the principal architect of three political parties: Antimasons, Whigs, and Republicans. Senator Walker of Mississippi captured the Jacksonian mantle from Van Buren and was a dominant Democratic manager during the latter part of the Van Buren Cycle. The national nominating conventions and the national committees were the new organizational creations, along with a single national election day.

Even as the parties were nationalizing themselves, regionalism persisted. Washington, a Southerner, had Adams, a Northerner, as his vice-president, and the North-South balance continued to be an aspect of party ticket-making. The Louisiana Purchase and westward migration added an unruly component to national politics, unsettling the regional balance of power. Southerners and their slaves migrated west as did Northerners with abolitionist principles. North-South economic and political rivalry intensified, led by eminent politicians on both sides. Stubborn regional factions arose within parties and eventually destroyed some of them. The regions finally turned to military means when Lincoln, a minority president from the West, was elected president.

The heroes were national, General Jackson becoming one in the Battle of New Orleans in 1815. Six years later the Jackson-for-President campaign began. Jackson saw himself primarily as a patriot and a champion of the underprivileged but never as a party leader. He left the work of political organization to the managers. He understood their thinking and never dealt with them capriciously. Only rarely did he go against their advice or appear to go over the heads of "the politicians." Initially his managers were a small group of Tennessee politicians who were especially adept at organizing the new electorate. When Senator Van Buren joined their efforts in 1826, the New Yorker provided much-needed leadership to the Jackson forces in Congress. A genius at organizations and procedure, Van Buren sought to have the Constitution amended so that if the top candidate fell short of a majority, the Electoral College would reconvene rather than have the question decided in the House of Representatives. In January 1827 he suggested that a national nominating convention be called to name the men to oppose Adams in 1828 and to achieve "the substantial reorganization of the old Republican Party," a suggestion taken up in 1832 (Remini 1959, pp. 130-31; Weston 1938, p. 88; Bassett 1928, p. 380).

After his inauguration, Jackson gave prompt attention to the political composition of his administration. The six states represented in his cabinet constituted one-third of the votes in the Electoral College as well as the principal sources of Jackson's popular support. His cabinet appointments were primarily administrative in character. For party counsel he turned to a personal political staff, the first "Kitchen Cabinet." Their advice encompassed campaign strategy, congressional relations, patronage, party organization, press relations, and the electoral implications of his policies. Although often in touch with the Kitchen Cabinet, Van Buren was apart from and senior to it, dealing with the president on a direct personal basis. By the end of Jackson's first term, Van Buren had rid the administration of the Calhoun faction, organized the first Democratic national nominating convention, and himself won its nomination for vice-president, all with Jackson's enthusiastic endorsement.

Between Jackson's reelection in 1832 and the end of Van Buren's first term as president in 1840, the organizational and electoral successes of the Democratic Party reached a high plane. State party machines were created or strengthened, nourished by presidential patronage. When Van Buren was nominated by the Democrats in 1836, the Whigs, successors to the National-Republican Party, did not bother to hold a national convention. However, economic depression and the slavery issue dogged Van Buren's tenure in the presidency and cost him the office in the election of 1840.

For Van Buren the creation of a national political party was essential and honorable work. He was indefatigable in his correspondence and personal contacts regarding the party.

But knowing, as all men of sense know, that political parties are inseparable from free governments, and that in many and material respects they are highly useful to the country, I never could bring myself for my part to deprecate their existence.... The disposition to abuse power, so deeply planted in the human heart, can by no other means be more effectively checked; and it has always struck me as more honorable and manly and more in harmony with the character of our People and of our Institutions to deal with the subject of Political Parties in a sincere and wiser spirit... (Cone 1950, pp. 124-25).

When he lost the election to Harrison in 1840, Van Buren became the first president under the national convention system to become an out-party leader. Characteristically, he took his titular leadership seriously. Lindenwald, his home in New York, became the party's informal national headquarters, whence he worked with candidates facing the 1841 and 1842 elections. In his *Autobiography*, Van Buren wrote that party organization is the greatest need of a party in defeat. In the past, "the rank and file of [an opposition] political party, taught by adversity the folly of their divisions, looked to a discontinuance of them to soothe its mortification..." (Cone 1950, pp. 193-94).

Van Buren was defeated by his successes in party organization. He failed to be renominated at the national convention of 1844, out-maneuvered by Senator Robert Walker and falling short of the two-thirds vote needed to nominate. The two-thirds rule had originally been established in 1832 to assure his own nomination for vice-president.

In his brief time in office President Harrison relied almost entirely on Clay, then Whig leader of the Senate, and Webster, who became his secretary of state. Tyler, a Virginia Democrat who had bolted, was the first vice-president to succeed upon the death of a president. Assuming a thoroughly nonpartisan posture and hobbled by constitutional issues surrounding the first vice-presidential succession, Tyler took up the project of retiring two old adversaries, Clay and Van Buren, from presidential politics.

Tyler's struggle with Clay began when the latter outlined his own legislative program in a Senate resolution presented on June 7, 1841: high protective tariff, internal improvements, and rechartering of the national bank. The Whig caucus, led by Clay, set out to promote the program. When Tyler vetoed a national bank bill, Clay suggested that the president resign if he could not conscientiously receive the instructions of Congress (Morgan 1954, pp. 40-43). When Tyler vetoed a second bank bill, his entire cabinet, with the exception of Webster, resigned. Two days later Tyler submitted names to fill the vacancies. The Whig caucus promptly issued a resolution regretting his "withdrawal of confidence from his real friends in Congress and from those by whose exertions and suffrages he was elevated to that office..." (Morgan 1954, p. 158). The Whig Party thus read Tyler, its own president, out of the party.

At the 1844 Whig national convention Clay was nominated by acclamation. On the Democratic side, the Virginia delegation, which included many of Tyler's home-state political friends, and Senator Walker generated a stalemate that prevented a two-thirds vote for Van Buren's renomination, led three other candidates to cancel each other out, and produced James K. Polk as the first "dark horse" nominee in convention history.

Polk turned his campaign over to Walker who set up a central committee in Washington, precursor of the first permanent national committee established four years later. Polk's election accomplished Tyler's objective; Clay and Van Buren were "retired." Polk's cabinet was made up of the party's most powerful state leaders: Robert Walker (Mississippi), James Buchanan (Pennsylvania), William L. Marcy (New York), George Bancroft (Massachusetts), John Y. Mason (Virginia), and Cave Johnson (Tennessee). Postmaster Johnson oversaw the removals and resignations of 11,000 of the government's 14,000 postmasters, far in excess of the 1-in-8 removals in the simpler patronage era of Andrew Jackson (Fowler 1943, Appendix III).

Polk announced early that he would be a one-term president. He comprehended the logic of the political vacuum created by this pledge, and he rejected suggestions that he himself stand for reelection in order to unite the Democratic Party. He deplored the maneuverings of his high-powered cabinet officers as they prepared for the next nomination. Of Congress, Polk wrote:

> I have a nominal majority of Democrats in both Houses of Congress, but am in truth a minority in each House. The disappointments about office among the members [in the distribution of patronage], and the premature contest which they are waging in favour of their favorites for the Presidency in 1848, are the leading causes of this lamentable state of things (Quaife 1910, Vol. II, p. 347).

Gideon Welles of Connecticut placed the blame squarely on Polk. "The administration has endeavored to acquire for itself a strong party character, but has failed to create a party attachment. It has trusted too much to organization, and [has] not [been] sufficiently mindful of principles" (Welles 1848). Nevertheless, organizational considerations prevailed. The national convention created its first national committee and chose its first national chairman.

The war with Mexico produced another military hero, General Zachary Taylor. Having made several statements opposing political parties and national conventions, Taylor found it necessary to declare publicly his Whig affiliation before a convention dominated by Clay supporters who would nominate him (Cole 1912, pp. 128-29). The nomination and Taylor's election were largely Thurlow Weed's accomplishments, the latter with an assist from Van Buren's third-party candidacy. The Taylor patronage was Weed's to distribute.

Taylor faced a hostile Congress that in turn was coping with an increasingly divided nation. As Clay forged the Compromise of 1850, Taylor died, Millard Fillmore succeeded to the presidency, Weed-Seward (the latter a senator from New York) adherents were removed from federal posts, and factionalism led to the Whig Party's terminal illness. Rejected by his own party in 1852, Fillmore was pleased to run four years later as the nominee of the American Party, the vehicle of nativist "know-nothingism" of that day.

The Democratic Party was also rushing toward chaos, divided between Northern "hunkers" who favored conciliating the growing Southern disaffection and the "barnburners" seeking to abolish slavery and keep the soil of the new West free of that institution. Franklin Pierce, another Mexican War general, became the second dark-horse nominee of the party and was offered to the electorate in the Jacksonian image as "Young Hickory of the Granite Hills." The campaign was listless. Whig self-destruction gave the election to Pierce. The patronage was mismanaged. The North-South conflict was straddled as civil war raged among the settlers of the Kansas and Nebraska territories. Control of the 1856 national convention was allowed to slip into the hands of James Buchanan's managers, who proceeded to win the nomination for him. Buchanan's Northern supporters insisted that second place on the ticket go to a young Southerner, John C. Breckinridge. The platform made no reference to the Pierce administration.

Of the 15 "slave" states, 14 supported Buchanan, who received only 45 percent of the national popular vote. Buchanan was beholden to the South in cabinet appointments and slavery policy. His principal challenger in the party was Senator Stephen A. Douglas of Illinois, whose antislavery position later split the party in 1860. Political parties were splitting, realigning, or disappearing throughout the nation as the slavery issue heated up. Buchanan's public nonpartisanship did not conceal his Southern inclinations and commitment to Breckinridge as his successor. The division in the 1860 Democratic national convention was close and adamant, leading to separate tickets, the election of a "free soil" Republican, and the most devastating armed conflict the world had yet witnessed. Chaos in the party system ended the Van Buren Cycle just as it had the Madison Cycle.

Despite the chaos, this cycle did leave permanent marks. Jackson and Van Buren had converted the presidency from a Whig monarchy to a partisan office. Presidents could now be heroic and assertively partisan. With the arrival of the national nominating conventions, the nationalization of party organization began to take a more deliberate course. The national conventions also emerged as the marketplace for transacting the deals that made national political coalitions possible, even producing a novel kind of presidential nominee, the "dark horse." However, the parties and the party system remained fragile, and the inability to put together a national coalition at the 1860 Democratic convention made civil war inescapable.

The Chandler Cycle
(1861 to 1884)

Lincoln had all he could do to preserve the Union and its presidency let alone the leadership of the new Republican Party. Lincoln and the nation needed a political party to hold together the 33 states, the far-flung and contentious sections, and the free-floating factions that called themselves Republicans, Whigs, Free Soilers, Americans, Radicals, not to mention National Democrats, Constitutional Democrats, War Democrats, and Peace Democrats. Few have been better politicians than Lincoln and few could find less of a party leadership role to play.

Amidst the party chaos, the Radical Republicans, among whose principal leaders was Senator Zachariah Chandler of Michigan, were the best organized, hardest hitting, and programmatically most stern. The Radicals carped at Lincoln's war management with partisan intent; only Republican generals were to be allowed to become electable heroes. The Radicals' Congressional Plan for Reconstruction of the South after the war was vindictive in the extreme, with partisan intent; only states with Republicans in power were to be readmitted to the Union. Former Democrat Andrew Johnson was to be removed from the presidency to which he succeeded upon Lincoln's assassination, by impeachment if necessary, with partisan intent; way had to be made for a Radical nominee. Congressional Radicals, later known as Stalwarts, had to help run the presidency, particularly under Grant, for partisan purposes; a vast patronage was there to be disbursed. Meanwhile, Democrats were preoccupied throughout the cycle with repairing their party, reincorporating the South into the Union, and finding winning candidates for Congress and the presidency.

New York's Senator William H. Seward, defeated by Lincoln at the 1860 nominating convention, was generally considered the senior Whig, now Republican, in Congress. Seward quickly assumed he would be "prime minister" to the new president, began to give unsolicited advice regarding cabinet appointments, and edited, without permission, Lincoln's drafts of resolutions to be submitted to Congress regarding the secession movement. When Lincoln hinted that Seward would not necessarily be a member of the cabinet and insisted that the cabinet would include ex-Democrats as well as ex-Whigs, Seward backed off and in time acknowledged Lincoln's party-building skills. Lincoln kept in touch with his party's national chairmen regarding cabinet personnel, convention arrangements, and campaign organization, but in a relatively quiet way.

The Radicals found allies in the Lincoln cabinet, held an anti-Lincoln majority in the Senate Committee on the Conduct of the War, supported a Fremont-for-President movement to oppose Lincoln in 1864, stole the Republican national committee from its chairman in 1866, masterminded the impeachment proceedings against Johnson in 1868, nominated and elected Grant in 1868 and 1872, and negotiated Hayes's victory in the disputed Hayes-Tilden election of 1876. When the Radicals won seats in the congressional elections of 1862, Lincoln realized that he would have to seek support for his policies and for reelection outside his party. He ceased making references to the Republican Party and tacitly encouraged the formation of "Union" and "Union Lincoln" clubs. The call for the Republican national convention of 1864 used the term "Union" in lieu of "Republican." This was the convention that put a War Democrat, Johnson, on the ticket.

Following Lincoln's assassination, Johnson had an even more difficult time as party leader. Having served as a minority member of the Committee on the Conduct of the War, he was well known to the Radicals, who would have none of him. What kind of national party could he head? Unionist (the label under which he was elected)? Republican? Democratic? As the 1866 midterm election approached, Johnson decided on two unprecedented tactics: conduct a special midterm national convention of all, whatever their party, who supported Johnson and his program, and hit the campaign trail in support of those congressional candidates who allied themselves with him, the first incumbent president to do this. The Radicals countered by calling their own convention on the same dates and by composing a new national committee to displace the incumbent pro-Johnson national chairman. Early in 1868 the Radicals in Congress came within one vote of impeaching Johnson for violating the Tenure of Office Act, thereby isolating him from both parties and assuring Grant's nomination at the Republican Convention.

A grateful citizenry attributed the conclusion of the Civil War to General Ulysses S. Grant and cared little about his party credentials (which had been Democratic and Union in previous elections) or lack of program. Convinced that the Radicals had beaten Johnson, whom he had served as secretary of war, Grant made himself available to the Republicans.

Party was never of compelling interest to Grant. At first, he appointed personal (several unsavory) friends to the cabinet and ignored Radical counsel on patronage. Using the leverage of the confirmation process and the Senate voting majority they possessed, a "Stalwart Cabal" (Radicals and state bosses for the most part) in the Senate took over the administration, left to Grant the pleasures but few of the responsibilities of office, dominated the patronage, renominated and reelected him, and drove Republican reformers into a new Liberal Republican Party. To his credit, Grant concluded his second term by insisting that party leaders in Congress resolve the explosive disputed Hayes-Tilden election in 1876 without resort to arms. In the outcome the Republicans won the presidency but lost the South.

The Liberal Republican defection of 1872, the Panic of 1873, loss of the House of Representatives in 1874 for the first time in 16 years to the Democrats, and scandals in the Grant White House made the reform Governor Hayes of Ohio acceptable to the Stalwarts in 1876. The price they exacted was the national chairmanship for Zachariah Chandler; the party machinery and the spoils were not to be given up lightly by the Stalwarts. As president, Hayes played a lone hand in party matters. His cabinet appointments, made without consulting Chandler, were aimed at bringing back the liberals and preserving as much of the Republican advantage in the South as possible. His withdrawal of federal troops, also without consulting Republican leaders, infuriated his colleagues but ended Republican dependency on a faulted Southern policy. Anticipating the Pendleton Civil Reform Act of 1883, Hayes issued a presidential order that no federal officeholder could be an officer of a political party, a rule he never applied to certain members of the Republican national committee.

The convention that nominated dark-horse James A. Garfield on its thirty-sixth ballot began as a stalemate between the Stalwarts and their state machines on the one side and James G. Blaine's

"Half-Breed" coalition on the other. To mollify the big-state leaders Garfield agreed to have Chester A. Arthur, the collector of the New York Port who had been removed by President Hayes for mismanagement, on the ticket. Calling attention to the "close and confidential relation" that must exist between the national committee and the nominees, Garfield suggested four factional moderates for the chairmanship; the one chosen promptly lost control of the campaign to the Stalwarts. Garfield soon engaged the state machines, particularly in New York, in struggles over cabinet and patronage appointments, a battle many considered as responsible for his assassination.

By the time Arthur came into office, the electorate had become evenly divided and firmly attached to the two major parties, local and state party organizations were strong and reminiscent of the hey-day of the Van Buren Cycle, and the national conventions and national committees became significant testing grounds of factional and leadership strength. The party role of the president had begun to be "inescapable," in Wilson's term, and Arthur, a well-known "spoilsman," was in the unenviable position of trying to hold a faction-ridden party together while at the same time supporting a purer politics, doing the latter with passage of the Pendleton Act. It was not enough, and Blaine defeated Arthur for the Republican nomination in 1884.

The tumultuous Chandler Cycle survived the Civil War, Reconstruction, the presidential election crisis of 1876, and two presidential assassinations. Instead of concluding with the chaos of earlier cycles, this one witnessed party loyalties well-established among the voters and party organizations sufficiently entrenched to engage in patronage and other excesses, enough to make "reformism" the theme of subsequent campaigns. The Chandler Cycle brought Congress back into the national party picture with a vengeance, revealed how a tightly organized and aggressively led faction could take over the national party and the presidency, and made reconstruction in the South a pawn in the party battle. At times party oligarchs ran the presidency, reflecting the tough machine politics that was thriving at the same time in many cities.

The Barnum–Hanna Cycle
(1885 to 1932)

William H. Barnum served as Democratic national chairman for 145 months between 1877 and 1889, the longest chairmanship tenure in either party. He worked in varying degrees of proximity with Samuel J. Tilden and Grover Cleveland, two highly partisan and activist leaders. Mark A.

Hanna, on the Republican side, was incumbent from 1896 to 1904. In fund raising, campaign organization, and patronage management, the two men contributed to the development of the national committees as significant agencies of presidential party politics. The cycle that bears their names here lasted well beyond their tenure and lives, manifest in the patterns of party behavior of presidents from Cleveland to Hoover.

Tilden, even before he became the Democratic presidential nominee in 1876, devoted most of his adult life to New York and national Democratic politics. He was thoughtful, practical, and innovative in dealing with issues of organization. He was skilled in negotiating with city machines and state bosses and enjoyed a larger personal following (including Chairman Barnum) throughout the party, all of which he was pleased to pass on to a talented successor, New York's Governor Cleveland.

As nominee and president, Cleveland paid careful attention to party management, with a "kitchen cabinet" of advisers inherited from Tilden, moneyed supporters flattered by party recognition, and issues chosen to demonstrate Cleveland's principled fighting style, particularly with regard to certain glowing issues of the times: reform, tariff, and free silver. Cleveland associates worked well to accommodate factional demands yet demonstrate ethical coolness to corrupt local bosses. By 1888, when Cleveland sought a second term unsuccessfully, Democratic clubs independent of the party had become popular (imitating a Republican organizational experiment) and functioned as both constraint upon a supplement to the party organization. Defeated by Benjamin Harrison despite his plurality in the popular vote, Cleveland retired to a law practice, pursued an unostentatious titular leadership role, engaged in a large correspondence on organizational and policy matters, and made plans for 1892.

Harrison owed his election to a coalition of powerful state bosses: Matt Quay of Pennsylvania, Tom Platt of New York, and Jim Clarkson of Iowa, not to mention his own organization in Indiana. Harrison appointed a Pennsylvania reformer, John Wanamaker, as postmaster-general, but Wanamaker's first assistant was Clarkson, who spoke of civil service as "the toy of a child" and proceeded to process 15,000 removals and resignations in his first year as patronage manager (Fowler 1943, pp. 214ff.; Clarkson letter, Michener Papers, 1890). Harrison was an experienced behind-the-scenes party strategist who was able to handle the competing ambitions of the Republican state bosses to head off the Blaine and McKinley opposition to his renomination in 1892. Governor McKinley's manager for this project was the wealthy Ohio industrialist, Mark Hanna.

Cleveland was less successful as party leader during his second term. The large Populist vote in 1892, the growth of farmers' organizations in the troubled agricultural regions, and the demand for free silver and cheap currency were developments he could not reconcile with his strong gold-standard position. As other Democratic leaders in increasing number responded to these trends, Cleveland lost support and patience. The nomination of William Jennings Bryan as the free silver candidate of the Democratic Party led Cleveland to endorse the nominee of the "bolter" Gold Democratic party.

McKinley was nominated by the Republicans as a protectionist favoring the gold standard and friendly to organized labor. Despite his wealth, Hanna, McKinley's national chairman, was also well known for his enlightened view of labor-management relations: "Organized labor and organized capital are but forward steps in the great industrial evolution that is taking place (Hanna 1902). It was an election in which only a strong labor vote could counterbalance the agrarian support that would undoubtedly go to the Democratic nominee.

The Republican national committee was organized by Hanna as never before. Hanna spent nine times the Democratic committee's budget, introducing modern accounting procedures, distributing 120 million pieces of campaign literature, keeping an army of 1,400 speakers on the road, and giving major attention to press relations. Once elected, McKinley relied heavily on his confidante, arranging a seat in the Senate for Hanna and making him responsible for distribution of the federal patronage. The patronage was disbursed through the national committee in conjunction with the regular Republican state organizations. Both McKinley and Hanna benefited from their close personal ties and mutually supportive mode of operation.

The arrival of the twentieth century found national party organizations modern and relatively stable, factionalism systematic and responsive to issues as well as to competing candidacies, and the president's party leadership explicit and meaningful for electoral as well as legislative purposes. Party chairmen and other senior party officers could expect to be consulted by the president. Factions could bolt for an election or two but not start a significant permanent party. The presidency, a rapidly expanding office, was beginning to propose entire legislative programs that would give advantage to the incumbent's party. The party role had been pushed high on the agenda of a president's concerns, like it or not, and some who followed McKinley in office did not like it.

Theodore Roosevelt, aware that no vice-presidential successor to a deceased president had yet won renomination in his own right, grasped the party reigns as soon as he assumed office to complete McKinley's second term. He appointed the vice-chairman of the national committee, a staunch supporter, to the postmaster-general position to make certain that the patronage worked in his behalf. Roosevelt then embarked on his public struggle against Big Business to fix his popular image as a trust-buster.

Hanna's death removed Roosevelt's principal potential opponent for the 1904 nomination. Roosevelt then installed an outstanding executive, Secretary of Commerce and Labor George B. Cortelyou, as national party chairman. To those who objected, he wrote: "I regard opposition or disloyalty to Mr. Cortelyou as being simply an expression of disloyalty to the Republican party" (New York *Times*, November 5, 1904). Finally, Roosevelt made certain that the Southern delegates to the national convention, mainly federal patronage beneficiaries, were in his corner, a tactic that served subsequent Republican presidents. Roosevelt was renominated, elected, and able to name his successor, William Howard Taft. Then, unhappy with the conservatism of Taft's administration, he was able to contribute to Taft's defeat in 1912 by himself running as the nominee of the Progressive Party. Observing all this, little wonder that Professor Woodrow Wilson thought so highly of party activists in the presidency!

As president, Taft's problems with his party's leadership were legion. He seemed to do the wrong thing in his cabinet appointments, his support of Speaker Cannon during the 1910 revolt of the House membership, his handling of the conservation issue, and his dealings with the Senate. The final judgment on Taft's ineptitude belonged to Roosevelt, who soon sought to regain control of the party and, failing that, bolted to the Progressives.

Wilson was one of the presidents most reluctant to work with party leaders. His fantasy was that the U.S. party system was parliamentary rather than federal in character (a belief perhaps reinforced by the strong support congressional Democrats gave his program in his first term). He distrusted city bosses and tried to handle patronage appointments personally at the outset. His penchant for "going to the people" over the heads of "the politicians" led to errors in legislative strategies, most notably his loss of the League of Nations struggle with Republican Senate leader Henry Cabot Lodge. Wilson was in the wrong country for the party leadership role he was performing.

Like Grant, Harding was the choice of an inner circle of Republican party leaders, the candidate of politicians in a smoke-filled room. A handsome man, he was also the beneficiary of women's suffrage, for this was the first presidential election in which women — most from upper socioeconomic brackets — voted. His administration, riddled with corruption, would have been a party disaster had he not died and been succeeded by Coolidge. "Silent Cal" worked successfully to renew public confidence in the presidency. Coolidge was the first major public figure to address the nation over a new device, the radio. The cabinet was reshuffled, and preparations were made for his nomination at the 1924 national convention.

Although Coolidge followed McKinley in avoiding the appearance of partisanship, he clearly recognized the political character of the presidency. In his autobiography he observed:

> Under our system the President is not only the head of the government, but is also the head of his party. The last twenty years have witnessed a decline in party spirit and a distinct weakening in party loyalty. While an independent attitude on the part of the citizen is not without a certain public advantage, yet it is necessary under our form of government to have political parties. Unless someone is a partisan, no one can be an independent.... Unless those who are elected on the same party platform associate themselves together to carry out its provisions, the election becomes a mockery... (Coolidge 1929, pp. 230-32).

Hoover also tried to be attentive to party affairs. He warned Southern Republicans to reorganize or lose the advantage of the anti-Smith vote in the Solid South as well as the federal patronage available to him. He tried to reshuffle the national committee and place it on a permanent basis. He ran into resistance and unexpected problems in both endeavors. He also ran into the Great Depression and thereby lost a large part of the party's progressive wing to the New Deal.

In conclusion, the Barnum-Hanna Cycle confirmed Wilson's recognition of the importance of presidential party leadership. The cycle also paved the way for the establishment of permanent natonal party headquarters as an essential, if not always well employed, aid in the performance of the president's growing party role.

The Farley Cycle
(1933 to 1980)

Franklin D. Roosevelt respected and enjoyed party politics. He brought with him to Washington as national chairman and postmaster-general an unusually popular party professional in the person of James A. Farley. Farley revitalized the party organization from top to bottom with Roosevelt's participation and support. Political intelligence, coalition building, distribution of a large patronage, convention management, fund raising, and other party functions were modernized in definition and management. The results persist to this day. It is no longer conceivable that either party would close down its national headquarters. It is no longer possible to ignore the value of headquarters functions. What has differed are the circumstances and styles with which contemporary presidents have approached their party leadership responsibilities. The presidents of the Farley Cycle, from Roosevelt to Ford, are of recent memory and are amply documented. They may be characterized briefly.

Roosevelt was a dedicated partisan throughout his career. He was concerned about party organization throughout the 1920s, even during his illness. In power, he actively strengthened constituencies, which included the labor movement, in order to strengthen the party. He worked closely with Democratic Congresses during his four administrations. He constructed the New Deal coalition that shaped national politics for more than four decades.

Truman was a worthy successor—an expressive Democrat, accustomed to dealing with bosses and machines, unassailable in personal integrity, masterful in his performances for the media, confident in the support he enjoyed of the newly established political machines of the labor movement, certain that the New Deal had produced a Democratic majority in the electorate that simply needed to be aroused. Wearied by the Cold War and the Korean War, disturbed by the civil rights divisions in his party, and unable to recruit General Eisenhower as his successor, Truman retired, leaving the party with a vigorous civil rights coalition, a dedicated titular leader in Adlai Stevenson, and an assertive foreign policy.

Eisenhower was ill at ease in his party role. He inherited Thomas Dewey's political organization and entourage and expressed his appreciation with cabinet appointments. In legislative matters he deferred to Senator Robert A. Taft and Speaker Joseph Martin. He viewed the national committee as a highly specialized technical agency. Vice-President Nixon seemed best able to handle the campaign work. Asked to describe his conception of the role of the president as the leader of his party, Eisenhower, in one interview, replied:

> He is the leader not of . . . the hierarchy of control in any political party. What he is is the leader who translates the platform into a legislative program. . . . And after that . . . I think it is his duty to use whatever means he deems most effective in order to get that program . . . translated into law (New York *Times*, June 9, 1957).

John F. Kennedy and his brother Robert were the children of Boston machine politics; they thrived on every aspect of party politics. As senator, Jack Kennedy developed a national following early in his career as well as impressive legislative skills under the tutelage of Sam Rayburn and Lyndon Johnson. In his brief and dramatic presidency, he and his brother launched exceptional efforts to motivate the black citizens of the South to take advantage of their newly won civil rights by registering and voting Democratic. Kennedy was a hard-working and hard-hitting partisan. In contrast, Johnson's talents and attention were mainly in the congressional arena to the neglect of the electoral. From a one-party state, Texas, where political struggles were factional rather than interparty, Johnson was less devoted to party images. This suited his legislative work, where he had to have political friends on both sides of the aisle. As a consequence, he gave little support to the national committee, and in fact cut its budget. His campaigns and leadership were more personal than partisan.

An extreme partisan from the start of his political career, Nixon sought to emphasize a statesmanlike image during his presidency. He campaigned untiringly for fellow Republicans while a senator and as vice-president. He also remained close to party organizational affairs. As Watergate demonstrated, Nixon's extreme partisanship never was far below the surface and to a large extent was his undoing. When Vice-President Spiro Agnew resigned, Nixon nominated a popular Republican, House Minority Leader Gerald Ford, for that post, giving further indication of his strong partisanship. Ford succeeded to the presidency upon Nixon's resignation, having barely enough time to organize his own forces against Ronald Reagan's challenge for the 1976 Republican nomination.

Carter in many respects had the same approach to party as Johnson. A former governor of a one-party state where his principal adversaries were in his own party, Carter had little feeling for the presidential party role. He was generally perceived as an "outsider" among the Washington Democratic establishment and only occasionally addressed himself to party problems. From time to time he called upon party officials to lend support for his programs but offered little in return. Carter's handling of Senator Edward M. Kennedy's opposition to his renomination in 1980 left hard feelings that may have cost him the election.

The Farley Cycle brought permanency, professionalism, and procedure to the national party organs. National headquarters came to have permanent addresses and continuing functions. National chairmen and their staffs, not to mention the party liaison staffs at the

White House, were increasingly expert and professional. As trends toward nationalization of the parties advanced, leadership—and presidential—concern with organizational procedure—from loyalty pledges to constituency representativeness—heightened, particularly in the Democratic Party. The cycle saw the arrival of opinion polls, voter studies, television, public relations firms, the spread of presidential primaries, fund raising-by-mail, political action committees—nearly all centrifugal forces in the evolution of party politics and the president's capacity to perform a party role.

A Reagan Cycle?

Ronald Reagan's nomination and election in 1980 were the culmination of nearly two decades of organizational effort by Republican conservatives. A network of conservative interest groups, think tanks, publications, and grass-roots organizations had grown in the fertile soil of motivation, money, and astute political management. At the national level, when William Brock became Republican national chairman, he found at his disposal a highly skilled staff, an ample treasury, and party leaders more than willing to watch him exercise his talents at grass-roots organization, candidate recruitment, and fund raising. The Republican National Committee raised an unprecedented $111 million in anticipation of the 1980 campaign (Saloma 1982; Broder 1981, p. 10).

Reagan's candidacy added ideology and personality to the partisan recipe. As president, Reagan appreciated, endorsed, and lent himself to the modernization and professionalization of the Republican National Committee and the congressional campaign committees as well. With full knowledge that the party holding the presidency nearly always loses seats in the House of Representatives in the midterm elections, Reagan campaigned vigorously and selectively for Republican candidates in 1982, thereby putting his own political standing on the line. Usually presidents leave the midterm hustings to others.

It remains to be seen whether the Reagan presidency has initiated a new cycle of presidential party leadership. There is little question that his is a partisan presidency. Given the recent increase in ideological commitment among the "regulars" in both party organizations—Republicans to the Right and Democrats to the Left—and given the ideological thrust of Reagan's symbols and policies, it may be that the long-awaited ideological national parties lie a short distance over the horizon. If there is indeed a Reagan Cycle, we may know much more about this tendency at its conclusion.

CONTEMPORARY PROBLEMS OF PARTISAN PRESIDENTS

We have seen how seven aspects of the presidential party role manifest themselves differently for each president. As this brief survey indicates, the differences are in large part a consequence of style and circumstances. During the latter part of the Farley Cycle, circumstances began to change in direction and to a degree that may have fundamental consequences for the president's future party role. The circumstances most readily observed have been the following.

1. *Increase in Independents.* In recent years there has been a substantial rise in the proportion of the voters who identify themselves as Independents rather than as Republicans or Democrats. This seems to reinforce the president's inclination to appear nonpartisan or openly acknowledge his need for support from some segment of the opposition party. Will this pattern stimulate more voter independence, leaving the two major parties to their most loyal and probably most ideologically extreme constituents?

2. *Presenting an image.* The mass media, particularly television, have assumed a dominant role in making and breaking candidates. Under pressure of time and costs, it is highly uncertain that a candidate's image, as projected, will actually reach his or her audience unedited and whole. Media partisanship, subtle and pervasive though it may be, is probably less a problem than the distortions that arise from the media's penchant for portraying conflict. Will it become increasingly difficult for the citizenry to see beyond the partial imagery to the personal qualities of its party leaders? Will the candidates find even less utility in tying themselves to party in creating and putting forth their own public images via television cameras?

3. *Winning the presidency.* Running for nomination and election has become a continuous and costly four- to eight-year effort that may be carried on in person or through the media, with or without the candidate's party. Circumventing one's party may sometimes reduce campaign costs, particularly if presidential primaries can be avoided. Does this mean that only the unemployed rich will be able to run for president? Are the opportunities for factional insurgency being diminished by the time and cost factors?

4. *Organizing coalitions.* A decline in the significance of the party platform and a rise in the number and resources of single-issue interest groups seem to be altering the traditional ways of bringing together coalitions. Will group fragmentation make it more difficult for presidential parties to bring together disparate interests into powerful coalitions?

5. *Reaching the grass roots.* With the demise of local organizations and the rise of national direct-mail means of getting in direct touch with voters, how will person-to-person contact be maintained? Will impersonality speed the pace of declining party loyalty on the part of party rank-and-file voters?

6. *New political institutions.* As President Eisenhower pointed out, the military-industrial complex may be reducing the capacity of our more

traditional institutions, such as Congress and the parties, to function as intended. Domestic parties will also soon need to find ways to relate to emerging supranational institutions such as transnational parties and international nongovernmental organizations (NGOs). How will these and other institutional developments affect the president's roles as commander-in-chief, world statesman, and party leader?

These and related questions may be asked and answered during the next presidential party leadership cycle. At the very least, what seems evident from today's vantage point is that new circumstances may diminish even further the president's need to tie himself tightly to his party, as well as his ability to lead the party when he is so inclined. Changes in the role behavior of presidents vis-a-vis their parties may be expected. However, we may also expect that these changes will fall within the patterns that have evolved gradually over the past 200 years.

NOTES

1. For example, surveys ranking presidents on scales of "greatness": the Chicago *Tribune* poll of 49 historians (January 10, 1982); David L. Porter's poll of 41 historians (1981); Arthur M. Schlesinger's polls of 1948 and 1962.

2. Other elements may be identified but have less prominence. For example, there is a growing awareness that the president's actions as a world leader may be increasingly significant for his role as party leader, for example, Johnson in Vietnam and Reagan as a foe of communism.

3. The Whig Party of eighteenth-century England was largely responsible for shaping the constitutional monarchy of that nation.

REFERENCES

Adams, Charles Francis. 1841. *Letters of John Adams Addressed to His Wife.* Boston, Little, Brown.

_____. 1850-56. *The Works of John Adams.* Boston: Little, Brown.

_____. 1876. *The Memoirs of John Quincy Adams.* Philadelphia: J. B. Lippincott.

Annals of Congress. Washington, D.C., 1798.

Bain, Richard C., and Judith H. Parris. 1973. *Convention Decisions and Voting Records*, 2d ed. Washington, D.C.: Brookings Institution.

Bassett, John Spencer. 1928. *The Life of Andrew Johnson.* New York: Macmillan.

Bowers, Claude G. 1925. *Jefferson and Hamilton.* Boston: Houghton Mifflin.

Broder, David S. 1981. "Introduction." In *Party Coalitions in the 1980s*, ed. Seymour Martin Lipset, pp. 3-13. San Francisco: Institute for Contemporary Studies.

Carroll, E. Malcolm. 1925. *Origins of the Wing Party.* Durham, N.C.: Duke University, Press.

Clarkson, James S. 1890. "Letter to Michener, May 29, 1890." Louis T. Michener (Harrison's personal manager) Papers, Library of Congress.

Cole, Arthur C. 1912. *The Whig Party in the South*. Washington, D.C.

Cone, Leon W., Jr. 1950. "Martin Van Buren: The Architect of the Democratic Party, 1837-1840." Ph.D. diss. University of Chicago.

Coolidge, Calvin. 1929. *The Autobiography of Calvin Coolidge*. New York: Cosmopolitan Books.

Cunningham, Noble E., Jr. 1957. *The Jeffersonian Republicans*. Chapel Hill: University of North Carolina, Press.

Dauer, Manning J. 1953. *The Adams Federalists*. Baltimore: Johns Hopkins University Press.

David, Paul T., Ralph M. Goldman, and Richard C. Bain. 1960. *The Politics of National Party Conventions*. Washington, D.C.: Brookings Institution.

Ford, Paul L. 1904-05. *The Works of Thomas Jefferson*. New York: G. P. Putnam's Sons.

Fornoff, Charles W. 1926. "Madison on the Nature of Parties." Ph.D. diss. University of Illinois.

Fowler, Dorothy G. 1943. *The Cabinet Politician; The Postmasters-General, 1829-1909*. New York: Columbia University Press.

Freeman, Douglas Southall. 1948-57. *George Washington*. New York: C. Scribner's Sons.

Goldman, Ralph M. 1951. "Party Chairman and Party Faction, 1789-1900." Ph.D. diss. University of Chicago.

_____ . 1966. *The Democratic Party in American Politics*. New York: Macmillan.

_____ . 1969. "Titular Leadership of the Presidential Parties." In *The Presidency*, ed. Aaron Wildavsky, pp. 384-410. Boston: Little, Brown.

Hanna, Mark A. 1902. "Industrial Conciliation and Arbitration." In *Annals of the American Academy of Political and Social Science* 20 (July): 21-26.

Lipscomb, Andrew A. 1905. *The Writings of Thomas Jefferson*. Washington, D.C.: Thomas Jefferson Memorial Association.

Madison, James. 1787. *The Federalist Papers*, Number 10.

_____ . 1792a. "A Candid State of Parties." *National Gazette*, September 27. Philadelphia.

_____ . 1792b. "Parties." *National Gazette*, January 23. Philadelphia.

_____ . 1867. *Letters and Other Writings of James Madison*. Philadelphia: J.B. Lippincott.

Morgan, Robert J. 1954. *A Whig Embattled; The Presidency Under John Tyler*. Lincoln: University of Nebraska Press.

Morse, Anson D. 1923. *Parties and Party Leaders*. Boston: Jones.

Pomper, Gerald M. 1966. *Nominating the President; The Politics of Convention Choice*. New York: W. W. Norton.

Quaife, Milo Milton. 1910. *The Diary of James K. Polk*. Chicago: A. C. McClurg.

Remini, Robert V. 1959. *Martin Van Buren and the Making of the Democratic Party*. New York: Columbia University Press.

Saloma, John S. 1982. "The New Political Order." San Francisco: Unpublished manuscript.

Weed, Harriet A., and Thurlow Weed Barnes. 1884. *Autobiography of Thurlow Weed*. Boston: Houghton Mifflin.

Welles, Gideon, 1848. "Selection of Candidate for President in 1848." In Welles Papers. Washington, D.C.: Library of Congress.

West, Willis M. 1918. *History of the American People*.

Weston, Florence. 1938. *The Presidential Election of 1828*. Washington, D.C.: Ruddick.

Wilson, Woodrow. 1908. *Constitutional Government in the United States*. New York: Columbia University Press.

PART II
PRESIDENT AND PARTY ORGANIZATION

3

THE PRESIDENT AND THE NATIONAL PARTY ORGANIZATION

Harold F. Bass

*T*he concept of *party* embraces three analytically separate structural elements: the party in the electorate, the party organization, and the party in the government. The president is chief among those office holders who have "captured the symbols of the party and speak for it in public authority" (Sorauf 1968, pp. 11-12). Initially, however, the presidency was envisioned and created as a nonpartisan office, owing both to the express intention of the framers of the Constitution and to the absence of organized political parties in 1787. Over the next half century, the emergence of national parties had two important and lasting effects on the presidency. First, to the expectations and requirements for presidential candidates, which heretofore had been considerable public service and esteem, was added party affiliation. Nomination became a *party* activity, a reward bestowed on party members. Second, the presidential nominee's status as head of the party ticket conferred on him the distinction of party leader. Combined with that of head of the executive branch, this status allowed the president to presume to be something more than the constitutionally stipulated chief executive. Indeed, there was now a basis for his claiming *government* chieftainship, with the idea and organization of *party* unifying separated national institutions under the leadership of the president (Remini 1976).

NATIONAL PARTY ORGANIZATION

National party organization appeared on the American scene as a Jacksonian era reform of party nomination methods. Its initial incarnation came in the form of the national party convention. The convention emerged out of dissatisfaction with and breakdown of "King Caucus," the initial procedure by which party nominees for president were selected by the party's representatives in Congress. Prior to the 1832 election, rank-and-file members of three parties—the Anti-Masons, the National Republicans, and the Democratic Rebuplicans—assembled to choose their presidential nominees (David, Goldman, and Bain 1960, pp. 17-19). The institution quickly took hold and has endured on a quadrennial basis aggregating delegations from state party organizations. In 1848 the Democratic National Convention inaugurated the practice whereby that body authorized and established a national party committee consisting of leaders of state parties headed by a party chairman* to conduct the presidential campaign and to guide the party's fortunes between conventions (Cotter and Hennessy 1964, pp. 13-15). During the decade of the 1920s, national party chairmen instituted permanent staffing of the national party headquarters (Bone 1958, pp. 36-37; Cotter and Bibby 1980). These constitute the components of the national party organization: the convention, the committee, the chairman, and the headquarters staff.

The national organization sits atop similarly constructed state and local party organizations in a decentralized, federal arrangement. At the outset, power within this hierarchy clearly rested with the state organizations. However, state party leaders and the factions they represented sought and vied among themselves for control of the national party, which was symbolized by the presidential nomination and, increasingly, by the national party chairmanship. In the years following the War Between the States, aspiring presidential candidates energetically sought the support of the party chieftains in order to attain the coveted nomination. For the most part, these party leaders operated and survived apart from the candidates they chose to sponsor for the presidential nomination; and they frequently sought the party chairmanship for themselves or their factions as a reflection of their influence. When the party nominee gained the White House, party managers within the government, under the supervision of the party chairman, attended to the party's interests and distributed sizable patronage largess to party workers. "By 1896," notes Goldman (1951, p. 75), the [party] chairmanship assumed the brightness

---

*The term "party chairman" is used because, until 1972, all were men. This usage throughout this chapter (or in other chapters) doesn't mean to demean or ignore the status of Jean Westwood as Democratic Party chairwoman, or of any other woman who has held a political position.

of a major star in the American political galaxy. It commanded public attention and, under victorious circumstances, vast political resources."

After the turn of the century, the party chairmanship continued to be a position of public visibility and political strength. Increasingly, it became linked with the cabinet office of postmaster general, the central billet within the government for distributing party patronage (Fowler 1943). Moreover, party chairmen came increasingly to be perceived and to act as subalterns and agents of the presidential nominees (Goldman 1951, p. 82; David, Goldman, and Bain 1960, pp. 72-73). The precedent had already developed that the presidential nominee could recommend a candidate for the party chairmanship and the national committee would ratify that choice. With this initiative coming to take the form of a prerogative, the recipient of the presidential nomination, and afterward the occupant of the presidential office, began to assume preeminence in party affairs over his putative sponsors, the state party chieftains who had earlier competed among themselves for dominance within the national party organization. During this power shift it was the national party chairman, a figure of imposing political stature, who firmly linked the party and the presidency by planting a foot in each camp. He was the party's representative in the presidency and the president's liaison with the party.

The position of the party chairmanship as an effective middleman between president and party reached a high-water mark during the long tenure of James A. Farley as Democratic Party chairman from 1932 until 1940. Farley's background, his personal style, and his political responsibilities conformed to and came to epitomize the traditional image and substance of that office (see Farley 1938, 1948). Yet Farley's experience and ultimate fate also portended a number of related organizational developments in the structures of the presidential campaign organization and the presidential office. In ensuing years they have come to estrange severely the president and his party and to diminish the status of the party chairman and the national party organization.

PRESIDENTIAL CAMPAIGN ORGANIZATION

The first development pertains to the structure of the presidential campaign organization. Theodore White (1975, p. 97) has observed that a presidential campaign "starts with a candidate, a handful of men, a theme and a plan. By November of election year it has enlisted hundreds of thousands of volunteers, politicians, state staffs, national staffs, media specialists and has become an enterprise." Such an endeavor requires organization and leadership. While there is an abundance of descriptive literature on presidential campaigns, relatively little analytical focus has been directed toward the structure of campaign organization. Notable exceptions include Lamb and Smith (1968), Ogden and Peterson (1968), Kessell (1968, 1980), and Kayden (1978). In these various accounts, presidential campaign organizations are characterized by a confusing profusion of titles and overlapping of responsibilities. Campaign managers, campaign chairmen, political directors, and strategy boards all contend for their respective nominees' ears and claim to speak and act authoritatively for them. A key question arises regarding the status of the party chairman and the national party organization within this array.

Traditionally, the campaign roles of the party chairman and the organization he heads were central to the presidential campaign. National party committees came into being in the mid-nineteenth century to provide campaign direction, and party chairmen customarily served as campaign managers. Indeed, the practice of allowing the presidential nominee to designate the party chairman developed to facilitate integration of the nominee's campaign with the national party effort. Thus, Franklin Roosevelt was conforming to established precedent when he named his preconvention campaign manager James Farley the national party chairman, whence Farley continued to exercise campaign management responsibilities. However, in recent years, most nominees have chosen instead to establish autonomous campaign organizations. Headquartered separately from the national party *their* principal advisers and strategists direct election efforts, with coordination and liaison with coterminous national party campaigns problematical. In such a situation the party chairman is ill-positioned to play his traditional linkage role on behalf of the party organization. A review of recent cases of chairman selection by nonincumbent presidential nominees indicates that an individual's talents and abilities in the realm of campaign management are only one among many selection criteria, some mutually reinforcing, others secondary, and still others contradictory (see Table 3.1).

One prevalent practice over the years has been for the nominee to reward someone who was instrumental in securing his nomination. This has taken two distinct forms. The first has been the designation of a personal loyalist from the preconvention campaign. For example, both Stephen Mitchell and Dean Burch had occupied leadership positions on behalf of the candidacies of Adlai Stevenson and Barry

TABLE 3.1: Campaign Party Chairmen Chosen by Nonincumbent Presidential Nominees, 1948–80

Name	Chosen by	State	Age	Religion	Political Background
Hugh Scott (R) (1948–49)	Dewey	Pennsylvania	47	Episcopalian	U.S. Congressman
Arthur Summerfield (R) (1952–53)	Eisenhower	Michigan	53	n/a	State Organization Leader
Stephen Mitchell (D) (1952–55)	Stevenson	Illinois[b]	49	Catholic	Personal Associate of Nominee
Paul Butler (D) (1955–60)	Stevenson[a]	Indiana	50	Catholic	State Organization Leader[a]
Thruston Morton (R) (1959–61)	Nixon[a]	Kentucky	51	Episcopalian	U.S. Senator
Henry Jackson (D) (1960–61)	Kennedy	Washington	48	Presbyterian	U.S. Senator
Dean Burch (R) (1964–65)	Goldwater	Arizona[b]	37	n/a	Personal Associate of Nominee
Ray Bliss (R) (1965–69)	Nixon[a]	Ohio	58	Episcopalian	State Organization Leader[a]
Lawrence O'Brien (D) (1968–69)	Humphrey	Massachusetts	51	Catholic	Federal Executive
Jean Westwood (D) (1972)	McGovern	Utah	49	Mormon	State Organization Leader
Robert Strauss (D) (1972–77)	Carter[a]	Texas	55	Jewish	State Organization Leader[a]
William Brock (R) (1977–81)	Reagan[a]	Tennessee	46	Presbyterian	Ex-U.S. Senator

[a] Nominees chose to retain the incumbent national party chairman.
[b] Nominees chose party chairmen from home state.

Goldwater, respectively. An alternative pattern has been the appreciative recognition of a party leader who has delivered crucial delegate support. After Arthur Summerfield, chairman of the large and influential Michigan delegation at the 1952 Republican convention, declared for Eisenhower at a strategic moment, his reward was the chairmanship (see Perlmutter 1952; David, Goldman, and Bain 1960, p. 64).

The nominee may use his prerogative to cultivate or mollify important party and electoral constituencies, with demographic factors taking on symbolic significance. Nominees can use the chairmanship to backstop efforts at geographic ticket balancing beyond the vice-presidential nomination or to recognize a regional center of party power. Summerfield's aforementioned selection also gave representation to the traditional Republican heartland. In 1960, Senator Henry Jackson, hailing from the Pacific Northwest, complemented a Democratic national ticket composed of Kennedy of Massachusetts and Johnson from Texas.

Within the Democratic Party, ethnic and religious background once constituted an informal elibigility limitation. For over three decades, from 1928 to 1960, every national chairman, whatever else he happened to be, was an Irish Catholic. This tradition paid homage to that powerful constituency within the party organization and also related to the absence, except for the ill-fated Al Smith, of a Roman Catholic among the party's presidential nominees. Since the Kennedy nomination in 1960, the relevance of this consideration has receded.

In 1972 a new factor, sex, was introduced. The selection of the first woman, Jean Westwood, as Democratic Party chairman symbolized the growing clout of women in party politics. Further, it indicated the emergence of new bargaining units at the convention superimposed amid the traditional state delegations: group caucuses reflecting group representation at the convention and new group pressure in the larger body politic (Sullivan et al. 1974, pp. 42-43).

The nominee may be pressured to retain the incumbent chairman, should such a figure have developed strong and vocal personal followings within the party organization during his tenure. This proved to be the case with respect to Paul Butler (D, 1956), Thruston Morton (R, 1960), Ray Bliss (R, 1968), Robert Strauss (D, 1976), and William Brock (R, 1980). Instead, he may offer the chairmanship as a consolation prize to an unsuccessful aspirant for a spot on the presidential ticket. In 1960 both Senators Jackson and Morton were leading contenders for their parties' vice-presidential nominations. Such a figure is likely to be an office holder as opposed to a personal aide of the nominee or a state organization leader. As such, he might be well situated to perform as chairman in the alternative campaign role of party spokesman, highly visible in the campaign, but largely divorced from the inner circle of advisers and decision makers. Whether the party chairman is expected to fill the traditional managerial role or the more contemporary role of spokesman is a final consideration to be taken into account by the nominee in recommending a candidate for that position.

While each campaign justifiably might be considered *sui generis*, an examination of the organizational vehicles for recent presidential campaigns illuminates diverse additional factors that have moved campaigns toward increased autonomy from the national party organization. In a number of instances, strategic considerations have mitigated against integration. Post-1932 Republican nominees, for example, were on several occasions hesitant to identify symbolically and organizationally *their* campaigns with the *minority* party under whose banner they ran. Richard Nixon's 1960 and 1968 efforts illustrate this phenomenon. The subsequent Nixon campaign, for his 1972 reelection as president, was even more autonomous, owing to his desire to appear above party, as president of all the people (see Nixon 1962, p. 322; T. White 1970, pp. 405-09; 1973, pp. 297-99). On the Democratic side, the autonomy of Adlai Stevenson's 1952 campaign can be attributed to his ongoing status as governor of Illinois, necessitating (or at least justifying) the establishment of campaign headquarters in Springfield, and his desire to separate his campaign from the "mess in Washington" where Democratic President Harry Truman remained ensconced (see Martin 1976, p. 766; Odgen and Peterson 1968, p. 102). More generally, presidential nominees, attempting to appeal to an American electorate decreasingly dependent on partisan sources and structures for political information, economic employment, and social services, and thus decreasingly inclined to make durable partisan attachments, are wary and even loath to rely on *party* organization as their electoral vehicle (see Agranoff 1976; Ripon Society and Brown, 1974, pp. 188-89).

From a different standpoint, party reform, and especially changes in the "rules" by which presidents are nominated and elected, have contributed to this shift toward autonomous campaigns. The advent of presidential primaries in the progressive era and their proliferation since 1968 have made the coveted presidential nomination increasingly attainable through an appeal to the party electorate rather than the party organization. Indeed, the contemporary role of the nominating convention appears to be one of ratifying the party's choice for the nomination as previously expressed in the primaries (see Davis 1967; Crotty 1977, pp, 193-237 passim; Keech and Matthews 1976, pp. 111-56 passim). This development contributes to autonomy in the campaign organization in that in order to contest the primaries, candidates have to assemble and have operational electoral organizations well in advance of the nominating convention. Moreover, federal election laws now mandate the establishment of separate candidate organizations to qualify for the public funding available and critical to the conduct of a presidential campaign (see Ranney 1978). Durng the preconvention period, the national party organization is expected to be at least nominally neutral, precluding integration; yet after the convention the candidate organization of the victor remains intact, both complicating integration and making relatively unnecessary reliance on the party apparatus.

Thus, current organizational arrangements have made the presidential campaign a weak foundation on which to build a mutually satisfactory relationship between the president and the national party organization. The trend toward autonomous campaign organizations both physically and psychologically separates the national party organization from the campaign and points toward a growing estrangement between the candidate for president and the party whose nomination is a means to that end. Moreover, it establishes an environment of uncomfortable tension between the victorious president-elect and his national party that carries over into the presidential transition and the administation.

STAFFING THE PRESIDENCY

After electoral victory, the president-elect turns his attention to the problem of staffing. He naturally looks to the campaign organization for the personnel nucleus around which to build his administration and the administrative apparatus to conduct the talent hunt. As noted, modern campaign organizations tend toward autonomy from rather than integration with the party organization, thus immediately reducing the party's potential influence in staffing. Moreover, due in large part to changes in the organization of the presidential office, the modern patterns for strategic placement of key campaign aides and conduct of personnel management have departed in important respects from traditional staffing procedures of earlier presidents. In turn, these departures have had a significant impact on the relationship between the president and the national party organization, contributing to a fundamental reorganization of both the process and substance of their interaction.

Two staffing trends are noteworthy. The first is the omission of the presidential campaign manager from the ranks of the cabinet secretaries, a departure from the long-standing practice of designating that figure either postmaster general or, more recently and less frequently, attorney general. The second is the transfer of the personal campaign into the White House Office, a modern development owing to the relatively recent establishment and expansion of that office.

The president's cabinet, composed of the executive department secretaries, has customarily included one or more key political advisers drawn from the campaign staff (Fenno 1959, pp. 67-71). From the outset of its establishment as a cabinet office during President Andrew Jackson's administration, the postmaster generalship was usually reserved for a leading campaign strategist. In the years before the Civil War, it was not uncommon for the new president to name his campaign manager as postmaster general where his demonstrated political acumen and loyalty could be put to fruitful use allocating the considerable resources of federal patronage available through the post office. With the strengthening of party organization in the post-Civil War period, the post office regularly was headed by a prominent party politician who had been active during the campaign. After the turn of the century it became accepted if not established practice not only to combine the campaign leadership positions of campaign manager and chairman of the national party committee, but also to install the director of that successful campaign in the cabinet as postmaster general (Bone 1958, p. 10; Fowler 1943, pp. 302-03).

Thus, party-presidential relations came to be managed by the shared efforts of the national party chairman, designated by the president and elected head of the national party organization, and the postmaster general, the "cabinet politician." These two offices linked party and presidency; and by the mid-1940s the common practice was to combine the offices in the same person, giving one individual both "hats." This arrangement formalized the traditional representation of the party's needs and interests by a "party manager" in the president's cabinet, and it gave the party organization, through its chairman, an organizational base within the government.

However, since the 1947 resignation of Robert Hannegan, once described by President Truman (1945) as the "political representative of the Democratic Party in the cabinet of the president," no subsequent party chairman has been accorded this dual institutional status. Once consonant, recruitment patterns and job requirements have diverged. Moreover, partisan considerations have come to have a diminished saliency in the cabinet arena; and the postmaster general is no longer a member. The more modern recruitment pattern locating the campaign manager in the cabinet as attorney general, itself now an anachronism, bypassed direct association with partisan concerns and interests (see Fenno 1959, p. 70; Staff of the New York *Times* 1973, pp. 387-89). The upshot has been the displacement of the party's designated advocate and manager from an official position within the administration, thereby removing the organizational anchor of stability and support such a base could provide and ensure.

An even more significant modern development involving the dispersal of the campaign organization has been the relocation of the nominee's personal campaign staff into parallel or compatible positions in the White House Office. Prior to its creation in 1939, presidents entering office who wished to staff the presidency with key campaign aides had to farm most of them out into the various cabinet departments. Since then, the availability of the expansive personal office structure has enabled modern presidents to retain close at hand and virtually intact the services of a considerable portion of their campaign teams. A list of White House staff assistants coming from campaign organizations would include the following notables: Sherman Adams and James Hagerty accompanying Eisenhower; Kenneth O'Donnell, Larry O'Brien, Theodore Sorensen, and Pierre Salinger under Kennedy; H. R. Haldeman, John Ehrlichman, and Dwight Chapin with Nixon; Hamilton Jordan and Jody Powell from the Carter campaign; Reagan aides James Baker, Michael Deaver, and Edwin Meese.

One result has been an alteration of the pattern of presidential party leadership. Responding to organizational opportunities, indeed imperatives, to minimize dependence and simultaneously expand power (see Thompson 1967, pp. 30-32; Wilson 1973, pp. 210-11), White House staff assistants have been assigned and have assumed major responsibility for the conduct of political operations and the management of party affairs. This turn of events has been facilitated and institutionalized by two practices that developed in the Truman-Eisenhower era. The first is the designation of a staff assistant as the president's personal liaison or contact with party and political leaders throughout the country, including the national party organization. The second is the employment of personnel and the establishment of an apparatus at the White House for handling political appointments. Each practice allows the president to internalize in the White House tasks and functions once clearly associated with the national party organization, both strengthening the White House operation and weakening that of the national party.

As liaison, a staff assistant ostensibly serves merely as a conduit, facilitating the transmission of advice and infomation, requests and demands, between president and party. However, insofar as he speaks and acts for the president on party matters, he inevitably supersedes and supplants the party chairman in what was once his central linkage role. The president's primacy and power as party leader have always encouraged elements within the party to focus their attention on the White House. However, the establishment of a sizable staff capacity there that is sufficient and willing to meet expectations has greatly enhanced this predilection. In conveying messages, power gravitates to the conveyer, the White House aide, whose presence not only encourages the bypass of national party headquarters, diminishing its prestige, but whose assignment includes monitoring the activities at party headquarters, diminishing its autonomy.

This configuration of White House staff management of president-party relations became apparent in the person and function of Matthew Connelly, President Truman's appointments secretary. All subsequent staffs have prominently featured at least one such figure. For most of Eisenhower's administration, Sherman Adams filled the role. Kenneth O'Donnell did so under Kennedy. Johson looked to Walter Jenkins and then Marvin Watson. In the Nixon White House, H. R. Haldeman supervised the liaison activities of several agents, among them Harry Dent, Murray Chotiner, and John Sears. Donald Rumsfeld and later Richard Cheney so served President Ford. Jimmy Carter relied mainly on Hamilton Jordan and Tim Kraft. In the Reagan staff arrangement, political operations have come under the general supervision of chief-of-staff Baker. Lyn Nofziger was initially designated the primary contact. After his departure from the staff in 1982, Nofziger was replaced in that position by Edward Rollins. During their years of service, many of these individuals, initially envisioned as operating with a "passion for anonymity," became widely known by the general public, thus overshadowing contemporaneous national party chairmen in public prominence as well as political responsibility.

Another characteristic of White House staff organization has been the deputation of a staff assistant to man an in-house personnel office managing presidential appointments (see Mackenzie 1982, pp. 79-88; Henry 1969). In the late 1940s Truman's adnimistrative assistant, Donald Dawson, set up such an office as a clearinghouse for information on jobs available and potential candidates to fill them. Subsequent presidents have maintained and institutionalized this administrative apparatus and function made possible by the presence of an expanded staff capacity to preempt what was once widely viewed as the province of the national party organization (see Cotter and Hennessy 1964, pp. 138-48; Mann and Doig 1965, pp. 77-78). Partially as a result, the national party organization has found its contemporary role in presidential appointments reduced from positive initiative to negative response: an occasional oopportunity to block proposed appointments by refusing political clearance.

Undoubtedly, the party's diminished patronage role can be accounted for in large measure apart from this organizational development. Years ago, presidential appointments placed large numbers of deserving partisans in low-level bureaucratic jobs. Such positions have become virtually blanketed by expanded civil service coverage (see Kaufman 1965; Mansfield 1965). Modern-era presidential appointments are largely restricted to relatively high-level executive slots atop the classified pyramid. Few such positions existed prior to the New Deal. Their number has vastly increased with the subsequent proliferation of executive agencies and staff (see Henry 1969; Mann and Doig 1965, p. 66). Thus, these offices were not available to be claimed by the party organization in its patronage heyday. Few would argue that the party unilaterally ought to assume the controlling role in handling these presidential appointments. Still, with respect to the relationship between the White House and the national party organization, White House self-reliance here, as with staff liaison, reduces the potential for a party contribution to presidential politics.

Thus, nonparty structures in the administration, as in the campaign, have supplanted the national party. In particular, the development of a sizable staff apparatus in the White House Office has both released the president from his dependence on officials at the national party headquarters and allowed him to extend comprehensive control over it. Now he can use his own personal staff to handle political assignments and party matters and to give detailed presidential supervision to the activities of those at party headquarters. The chief impact of this lessened dependence and expanded surveillance on the part of the White House has been to reduce both the potency and autonomy of the party operation. Rather than serving as an ally and complement of the presidential power, it has been rendered superfluous and submissive to that power.

FORMS OF INTERACTION

This outline of historical and organizational developments frames the consideration of forms of interaction between the president and various elements of the national party organization. These include

EDITOR'S PERSPECTIVE

LBJ, Chairman Bailey, and Discontent in the Party Ranks

Presidents have often been accused of neglecting their party organizations, but seldom have they been more roundly and publicly criticized for their neglect by other party officeholders than Lyndon Johnson was. In December 1966 a group of Democratic governors meeting in White Sulphur Springs, West Virginia, went public with criticism of the Democratic National Committee's (DNC) neglect of the governors, and the president's seeming lack of interest in providing effective leadership for strengthening the DNC. The target of the criticism — along with LBJ himself — was party chairman John M. Bailey. The dispute — and its causes — were the basis for the following "Inside Report" column by Rowland Evans and Robert Novak, which appeared in the Washington *Post* on December 21, 1966.

Later Than LBJ Thinks

Not even the angry slap at President Johnson by the Democratic Governors last week seems destined to force the political reform of the President's Party so badly needed both within the White House and the Democratic National Committee. . . .

"The Democratic Party hasn't been in such bad shape for 30 years," confides an old pro with intimate connections to the President and no sympathy whatsoever for the anti-Johnson recriminations now coming so boldly from the politicians.

Why, then, is it unlikely that the President will take the necessary steps to rejuvenate his Party? Part of the answer undoubtedly lies in Mr. Johnson's parochial political heritage. As a Texas Democrat and leader of his Party in the U.S. Senate, Mr. Johnson spent eight years fighting off political attack from the Democratic National Committee. Mr. Johnson's perennial warfare against the late Paul M. Butler, then Democratic National Chairman, led to one of Washington's celebrated feuds in the 1950s.

With some justification, this intra-party battle left Mr. Johnson with a low opinion of the national committee. And today, the softest spot in the Party's armor is right there in the National Committee, still headed by the amiable John M. Bailey.

Mr. Johnson seems to be afraid that if he replaces Bailey with a tough-nosed political manager, the National Committee might be built into a power center capable of challenging the White House.

This is, of course, preposterous, but to non-Northern Democrats the National Committee has always represented a center of big-city power

EDITOR'S PERSPECTIVE (continued)

politics. And with the Johnson and Kennedy wings of the Party more suspicious than ever of each other, Mr. Johnson apparently does not want to give the committee an independent power of its own. . . .

In the White House itself, the President's man Bill Moyers has more and more become the bridge between the Northern organization Democrats and Mr. Johnson. . . .

This is true despite the fact that White House appointment Secretary W. Marvin Watson, Jr., the conservative Texas politician and former steel man, is the President's designated agent to the politicians. Watson doesn't talk the language of the big-city, big-state Democratic politicians. And they don't appreciate his tight-budget, cost-accounting methods of running their Party. . . .

In spite of continuing criticisms of Bailey's leadership and calls for his replacement, Johnson kept him at the helm of the DNC until August 1968, when newly nominated candidate Hubert Humphrey named Lawrence O'Brien as his party chairman and campaign manager.

chairman selection and deployment, headquarters management, financial and organizational collaboration, convention outcomes, and nomination and election campaigns.

The party chairmanship remains the hub of the relationship. The practice of allowing and expecting the presidential nominee to recommend to the national committee his candidate to chair the party carries over to the victor's term in office. This makes the chairmanship in effect a presidential appointment and maintains control over the party organization by the head of the party-in-office. Since the average tenure for post-World War II national chairmen of the party controlling the White House is about two years, virtually all presidents have had this opportunity to interact with and influence the national committee. Among modern presidents only Lyndon Johnson never had occasion to choose a party chairman. Customarily when a vacancy exists, perhaps at the instigation of the president, the national committee sends a delegation to the White House to be notified formally of the president's choice. Then it convenes to elect the individual. Having done so, the committee's subsequent interaction with the president is limited to occasional presidential addresses and receptions scheduled in conjunction with regular meetings of the committee.

In the years since World War II, presidents-elect and incumbents have selected 16 national party chairmen (see Table 3.2). Chairmen have been recruited from diverse political backgrounds, but state organization leaders and legislators have predominated. All have been identified with the political causes and campaigns of their presidents, but only William Boyle qualifies purely as a close personal associate. Geographically, most of these chairmen have come from the East and the Midwest. Two came from the same state as their presidential sponsors, five from the same region, and nine from different regions. Most of the Democratic chairmen were Catholics, while Methodists and Episcopalians numbered prominently in the Republican group. Gerald Ford chose the only woman.

A number of circumstances have triggered the departures of party chairmen during their president's terms. A few have resigned for personal reasons or to pursue their own political interests. On other occasions the presidents have created the vacancies by appointing chairmen to high-level government positions. Truman designated McGrath attorney general; Nixon chose Rogers Morton to be secretary of the interior; and Ford made Bush the head of the U.S. Liaison Office in the People's Republic of China. These appointments suggest an additional presidential staffing tendency: to bring associates of proven trust and value into the administration, while

TABLE 3.2: National In-Party Chairmen, 1945–82

Name	Chosen by	State	Age	Religion	Political Background
Robert Hannegan (D) (1944–47)	Roosevelt	Missouri	41	Catholic	State Organization Leader, Federal Executive
D. Howard McGrath (D) (1947–49)	Truman	Rhode Island	44	Catholic	U.S. Senator
William Boyle (D) (1949–51)	Truman	Missouri	47	Catholic	Personal Associate of President
Frank McKinney (D) (1951–52)	Truman	Indiana	47	Catholic	State Organization Leader
C. Wesley Roberts (R) (1953)	Eisenhower	Kansas	49	Methodist	State Organization Leader
Leonard Hall (R) (1953–57)	Eisenhower	New York	53	Episcopalian	Ex–U.S. Congressman
Meade Alcorn (R) (1957–59)	Eisenhower	Connecticut	50	Congregationalist	State Organization Leader
Thruston Morton (R) (1959–61)	Eisenhower	Kentucky	51	Episcopalian	U.S. Senator
John Bailey (D) (1961–68)	Kennedy	Connecticut	57	Catholic	State Organization Leader
Rogers Morton (R) (1969–71)	Nixon	Maryland	55	Episcopalian	U.S. Representative
Robert Dole (R) (1971–73)	Nixon	Kansas	48	Methodist	U.S. Senator
George Bush (R) (1973–74)	Nixon	Texas	49	Episcopalian	Federal Executive
Mary Louise Smith (R) (1974–76)	Ford	Iowa	59	Protestant	State Organization Leader
Kenneth Curtis (D) (1977–78)	Carter	Maine	45	Protestant	Ex–Governor
John White (D) (1978–81)	Carter	Texas	54	Baptist	Federal Executive
Richard Richards (R) (1981–83)	Reagan	Utah	49	Presbyterian	State Organization Leader
Paul Laxalt (R) (1983–)*	Reagan	Nevada	60	Catholic	U.S. Senator
Frank Fahrenkopf (R) (1982–)	Reagan	Nevada	43	Catholic	State Organization Leader

* General chairman.

assigning a lower priority to the maintenance of the party apparatus (compare Wallerstein 1969). Alternatively, presidential dissatisfaction can be a factor. Taints of scandal have been associated with the resignations of Boyle and Roberts (See Donovan 1982, pp. 338-39; Leviero 1953); and more recently, Curtis and Richards have departed amid media speculation suggesting conflict with the White House as the chief cause (See Bruno 1977; Smith 1977; Taylor and Cannon 1982).

Installed in office by the president, and serving at his pleasure, national chairmen encounter their party leader in circumstances that vary considerably in both frequency and substantive significance. The clear tendency is toward infrequent meetings in rather formal, ceremonial settings. To be sure, President Truman had a standing appointment every Wednesday afternoon with the Democratic Chairman to discuss party politics (Johnson 1974, p. 52; Steinberg 1962, p. 350). Eisenhower regarded the party chairman as the "alter ego on party matters of the president" (Ferrell 1981, p. 357), and he genuinely expected the chairman to be the "political expert" in the presidential allocation of administrative responsibilities and advisory roles (See Wilder n.d.). Still, an anecdote shared by one-time Republican Party chairman Robert Dole, allowing only slightly for exaggeration, better portrays the contemporary character of the relationship. Senator Dole recalls receiving a telephone call from the White House informing him that his long-standing request to see President Nixon was about to be granted, if he would tune his television set to the proper channel to receive the president's scheduled campaign address (T. White 1973, p. 61n).

Although no party chairman has simultaneously held a cabinet secretaryship since 1947, several of them have made individual arrangements to attend meetings of the cabinet on a regular or intermittent basis. At these sessions, party chairmen have been kept informed of the administration's public policy proposals, have assessed their partisan ramifications, and have sought to establish clearance procedures for political appointments. While the chairman's physical presence at cabinet meetings provides him with an avenue of access to the president, it undoubtedly has greater symbolic than substantive significance.

The propensity of some modern presidents to name incumbent legislators party chairmen has been accompanied by the introduction of a new arena for interaction: the weekly congressional leadership meetings. Although none of these dual incumbents has been a ranking member of his party's congressional hierarchy, several of them along with some of their nonlegislative brethren have requested that they be present at these sessions where legislative strategy is planned and progress is monitored. The presence of the party chairman both enables him to coordinate impending developments in the legislative arena with his own organs of party policy and publicity and provides him with a forum to bring his point of view directly to the president.

However, the greater significance of this staffing trend rests not so much in the opening up of a new access opportunity as in the shifting presidential expectations regarding the role of the party chairman. In years past, his managerial responsibilities were primary. As these responsibilities have increasingly come under White House control, an alternative role has emerged for the party chairman: that of party spokesman, articulating, though not necessarily determining, party positions for the benefit of the media and the public and campaigning for party nominees for public office. Incumbent legislators tend to be well prepared to fill this particular role. At the same time, it is often unsettling to the national committee members and state party leaders who make up the party organization to have a legislator as their designated leader. Recall the analytical distinction between party-in-office and party organization. Party organization activists tend to resent the idea and reality of an interloper, and necessarily a part-time one at that, wielding authority over their prescribed domain. They generally believe their interests to be best represented by one of their own kind occupying the chairmanship full time (See Evans and Novak 1972, p. 363). As a result, in the 1970s both national party committees established their chairmanships as full-time, salaried positions.

This eligibility requirement complicated President Reagan's replacement of Richard Richards with Paul Laxalt, one of his oldest political allies and U.S. senator from Nevada. At the behest of the White House, the Republican National Committee created a new position, general chairman of the Republican Party, especially for Laxalt. In that role, Laxalt was made nominally responsible for supervision and coordination of Republican Party political operations on Capitol Hill, at party headquarters, at the White House, and in the forthcoming presidential campaign. However, party officials attending Laxalt's installation generally acknowledged that the influence of the White House Office at party headquarters would not be diminished. Meanwhile, to conform with party rules, the national committee elected Frank Fahrenkopf, a Laxalt protégé and former Nevada state GOP chairman, as its titular, salaried chairman with responsibility for party headquarters management (See Hoffman 1982; Peterson 1983; Raines 1983).

Ostensibly, staffing and management of the national party headquarters would appear to be a primary responsibility of the chairman, acting in his capacity as "administrator (Cotter and Hennessy 1964, p. 78). In fact, relatively few chairmen have demonstrated interest in personally managing the headquarters. The burdens of additional roles assigned a higher priority and other institutional and professional affiliations serve to conflict with and preclude that of administrator. The accepted procedure has been for the chairman, should he so wish, to delegate managerial authority to one of his chosen assistants, leaving himself free in varying degrees to engage in other activities. In effect, General Chairman Laxalt was expected to do just this; so the unanticipated impact of the full-time salaried chairman rule appears to have been to limit and diminish the titular chairmanship.

However, on several previous occasions in recent years, the White House has developed a presidential agent at party headquarters in a position nominally subordinate to the chairman but vested with managerial authority. That individual has then served as the channel of communication with the White House staff assistant in charge of party liaison, facilitating White House surveillance and supervision of the day-to-day activities of the headquarters. Such a situation developed during the Truman presidency when Truman's old Missouri political aide William Boyle was named executive vice-chairman of the Democratic National Committee then headed by Senator J. Howard McGrath (Leviero 1949). In his first months in office, Richard Nixon sought to perpetrate an analogous arrangement at the Republican National Committee. He promised a position there to long-time associate Murray Chotiner with the understanding that Chotiner would have responsibility for running the headquarters operation with a commensurate title under a figurehead chairman. When the designated chairman, Representative Rogers Morton, balked, the plan fell through; but Nixon later successfully established a similar format at the outset of the tenure of Morton's successor, Senator Robert Dole (See Gregory 1970; Evans and Novak 1972, pp. 71-74, 364).

Party chairmen who were not legislators have also been subjected to this treatment. While retaining Kennedy-designate John Bailey as party chairman, Lyndon Johnson sent his Texas operative Clifton Carter to the Democratic National Committee to represent his interests there (See T. White 1965, pp. 416-17; Lamb and Smith 1968, pp. 153-59). Jimmy Carter assigned fellow Georgian Phil Wise to the staff of party chairman Ken Curtis as executive director, although after the appointment was announced, Wise decided not to accept it (Weaver 1977). Even though this demonstration of White House control does not require a legislator in the chairman's office, such a designation facilitates it; in doing so, the president may simultaneously assuage the fears of elements within the party organization that their interests are not being adequately represented.

Laxalt and Fahrenkopf notwithstanding, this pattern strongly suggests contemporary presidential tendencies to view the titular chairmanship in nonmanagerial terms and to bring about close presidential oversight and management of party headquarters. From the party chairman's perspective, while headquarters administration is not likely to be assigned preeminence, it is still an integral part of his overall responsibility. When the White House takes steps to place a presidential agent at the headquarters, even with the chairman's knowledge and consent, this compromises the chairman's authority and status with the White House, the party, and the public.

Clearly, not all White House-national committee interaction produces estrangement and reduces national party prestige and autonomy. Controversy does not lurk at every intersection. Congenial accommodation characterizes a great deal of activity by the national party organization on behalf of the White House. Routinely, the financial and organizational structures of the national committee are utilized to front what are really White House programs. An obvious example is the White House practice of billing the national committee for any travel and living expenses incurred by the president when he is visibly attending to his responsibilities as party leader. Such situations include presidential campaigning for himself and other party candidates and his appearances at party-sponsored affairs such as fund-raisers and rallies, including the national convention.

Occasionally, the national committee can be prevailed upon to carry on its payroll individuals who actually work for the White House. For example, prior to and during the 1948 presidential campaign, the Research Division of the Democratic National Committee was set up only nominally under the organizational umbrella of the party headquarters. It was housed separately and functioned as an adjunct of the Truman White House under the direction of White House aides (Ross 1969, pp. 80-81, 163). Stephen Hess (n.d.) reports that in September 1958 he was hired by the White House to write speeches for the president during the midterm campaign. He was assigned an office at the White House. However, because of budgetary restrictions and the limited and temporary role he was to play, he was formally employed by the Republican National Committee.

Another commonplace arena of interaction involves the preparation by the national committee staff of a partisan publication to serve as a publicity organ for the administration and to flay the opposition. The White House staff is in a position to furnish the party headquarters with data and inside information to make the publication attractive, relevant, and substantive, so such assistance is both sought and welcomed by the party headquarters. However, even here an active White House role in supplying editorial guidance may lead to its monitoring and controlling the output. During the Nixon administration, reports Clifford W. Brown (Ripon Society and Brown 1974, p. 230), the Republican National Committee publication *Monday* became "so popular with the president that the White House staff, in effect, snatched it away from the national committee staff." The White House-designated editor, John Lofton, "turned a credible and informative publication into a noncredible smear sheet."

An impending national nominating convention provides the setting for a great deal of interaction between the White House and the national party organization. When the party is out of power, the national committee operation is supposed to be neutral toward competing candidates for the nomination. However, when there is an incumbent president available and seeking the nomination, the logical assumption is that the party headquarters over which he has established his control will be both strongly supportive of his candidacy and in a strategic position to assist in his nomination. Moreover, when the incumbent is not himself a candidate, the party machinery can be expected to support such efforts as he may undertake to influence the party's choice as his successor.

The exercise of presidential party leadership at conventions has been associated with a long string of successful outcomes. Not since Chester Arthur in 1884 has an incumbent who formally sought his party's nomination been denied it. Indeed most of his successors have been nominated with consummate ease. However, very recently two consecutive rather strong challenges have been mounted, suggesting that post-1968 reform of convention delegate selection methods have had the impact of partially offsetting the advantages accorded the incumbent through his control of the party machinery (See Ranney 1978).

On these occasions when the incumbent president is not a candidate for the nomination, he is naturally interested in his party's choice as his successor; and he likely has his own preference. The convention system of presidential nomination has produced very few instances of successful transfer of the nomination from a retiring incumbent to a designated understudy (David, Goldman, and Bain 1960, p. 116). However, in recent years two clear inheritances have occurred: Eisenhower-Nixon in 1960 and Johnson-Humphrey 1968. In addition, Truman endorsed Stevenson's successful nomination in 1952.

On each of these occasions, the retiring president had aides monitoring convention arrangements and deeply involved in maneuverings on his behalf during the proceedings (see Leviero 1952; Kessell 1962; Herbers 1968; Humphrey 1976, pp. 388-89). Here again an expanded staff capacity has enabled incumbents to maintain control.

Traditionally, the national party has convened only to nominate its presidential candidate, with other activities subordinated and occurring in the context of this major function. In 1974 the out-of-power Democrats met in Kansas City for an issues conference midway through the presidential term. Four years later, with Democrat Jimmy Carter in the White House, another conference was held in Memphis, providing an unprecedented opportunity for White House-national party organization interaction. On this occasion the Carter White House and his appointees at the national party headquarters designed and controlled the agenda and mounted a monitoring operation of the floor of the convention to ensure that the administration's positions would prevail against intraparty challenges (Cook 1978). The effort replicated the typical White House pattern of surveillance and supervision repeatedly demonstrated at the nominating conventions.

The adjournment of the nominating convention inaugurates the general election phase of the presidential campaign. Regardless of whether the incumbent is the nominee, his very presence constitutes a consideration of critical significance with respect to the role and status of his party's national organization in that campaign. When incumbents have been nominated, they have ordinarily declined to exercise their prerogatives of chairman selection. Rather, in anticipation of nomination, they have installed their choices as party chairman well in advance of the conventions, and have retained them at least through the conclusion of the campaigns. Interestingly, this arrangement has not produced an abundance of integrated presidential campaign organizations, despite its logistical attractiveness given the president's staffing prerogatives at party headquarters. Rather, the White House staff has emerged as the dominant organizational entity in modern reelection campaigns, seconded by personal campaign organizations (see the following descriptions of incumbents' presidential campaign organizations: Ross 1969, pp. 81, 165, 171-72; Phillips 1966, p. 225; Adams 1961, pp. 224-34; Ogden and Peterson 1968, pp. 98-101; T. White 1965, pp. 413-21; Ripon Society and Brown 1974, pp. 63-70; Witcover 1977, pp. 537-38; Bonafede, Malbin, and Walters 1976; Bonafede 1976; 1980; Light 1980).

For retiring incumbents, transfers of party leadership to heirs have been complicated by mutual misgivings that affect the status of the national party organization. The nominee's prerogative of selecting the party chairman and taking over the party machinery is potentially difficult to exercise since it entails replacing loyalists of the sitting president. Such a sensitive decision can be a crucial consideration affecting campaign integration or autonomy. In turn, while the retiring incumbents have not questioned the nominees' "rights" to so claim party leadership, neither have they shrunk from continuing to conduct their own liaison on a limited scale. For example, Harry Truman, while unenthusiastic about Adlai Stevenson's choice of Stephen Mitchell as party chairman, maintained his practice of meeting weekly with the chairman and put himself at the disposal of the national committee for campaign involvement (Truman 1965, p. 561; W. White 1952; "Truman is 'Buck Private' " 1952). In 1960 President Eisenhower personally attended to the placement of Fred Scribner in the position of manager at the Republican National Committee headquarters in the absence of party chairman Thruston Morton, an Eisenhower holdover, who took on extensive campaigning assignments (Scribner n.d.). Interestingly, the most perfunctory of these retiring presidents in his party relations was Lyndon Johnson (see Hawthorne 1968; Fleming 1968), who had been perhaps the most heavy-handed in his supervision to that point (see Reed 1967; Evans and Novak 1968, p. 598; T. White 1970, pp. 129-30). In the relationship between a president and the national party organization, this postconvention liaison concludes the interaction that began with his initial nomination.

CONCLUSION

This inquiry into the relationship between the president and the national party organization has revealed a common thread throughout diverse presidencies: White House dominance, facilitated through presidential staffing prerogatives at the party headquarters and supervision of those agents by the White House staff. While the tone of the relationship has varied according to a particular president's partisan background, character, and style, the basic structural pattern has remained constant for over three decades.

A major casualty of this modern pattern of party-presidential relations has been the national party chairman. His public standing has decreased as nonorganizational recruits personally loyal to the president increasingly have replaced him in such pivotal linkage roles as campaign manager, patronage dispenser, cabinet politician, and political adviser and operator. A contemporary party chairman undertaking such roles would be regarded as a conspicuous exception to the norm. More often, his modern role in presidential politics has proved to be that of a figurehead-spokesman, estranged from the president's inner circle and bypassed in the party relations conducted by the White House aides at party headquarters and with lesser party chieftains.

Generations of presidency scholars have viewed weak national party organization as a major limitation on presidential leadership (see Herring 1940, pp. 22-23, 74-75; Burns 1967, pp. 325-30; Hargrove 1974, pp. 295-98; Cronin 1980, pp. 138-174). This analysis indicates that presidential party leadership is partially responsible for national party weakness. First in the campaign and later in the White House, party leadership has manifested itself in an unwillingness to tolerate interference and rivalry from party organization representatives not solely and wholly tied to presidential perspectives and interests. An organizational dynamic at the White House has produced not merely inattention but also deliberate and systematic efforts to undermine the development and maintenance of the stronger national party organization. The destructiveness of presidential leadership toward its object, the national party, is clearly not in keeping with Neustadt's (1960) conventional conception as the exercise of personal bargaining and persuasion.

Meanwhile, the displacement of the national parties from their previously significant station within the presidency has been accompanied by their fundamental reorientation of organizational tasks and priorities in the direction of party building. These efforts have met with unprecedented success. Party organization power, influence, and authority increasingly have become centralized at the national level, and national parties have become potent institutions on the political scene (see Cotter and Bibby, 1980). However, these advances have come to pass mainly during periods when the party has been out of power (see Cotter and Hennessy 1964, pp. 211-24; Sundquist 1968, pp. 405-15; Bibby and Huckshorn 1968; Crotty 1978; Bibby 1980; Polsby 1983, p. 36). Further, they have tended to stall when the party's nominee enters the White House (see Cotter and Hennessy 1964, p. 223; Saloma and Sontag 1972, p. 99). Ironically, while the capture of the presidency is the manifest objective of the national party organization, achievement of the goal is accompanied by reduced organizational antonomy and power. Paradoxically, avoidance of presidential leadership appears to be the route to party development.

Turning finally to the impact of presidential party leadership on the presidency, the assumption by the White House of responsibility for the management of party relations has undoubtedly strengthened the position of the White House staff within the presidency. However,

EDITOR'S PERSPECTIVE

Might the Parties be Better Off without Presidents?

It is commonly assumed that the national party organizations are strengthened when the party holds the White House. Recent experience indicates that the organization may actually be strengthened more when the party is out of the White House. Bibby (1980) and Cotter and Bibby (1980) have documented the rejuvenation of the Republican Party's national organizaton while Jimmy Carter was in the White House. Clay F. Richards suggested in a July 1982 newspaper column that the same may have been happening to the Democratic Party with Ronald Reagan in the presidency. That column follows in its entirety.

Democrats rebuild party ties

by Clay F. Richards, United Press International

WASHINGTON—Having a president in the White House is not necessarily in the best interest of a political party.

The Republican Party was pretty nearly sucked dry by the Nixon years and Jimmy Carter did the same thing to the Democrats during his four years in office.

That the two major parties survived is in large part due to the leadership of two national chairmen—Bill Brock, who rebuilt the GOP while Carter was in office, and Charles Manatt, who is doing the same kind of job right now while President Reagan is in office.

While the Reagan administration is somewhat of a drain on the resources of the Republican National Committee right now, he is not hurting the party badly for several reasons.

First among them is that the Republicans are drawing in so much money that there is enough to finance both the White House's political activity, and the party's 1982 election efforts at the same time.

Second, Republican Chairman Richard Richards is a prudent leader devoted to the nuts and bolts activities of building the party at the grass roots level rather than being a grandstanding party leader with the party crumbling beneath him.

The leaner Democrats devoted a considerable portion of their limited finances to supporting the political activities of the Carter administration. And Carter had almost a disdain for the party, refusing to do the kind of fund-raising activity that would have replenished what he was spending.

Even though he is gone, Carter is still burdening the party with some of his leftover campaign debt.

Manatt has moved swiftly and surely to overhaul the party operation.

EDITOR'S PERSPECTIVE (continued)

The bridges to their natural allies in labor, burned by George McGovern in 1972, were quickly rebuilt by adding 20 union leaders to the Democratic National Committee, five of them to the executive committee.

The delegate selection process was overhauled so that more party leaders and fewer party bombthrowers will pick the 1984 candidate and write the platform.

A direct mail operation was started that in a few years, if properly pursued, will make the Democrats capable of competing with the GOP dollar for dollar.

Democratic members of Congress, somehow viewed for years as really not part of the Democratic Party, have been openly courted and brought into active roles in running the party.

The party finally entered into a financial arrangement that wiped out the longstanding debt it owed on the presidential campaigns of Robert Kennedy and Hubert Humphrey.

Democrats were able to hold a midterm convention in Philadelphia last month where the enemy was Ronald Reagan, and not fellow Democrats as had been the case in the two previous such meetings.

Before he is out of office, Manatt has vowed to achieve another goal — a home for the party in a building it owns, instead of the rented space it now occupies in downtown Washington.

In short, nothing builds a party like being out of office.

this is not to say that it has strengthened the presidency in any meaningful way. Rather, the minimization of dependence and enhancement of control ostensibly afforded by this internalization may be merely illusory. Instead, it may have isolated and alienated this source of traditional support from the president, leaving him more vulnerable than in the past to the tides of fortune. Thus, the real victim in the relationship between the president and the national party organization may be the president.

REFERENCES

Adams, Sherman. 1961. *First Hand Report.* New York: Harper.

Agranoff, Robert. 1976. "The New Style of Campaigning: The Decline of Party and the Rise of Candidate-Centered Technology." In *The New Style of Election Campaigns,* 2d ed., ed. Robert Agranoff, pp. 3-47. Boston: Holbrook.

Bibby, John F. 1980. "Party Renewal in the National Republican Party." In *Party Renewal: Theory and Practice,* ed. Gerald Pomper, pp. 102-15. New York: Praeger.

_____, and Robert J. Huckshorn. 1968. "Out-Party Strategy: Republican National Committee Rebuilding Politics." In *Republican Politics: The 1964 Campaign and its Aftermath for the Party,* ed. Bernard Cosman and Robert J. Huckshorn, pp. 205-33. New York: Praeger.

Bonafede, Dom. 1976. "Campaign Report: A Glimmer of Hope Burns in the Heart of the PFC." *National Journal,* October 2, pp. 1379-80.

_____. 1980. "White House Report: It's Extravagant, It's Majestic, It's Carter on the Campaign Trail." *National Journal,* October 25, pp. 1790-94.

_____, Michael J. Malbin, and Robert Walters. 1976. "Campaign Report: Will It Be Hard for Americans to Say 'No' to a President?" *National Journal,* August 28, pp. 1198-1213.

Bone, Hugh A. 1958. *Party Committees and National Politics.* Seattle: University of Washington Press.

Bruno, Hal. 1977. "Democrats in Disarray." *Newsweek,* December 17, pp. 25, 28.

Burns, James M. 1967. *The Deadlock of Democracy: Four Party Politics in America.* Englewood Cliffs, N.J.: Prentice-Hall.

Cook, Rhodes. 1978. "New Party Rules: The Real Memphis Legacy." *Congressional Quarterly Weekly Report,* December 16, pp. 3533-35, 3455.

Cotter, Cornelius P., and John F. Bibby. 1980. "Institutional Development of Parties and the Thesis of Party Decline." *Political Science Quarterly* 95: 1-27.

Cotter, Cornelius P., and Bernard C. Hennessy. 1964. *Politics Without Power: The National Party Committees.* New York: Atherton.

Cronin, Thomas E. 1980. *The State of the Presidency,* 2d ed. Boston: Little, Brown.

Crotty, William J. 1977. *Political Reform and the American Experiment.* New York: Crowell.

———. 1978. *Decision for the Democrats: Reforming the Party Structure.* Baltimore: Johns Hopkins University Press.

David, Paul T., Ralph M. Goldman, and Richard C. Bain. 1960. *The Politics of National Party Conventions.* Washington, D.C.: Brookings Institution.

Davis, James W. 1967. *Presidential Primaries: The Road to the White House.* New York: Crowell.

Donovan, Robert J. 1982. *Tumultuous Years: The Presidency of Harry S. Truman, 1949-1953.* New York: W. W. Norton.

Evans, Rowland, and Robert Novak. 1968. *Lyndon B. Johnson: The Exercise of Power.* New York: New American Library.

———. 1972. *Nixon in the White House: The Frustration of Power.* New York: Random House.

Farley, James A. 1938. *Behind the Ballots: The Personal History of a Politician.* New York: Harcourt, Brace.

———. 1948. *Jim Farley's Story: The Roosevelt Years.* New York: Whittlesey.

Fenno, Richard. 1959. *The President's Cabinet: An Analysis in the Period from Wilson to Eisenhower.* New York: Vintage.

Ferrell, Robert H., ed. 1981. *The Eisenhower Diaries.* New York: W. W. Norton.

Fleming, Thomas J. 1966. "Selling the Product Named Hubert Humphrey." New York *Times Magazine*, October 13, pp. 45-47.

Fowler, Dorothy G. 1943. *The Cabinet Politician: The Postmaster General, 1829-1909.* New York: Columbia University Press.

Goldman, Ralph M. 1951. "Party Chairman and Party Faction, 1899-1900." Ph.D. diss. University of Chicago.

Gregory, Neal. 1970. "CPR Report: Republican National Committee Finds Defending President a New Role." *National Journal*, May 2, pp. 741-45.

Hargrove, Erwin C. 1974. *The Power of the Modern Presidency.* New York: Knopf.

Hawthorne, Mark. 1968. "Democrats Map Staff Changes: Convention Manager Leaving." New York *Times*, September 6, p. 34.

Henry, Laurin. 1969. "The Presidency, Executive Staffing and the Bureaucracy." In *The Presidency*, ed. Aaron Wildavsky, pp. 529-57. Boston: Little, Brown.

Herbers, John. 1968. "Johnson Seen Calling Tune." New York *Times*, pp. 1, 30.

Herring, Pendleton. 1940. *Presidential Leadership: The Political Relations of Congress and the Chief Executive.* New York: Rinehart.

Hess, Stephen. n.d. Oral History Transcript, Columbia University-Eisenhower Library, Abilene, Kansas.

Hoffman, David. 1982. "New GOP Chief Takes Job Believing Reagan Will Run in 1984." Washington *Post*, November 7, p. A3.

Humphrey, Hubert H. 1976. *The Education of a Public Man.* Ed. Norman Shearer. Garden City, N.Y.: Doubleday.

Johnson, Richard T. 1974. *Managing the White House.* New York: Harper.

Kaufman, Herbert. 1965. "The Growth of the Federal Personnel System." In *The Federal Government Service*, 2d ed., ed. Wallace S. Sayre, pp. 7-69. Englewood Cliffs, N.J., Prentice-Hall.

Kayden, Xandra. 1978. *Campaign Organization*. Lexington, Mass.: D.C. Heath.

Keech, William R., and Donald R. Matthews. 1976. *The Party's Choice*. Washington, D.C.: Brookings Institution.

Kessel, John H. 1962. "Political Leadership: The Nixon Version." In *Inside Politics: The National Conventions, 1960*, ed. Paul Tillett, pp. 39-54. Dobbs Ferry, N.Y.: Oceana.

_____. 1968. *The Goldwater Coalition: Republican Strategies in 1964*. Indianapolis: Bobbs-Merrill.

_____. 1980. *Presidential Campaign Politics: Coalition Strategies and Citizen Responses*. Homewood, Ill.: Dorsey.

Lamb, Karl A., and Paul B. Smith. 1968. *Campaign Decision Making: The Presidential Election of 1964*. Belmont, Calif.: Wadsworth.

Leviero, Anthony. 1949. "Truman Gives Post to Campaign Aide." New York *Times*, February 9, p. 30.

_____. 1952. "Truman Reserves Key Role in 'Wide Open' Nomination." New York *Times*, July 20, sec. 4, p. E5.

_____. 1953. "Roberts Resigns; G.O.P. Head Scored by Kansas Inquiry." New York *Times*, March 28, pp. 1, 11.

Light, Larry. 1980. "Gift for Electoral Politics: Carter's Style of Campaigning Provides Tough Competition." *Congressional Quarterly Weekly Report*, September 13, pp. 2702-08.

Mackenzie, G. Calvin. 1981. *The Politics of Presidential Appointments*. New York: The Free Press.

Mann, Dean E., and Jameson W. Doig. 1965. *The Assistant Secretaries: Problems and Processes of Appointment*. Washington, D.C.: Brookings Institution.

Mansfield, Harvey C. 1965. "Political Parties, Patronage, and The Federal Government Service." In *The Federal Government Service*, 2d ed., by Wallace S. Sayre, pp. 114-62. Englewood Cliffs, N.J.: Prentice-Hall.

Martin, John Bartlow. 1976. *The Life of Adlai Stevenson*, Vol. 1: *Adlai Stevenson of Illinois*. Garden City, N.Y.: Doubleday.

Neustadt, Richard E. 1960. *Presidential Power: The Politics of Leadership*. New York: John Wiley.

Nixon, Richard M. 1962. *Six Crises*. Garden City, N.Y.: Doubleday.

Odgen, Daniel M., Jr., and Arthur L. Peterson. 1968. *Electing the President*, rev. ed. San Francisco: Chandler.

Perlmutter, Nathan. 1952. "Eisenhower's Choice." *Nation*, September 6, pp. 191-92.

Peterson, Bill. 1983. "Republicans Endorse Reagan-Bush in 1984, Put Laxalt in Charge." Washington *Post*, January 29, p. A7.

Phillips, Cabell. 1966. *The Truman Presidency: The History of a Triumphant Succession*. New York: Macmillan.

Polsby, Nelson W. 1983. *Consequences of Party Reform*. New York: Oxford University Press.

Raines, Howell. 1983. "Laxalt and Political Ally Chosen for G.O.P. Posts." New York *Times*, January 29, p. 10.

Ranney, Austin. 1978. "The Political Parties: Reform and Decline." In *The New American Political System*, ed. Anthony King, pp. 213-47. Washington, D.C.: American Enterprise Institute.

Reed, Roy. 1967. "Johnson's Traffic Cop One of the Most Important Men in the Capital." New York *Times*, September 17, p. 70.

Remini, Robert V. 1976. "The Emergence of Political Parties and Their Effect on the Presidency." In *Power and the Presidency*, ed. Philip C. Dolce and George H. Skau, pp. 24-34. New York: Scribner's.

Ripon Society, and Clifford W. Brown, Jr. 1974. *Jaws of Victory: The Game Plan Politics of 1972, the Crisis of the Republican Party, and the Future of the Constitution*. Boston: Little, Brown.

Ross, Irwin. 1969. *The Loneliest Campaign: The Truman Victory of 1948*. New York: New American Library.

Saloma, John S. III, and Frederick H. Sontag. 1972. *Parties: The Real Opportunity for Effective Citizen Politics*. New York: Knopf.

Scribner, Fred. n.d. Oral History Transcript. Columbia University-Eisenhower Library, Abilene, Kansas.

Smith, Terence. 1977. "Democrat Leader Denies White House Forced Him to Quit." New York *Times*, December 9, p. 12.

Sorauf, Frank J. 1968. *Party Politics in America*. Boston: Little, Brown.

Staff of the New York *Times*, eds. 1973. *The Watergate Hearings: Break-in and Cover-up*. New York: Viking.

Steinberg, Alfred. 1962. *The Man from Missouri: The Life and Times of Harry S. Truman*. New York: Putnam.

Sullivan, Denis G., Jeffrey L. Pressman, Benjamin I. Page, and John J. Lyons. 1974. *The Politics of Representation: The Democratic National Convention, 1972*. New York: St. Martin's.

Sundquist, James L. 1968. *Politics and Policy: The Eisenhower, Kennedy, and Johnson Years*. Washington, D.C.: Brookings Institution.

Taylor, Paul, and Lou Cannon. 1982. "RNC's Embattled Richards Resigns; Timing and Performance Questioned." Washington *Post*, October 5, p. H5.

Thompson, James D. 1967. *Organizations in Action*. New York: McGraw-Hill.

Truman, Harry S. 1945. "The President's News Conference of October 31, 1945." In *Public Papers of the President of the United States*, pp. 450-57. Washington, D.C.: U.S. Government Printing Office.

_____. 1965. *Memoirs*, Vol. 2: *Years of Trial and Hope*. New York: Doubleday.

"Truman is 'Buck Private,' But Awaits Tour 'Go.'" 1952. New York *Times*, August 3, p. 51.

Wallerstein, Immanuel. 1969. "The Decline of the Party in Single-Party African States." In *Political Parties and Political Development*, ed. Joseph LaPalombara and Myron Weiner, pp. 201-14. Princeton, N.J.: Princeton University Press.

Weaver, Warren, Jr. 1977. "Carter Campaign Aides Leading Democratic Staff." New York *Times*, January 19, p. 21.

White, Theodore H. 1965. *The Making of the President, 1964.* New York: Atheneum.

_____. 1970. *The Making of the President, 1968.* New York: Atheneum.

_____. 1973. *The Making of the President, 1972* New York: Atheneum.

_____. 1975. *Breach of Faith: The Fall of Richard Nixon.* New York: Atheneum.

White, William S. 1952. "Mitchell Stresses Role of President." New York *Times*, August 21, p. 1.

Wilder, Philip S. n.d. "The Republican National Committee Chairmanship under Eisenhower." Unpublished manuscript.

Wilson, James Q. 1973. *Political Organizations.* New York: Basic Books.

Witcover, Jules. 1977. *Marathon: The Pursuit of the Presidency, 1972-1976.* New York: Viking.

4

THOUGHTS OF A DEPARTING NATIONAL CHAIRMAN: INTERVIEW WITH RICHARD RICHARDS

From an Independent Network Interview with Richard Richards

*R*ichard Richards was selected by Ronald Reagan to replace William Brock as chairman of the Republican National Committee following the 1980 election. Richards served until January 1983. After announcing in October 1982 that he would not seek another term as chairman, and just before the November elections, Richards was interviewed on the Independent Network's "From the Editor's Desk" by producer and moderator Richard Heffner, Associated Press executive editor Lou Boccardi, and *Wall Street Journal* editorial writer Susan Lee. Portions of the interview deal with the relationship of the party to the White House and with presidential midterm campaigning, and are illustrative of themes developed in this book. The following excerpts were selected by the editor and are published here with the permission of Mr. Richards, the panel participants, and New York television station WPIX.

*   *   *   *

HEFFNER: Our guest, in Washington, is Richard Richards, selected by Ronald Reagan to be chairman of the Republican National Committee after his 1980 presidential victory.

A year ago, it was rumored that opponents in the Reagan White House wanted to push Mr. Richards out of his job. He denied that, he said he had the president's confidence, planned to stay the course, and, as for another term, said, "I have to see how bloody I am at the time."

Well, now, even before that time, even before the coming elections, Mr. Richards has announced he will not serve again. Perhaps, then, we ought to find out today how bloody the Republican National chairman is.

Mr. Richards, is that a fair question to ask you? You have a reputation for being quite candid, and at the time of that statement last year, indeed, you said, "I'm a very candid and straightforward guy; I don't lie to people." And that's your reputation—as a straight shooter. Why won't you be there where you have been for the last two years?

RICHARDS: Well, Richard, I think primarily for two reasons. Number one, the president did not specifically ask me to stay on. And number two, this is a tough job and it's an especially difficult job when you have the White House and when, as I indicated earlier, every clerk in the White House thinks he can do my job better than I can—and they don't even know what it is. The combination of those things, I think, just makes it attractive to do something else in 1983 and 1984. And I have to assume, Richard, that maybe the president wants to reorganize the committee more along the line of a reelection committee than the way we've been operating in 1981 and 1982. At any rate, he did not ask me to stay on and I did not ask him to [let me] stay on and I've made a decision to get out.

LEE: Previously, you've complained that the White House staff pushed you out because you weren't glamorous enough. Now, if that's true—and you seem quite glamorous to me—what kind of advice would you—will you give your successor on how to deal with the White House staff?

RICHARDS: Well, [I'll tell you what] I think we really need to do, Susan, in order to accomplish the things that I think need to be done with the White House and with the National Committee. I think the political operation of the reelect Reagan effort, if that's what it is, ought to be in the Republican National Committee and not in the White House. I think when you have a political shop down there, automatically you set up a buffer between the primary movers in the White House and the Republican National Committee, and that creates some problems that you really don't need.

LEE: Well, at one time, you said perhaps there should be no buffer from the White House. Would you go with that?

RICHARDS: Have no buffer from the White House—certainly; I think the national chairman really ought to be able to talk to the president and the chief of staff and the other political operatives in the White House—and I'm speaking of the top echelon—without going through a political operation, as such.

BOCCARDI: If we could stay with that for just a second, have you told the president that? And what's his view of it?

RICHARDS: I haven't told that to the president, but I have discussed it with Jim Baker and Mike Deaver. I don't know what their view of it is. I didn't ask them their opinions. I simply indicated that I thought that was a reasonable thing to do; and hopefully I'll get a chance to do it. As a matter of fact, I plan to be with the president next week on the campaign trail, and then on election eve, so I'm sure I'll get a chance to say that and I will indeed do it.

BOCCARDI: Speaking of the campaign trail, you said a few weeks ago that you didn't think the president was scheduled for enough campainging. Are you satisfied now that he's doing enough?

RICHARDS: I think the president is doing about all he can do. As a matter of fact, I'm very pleased that he's on the road to the degree that he is. I think he's going to help a lot of our gubernatorial candidates who are in close races. I'm certain that he's helping many of our senatorial candidates. I was with the president the other day in Peoria, and he did a great job for Bob Michel and, I think, gave him a real boost in his home town.

.   .   .   .   .

LEE: I'd like to ask Lou's question in a slightly different way. I remember, back last summer, you were really behind the strategy of getting the president committed to this coampaign, even though midterm elections are usually local affairs. Well, now, four months have passed, and there of course have been unremittingly bad economic statistics, and quite recently we've had a picture of Republican candidates trying to distance themselves somewhat form the president and from the national Republican program. Do you still think that your strategy of getting the president out there to make this sort of a referendum on Reaganomics was the correct strategy?

RICHARDS: Susan, I have to say that I think unquestionably the best thing going for the Republican Party today is Ronald Reagan. Although everyone does not accept Reaganomics, the president personally is very popular; he's very strong. There may be a few candidates that want to separate themselves a little bit on the issues, but I'll tell you one thing: I don't know any candidate that wouldn't give his right arm to get the president out in his district and campaign for him. We're getting a lot of requests to get the president out. If the president can't come, they want a videotape; they want him on radio; they want him any way they can get him. So I really don't think it's an accurate statement that they're trying to distance themselves or run away from the president. I think quite the contrary.

LEE: Well, there's a Republican in Rhode Island who in fact is running against the president.

RICHARDS: Well, that's a rare case, and I've been out with the president on the campaign trail in a race like that of Millicent Fenwick [of New Jersey], who has not really supported the president down the line on legislation; but the president doesn't require everyone [to] go down the line with him, 100 percent. There is no litmus test in the party. You have to pass a certain level of support before you get our money and our effort. We expect and would hope that Republicans are with us on the big issues, on the fundamental issues. Certainly we're planning for that first vote in the House of Representatives or the first vote in the Senate that organizes that particular legislative body.

LEE: I can't resist asking you what that litmus test that Gary Arnold [congressional candidate from California] didn't pass, so he didn't get funds [from the national Republican Party].

RICHARDS: Well, I'll have to be candid with you, Susan. On a lot of these tests—and I'm reluctant to do it, but my attitude has always been to be candid and straightforward—we look at candidates as we go into the campaign, and we look at some that we think cannot lose in any event, because they're very popular, they're in a very good district, they've got a good record in the district, and we don't worry about them. On the other hand, we look at some candidates that we don't think can really win—candidates that haven't put together a campaign team, haven't organized, and haven't raised any money, and we almost have to write them off at the outset. When we find either of those two categories, we don't make financial commitments to them.

BOCCARDI: What about the Senate race in California? There were several stories this week that said the the president was being asked not to come into California, for fear of hurting Pete Wilson. Were those stories untrue?

RICHARDS: Well, I haven't talked to anyone who knows. I've read that in the press. But I'll tell you Pete Wilson was anxious to get the president in there, before. He's been there. He's helped Pete in the campaign. The president, of course, is very popular in California. There is such a thing as overkill, and a lot of the opposition, when you bring in too many of our big guns, talk about bringing in the outsiders rather than letting the local folks made up their mind. There may have been some of that in the strategy. But I'm sure Pete Wilson was delighted to have the president out there for him when he was there, earlier.

. . . . .

[After concluding the interview portion of the progam, the panelists were asked to comment on Mr. Richards's remarks. Excerpts follow.]

HEFFNER: Susan and Lou, you're the gatekeepers. How are you going to interpret what we've just heard to the American people? Susan?

LEE: Well, I actually thought what I found most interesting is the sort of scapegoat notion. If the Republicans lose very big, in [November], they're going to need a scapegoat, and what is more perfect than the chairman of the Republican National Committee? However I think what Richards has done is that he's removed himself as a scapegoat by simply resigning or allowing himself to be pushed out or, at the very least, announcing it a week before the election. It was a sort of an interesting preemptive strike — one you don't often see in Washington — I think it was very slickly done. And it's interesting, in what he said — he's been very, very optimistic all along, on the Republican prospects; and one of the reasons, apparently, the White House staff has been annoyed and irritated with him is his optimism. I think the fact that he's sort of taking himself out of the running as a scapegoat, on the one hand, and some scaling down of his optimism, on the other, makes me think that perhaps the Republicans are pretty nervous.

BOCCARDI: Well, he may have jumped, as he said, but I think it's clear that somebody handed him a parachute. . . .

5

THE GAVELS OF AUGUST: PRESIDENTS AND NATIONAL PARTY CONVENTIONS

Howard L. Reiter

V. O. Key once wrote that "in a fairly real sense, the national convention is the national party" (1964, p. 431). If this is so, then there is no better way to observe the opportunities and dilemmas of presidential party leadership than at those quadrennial events. Conventions can serve as barometers of many political trends, from the state of party organization to the status of social groups to the influence of the chief executive on those who are nominally in his corner. Here, our task is to ask three basic questions: What resoures does a president have to influence the actions and outcomes of national conventions? What significant barriers are there to the exercise of his leadership? Have those barriers grown stronger or weaker in recent years?

Before addressing these questions, though, we must first consider some important contextual factors that help to shape the relationship between the president and the convention. The nominating process itself has undergone major changes in the past few decades, and it is important to recognize those changes in order to assess their possible impact on the role of the president. The delineation and assessment of these changes has spawned a sizable literature, and for our purposes we need not delve very deeply into it. It will be sufficient to note, first of all, that power at both parties' national conventions has devolved from organizational leaders to candidate-centered cadres, with issue-oriented caucuses playing a secondary role, particularly within the Democratic Party. In other words, the past pattern of party leaders assembling in smoke-filled rooms to wheel and deal over the nomination has been superseded by the arrival at the convention of the candidate who has won a majority of the delegates in a long process of primaries, caucuses, and state conventions.

The source of this change has been attributed to two underlying trends. One is the gradual weakening of party organization over many decades and at all levels of government (Crotty and Jacobson 1980). This party decline has in turn been linked to the electronic mass media, which have replaced party organization as the primary mode of political communication; to the rise of national interest groups, which provide campaign funds to candidates; to the assimilation of the American electorate into the middle class, which deprived traditional party machines of an electoral base dependent on their favors; and to political reforms such as the direct primary and civil service, which weaken the control of party organization over, respectively, nominations and patronage. Whatever the causes, the effect of these changes on the presidential nominating process seems clear: State and local party leaders, lacking the resources to control their own organizations, are less equipped than they used to be to bring well-disciplined delegations to national conventions. Instead of being pawns ready to vote as their leaders dictate, delegates have become free agents eager to vote for the candidates of their choice, regardless of the whim of the local leader.

The second factor that has influenced changes at national conventions has been the series of changes in the rules that have affected both parties for nearly two decades. The Democrats' loyalty oath and racial discrimination controversies of the 1950s and early 1960s were succeeded by the brawling, bloody 1968 convention, which established two commissions to reform the rules in time for the 1972 convention. The more prominent commission, widely known as the McGovern-Fraser Commission, produced a report that advocated many changes intended to achieve procedural fairness in the delegation selection process, adequate representation for each candidate's supporters, and more women, blacks, and young people as delegates (*Mandate for Reform* 1970). Subsequent commissions established a party charter, midterm party conferences, and proportional representation for candidates' partisans. Perhaps the most important unintended consequence of the reforms was a proliferation of delegate selection primaries, which many states decided would be the easiest way to comply with national party guidelines. By 1980, three-quarters of both parties' delegates were chosen in primary states.

For our purposes one of the most important developments concerns the ability of a president to win his party's nomination. Here we can see some clear historical patterns. From 1792 through 1840, every president won the right to seek a second term. From 1844 through 1884, only Lincoln and Grant received a second nomination. Since 1888, every president who has fought for the nomination has succeeded in capturing it. However, there have been signs in recent years that the struggle is becoming more difficult. Until 1976, only three twentieth-century presidents have been opposed by as many as 10 percent of the national convention delegates: Taft in 1912, Franklin Roosevelt in 1940, and Truman in 1948. In addition, Truman in 1952 and Lyndon Johnson in 1968 showed every sign of running until disappointing showings in the New Hampshire primary; and they may have been harbingers of the more recent trend of serious opposition to incumbents' bids for second terms. Ford in 1976 and Carter in 1980 faced strong opponents who ran ahead in early polls and won a number of primaries. At their respective conventions, Ford won only a bare majority of delegates, and Carter netted fewer than two-thirds — the worst incumbent showings since 1912.

Presumably the factors that explain why the power of party leaders in general has declined can help us understand why presidential power seems to have diminished in this area. The gradual weakening of parties, and new rules that give insurgents more of a chance to win nominations, have certainly played a role here. Perhaps the proliferation of primaries has been especially important. Since the concern of this chapter is the convention itself, however, we must bear in mind the important distinction between presidential weakness in the nomination race as a whole, and presidential strength or weakness at the convention. In other words, Ford's and Carter's difficulties had little to do with their conventions per se, but rather with the primaries and other events that preceded the convention. Once these presidents arrived at the convention in a weaker position than most of their twentieth-century predecessors, however, were they able to compensate for those weaknesses by successful manipulation of the convention itself?

In order to answer this paramount question, we must decide how to measure the extent to which the president, or any other party leader, controls a convention. Without delving into complex questions of the meaning of power and how to tell when it is being exercised, we shall focus on several discrete decisions affecting the convention. They include the selection of the time and place of the gathering; the designation of convention managers, major speakers, and committee chairs; the adoption of convention rules; ruling on delegate credentials challenges; the drafting of the platform; and of course the selection of the nominees. Above all, there are the overall questions of convention management: Who if anyone runs the convention? How much party harmony is projected to the nation? Who decides on the themes the party will present to the public?

SIX CONVENTIONS IN SEARCH OF A THEORY

In addition to these factors, there is a wide variety of circumstantial factors involving the role of the incumbent at a national convention. The ability of the president to control a convention depends in large part on two factors: whether he is a candidate himself, and whether the nomination is contested. Hypothetically a president will have the most control over convention activities when he is the nominee and has no significant opposition, and the least control when he is not running and there is a wide open race for the nomination. Of course, even in an uncontested situation, strong leadership of the party may help to present an orderly and united front, which can be an asset for the fall campaign. Reviewing all of the in-party conventions from 1960 to 1980 gives us six conventions with a good partisan and circumstantial mix: two presidents nominated by consensus (Johnson in 1964 and Nixon in 1972), two nominated over serious opposition (Ford in 1976 and Carter in 1980), and two who did not run (Eisenhower in 1960 and Johnson in 1968). Conveniently, each pair of conventions includes one Democrat and one Republican. Before examining specific opportunities for presidential influence, a brief synopsis of each convention is in order.

Uniting Behind the Incumbent

Lyndon Johnson in 1964 and Richard Nixon in 1972 faced very similar strategic circumstances: Their parties were united behind them, despite some discontentment expressed in the primaries, and the out-party had nominated a relatively ideological opponent whose convention victory had created widespread dissension. Each incumbent decided to use the convention to present an image of a responsible and sober president, beloved by his party, in order to attract as many disaffected members of the other party as possible.

In Johnson's case, the main task was to maintain control over the two matters that were in question: the vice-presidential nominee and the fight over the Mississippi delegation. Having ruled out Attorney General Robert Kennedy as his running mate, Johnson precluded a convention groundswell for Kennedy by scheduling a film on President John F. Kennedy after the vice-presidential balloting. The Mississippi conflict was solved by a compromise engineered by Johnson and intended to placate both civil-rights advocates and white Southerners. Johnson designated the vice-presidential frontrunner, Senator Hubert Humphrey, to engineer the compromise, and his success at getting what Johnson wanted secured his place on the ticket. Otherwise the convention was carefully stage-managed by Johnson's ally Marvin Watson, of whom it was said by Lawrence O'Brien (1975, p. 178): "A delegate could scarcely go to the bathroom without his okay." The appearance of consensus was fostered by the lack of any roll-call votes, the first Democratic National Convention in history of which that can be said (Bain and Parris 1973, pp. 314-17; Evans and Novak 1966, pp. 440-62; Pomper 1966; Tillett 1966, pp. 22-36; White 1965, pp. 246-93).

For Nixon, the convention involved even less controversy. His vice-president had been selected four years earlier, and the only division at the convention was over the delegate apportionment formula for 1976. In that fight the White House played no visible role, despite tacit support for party convervatives (*Congressional Quarterly Weekly Report* [hereafter *CQWR*] 1972, p. 2044). The convention became an extravaganza to display the administration in the best light. To maintain viewer interest it was shortened to three days, and as Nixon's aide Jeb Magruder later wrote, the convention was "virtually flawless as a PR effort [because] we realized we must minimize the 'convention' aspects of our convention, and treat it instead as a television show." Like any television show, it had a script that included instructions to speakers as to exactly what times to pause, to nod, and to expect "spontaneous" demonstrations to begin (Crouse 1973, pp. 165-66; see also Bain and Parris 1973, pp. 338-43; May and Fraser 1973, pp. 171-76; Schell 1976, pp. 273-79).

The Incumbent Steps Down

Eisenhower in 1960 and Johnson in 1968 were at the end of their administrations, and each with mixed emotions saw his vice-president nominated by the convention. There the resemblance between those conventions ends, and two factors are crucial in explaining the difference: the degree to which each president involved himself in party affairs, and the extent of division in the party over who his successor should be. The 1960 Republican Convention nominated Richard Nixon over virtually no opposition, with Eisenhower playing little visible role. The 1968 Democratic Convention was torn apart by controversy over the Vietnam War and the strong-arm tactics of the convention managers, and while Johnson never showed up, his aides exerted firm control over the convention. By the time Hubert Humphrey was nominated, his campaign was mortally wounded.

The combination of Dwight Eisenhower's desire to keep himself "above politics" and his apparent reservations about the qualifications of his vice-president kept him out of the preconvention jockeying. When he did endorse Nixon, his statement sounded unenthusiastic to many (Broder 1971, p. 1-15; Hinderaker 1962, pp. 18-20; Lyon 1974, p. 837; Parmet 1972, p. 565; Robinson 1974). His aides played a key role in the only controversy at the convention, that over the platform, and Eisenhower himself gave Nixon suggestions for the vice-presidential selection (Nixon 1962, pp. 341-42; Parmet 1972, p. 567). By and large, though, the incumbent's attitude was summarized by his comment to reporters at the convention: "Maybe you've forgotten, but there is a political campaign on and us old fellows are supposed to be forgotten" (Kessel 1962, p. 43n; see also Bain and Parris 1973, pp. 306-09; David 1961; Lamb 1962; Tillett 1961; White 1961, pp. 239-46).

"No one," Hubert Humphrey (1976, p. 356) later wrote, "played a more important role in my receiving the nomination for the presidency" than Lyndon Johnson, but that was a mixed blessing at best. Johnson, after all, was a man whose idea of party leadership was personal domination (Broder 1971, pp. 40-77; Robinson 1974). His staffers stage-managed the 1968 Democratic Convention as thoroughly as they had run the 1964 convention, controlling scheduling, tickets, and hotel rooms as well as politics. Humphrey's campaign manager, Lawrence O'Brien (1975, p.252), later wrote that "nobody in the Humphrey organization had the remotest influence on the planning of the Convention. . . . I found it ironic when the McCarthy camp began complaining that they were being discriminated against, being frozen out in favor of Humphrey, because we were receiving exactly the same treatment." Most important was Johnson's refusal to accept a compromise over the Vietnam platform plank, which severely damaged Humphrey's chances of reuniting the party. Most ironic was Johnson's disclaimer to the press: "I am not talking to the convention. I am not sending any emissaries. I don't have anyone reporting to me other than Cronkite. . . . I am not involved in any of the fights, the rules, credentials, or platforms or personalities" (*Congressional Quarterly* 1968, p. 2402; see also Bain and Parris 1973, pp. 322-28; Chester, Hodgson, and Page 1969, pp. 519-42; *CQWR* 1968; White 1970, pp. 325-81). Clearly the 1968 Democratic National Convention violates the expectation that compared to other types of conventions, the incumbent will have the least influence over a convention in which he is not running and there is serious division.

The Incumbent Fights for Nomination

Gerald Ford and Jimmy Carter must have viewed wistfully the resentment at Johnson's heavy-handedness, for they were the most threatened presidents in recent times. Each was challenged by an articulate long-time party hero who accused the president of wandering from the party's true mission, each began the campaign low in the polls, and each bounced back by winning a majority of primaries. By the time of the convention, the challenger was reduced to desperate attempts to change the rules.

As Ronald Reagan saw his chances for the nomination slipping away in the weeks before the 1976 Republican Convention, he startled observers by announcing that if nominated, he would chooose Senator Richard Schweiker as his running mate. Reagan's adviser John Sears then devoted his energies to trying to get the convention to adopt a rule forcing Ford to announce *his* running mate, an effort that failed. In other ways, however, Ford made obvious attempts to placate the conservatives for the sake of party unity: He accepted nearly all of the conservatives' platform proposals, even those implicitly critical of his policies, he gave Reagan a veto on the vice-presidential nomination, and he paid lavish tribute to the Californian when he accepted the nomination. Conservatives won everything at the convention except the nomination, which Ford carried narrowly. As one journalist put it, "Though he was the incumbent, Ford was treated almost as if he were an interloper" (Witcover 1977, p. 510; see also Arterton 1977-78; Drew 1977, pp. 358-86; Moore and Fraser 1977, pp. 14-15; Nakamura 1977-78; Pomper 1977, pp. 26-29; Sullivan 1977-78; Weinberg 1977-78).

At the 1980 Democratic Convention, Edward Kennedy tried to break Carter's hold on the delegates by asking the convention to free all delegates from commitments they had made in the primaries. While that effort failed, Kennedy won Carter's consent to address the convention in prime time during the debate over economic planks of the platform. The combination of the popularity of some of the planks, Kennedy's eloquence, and the support of various interest groups and issue activists gave Carter some platform defeats and forced him to fight hard to win on other planks. Like Ford, he acquiesced on some major issues and praised his opponent during his acceptance speech. On the other hand, his nomination was even less in doubt than Ford's had been (Drew 1981, pp. 224-57; Malbin 1981, pp. 117-31; Moore 1981, pp. 169-76; Polsby 1981; Pomper 1981, pp. 21-32).

PRESIDENTIAL RESOURCES

To what extent, and in what ways, were these presidents able to influence the outcomes of the past six national party conventions? Are any of their tools less effective than they once were, and can this explain Ford's and Carter's problems at the 1976 and 1980 conventions? We turn now to an enumeration of the convention resources at a presidents's disposal, in an attempt to determine which, if any, have eroded over time.

The National Committee

Most of the advantages an incumbent has in an intraparty battle rest on his control of the national party machinery. The national committee issues the call to the convention, which includes the ground rules; establishes when and where the convention is to meet; allocates tickets, hotel rooms, and seating on the convention floor; and appoints the key personnel of the convention—chairpersons of the convention and its committees, and featured speakers. The president, in turn, controls the national committee, whose chairperson is chosen by the White House. The party chairperson at each of the contested conventions under consideration—the Democrats in 1968 and 1980 and the Republicans in 1976—made no pretense of being anything other than a fervent partisan of the administration.

One example of how the president can influence national committee control over the convention occurred when President Kennedy and his advisers settled on a new delegate apportionment formula for the 1964 convention. The rule, which had the effect of a long-term decrease in the South's share of delegates, was duly adopted by the Democratic National Committee at its next meeting (White 1965, pp.28-29; Tillett 1966, pp. 30-31). In advance of the more divided 1976 Republican Convention, on the other hand, the Ford-controlled Republican National Committee voted down Ronald Reagan's proposal to require presidential candidates to name their vice-presidential choices before the balloting, and also rejected a Reagan plan to have both Ford and Reagan address the convention (Witcover 1977, p. 508; New York *Times* 1976b). While the conventions in question could have reversed these national committee decisions, having them decided in the president's favor gave the incumbent a definite tactical advantage. This edge has become especially important in recent years in the Democratic Party, where reform commissions under the auspices of the Democratic National Committee have labored long and hard to lay the groundwork for national conventions and midterm party conferences. The Carter administration was able to secure the passage of rules governing the 1978 conference that would limit the number of delegates, require minority reports to get one-quarter of the delegates' signatures to reach the floor, and stipulate that a majority of all delegates, not only those present, would be needed to pass resolutions.

EDITOR'S PERSPECTIVE

The President's Man in the Chairmanship

An unwritten rule in the president-party relationship is that presidents can name their own national party chairs. This could be seen as giving added leverage to the party in its relations with the White House, but even more it strengthens presidential control over the operations of the party organization. When presidential interests are not consistent with the interests of others in the party, it is the others who normally suffer. Such is the case when the party chair is "the president's man (or woman)," and the chair oversees the distribution of important party resources. That can be particularly important when a president faces intraparty challenges to renomination.

In January 1978, Jimmy Carter and the DNC replaced party chairman Kenneth Curtis, who had resigned, with former Deputy Secretary of Agriculture John C. White. The following is excerpted from a May *Texas Magazine* article by Cragg Hines, based in part on an interview with White.

> White succeeded former Maine Gov. Kenneth Curtis, who in the eyes of Carter political strategists was giving the liberal carpers in the party too much rein.
>
> Another Texan, former national chariman and Carter confidante, Robert S. Strauss of Dallas, assured the president that White would do the White House's bidding.
>
> And he has.
>
> "I don't know of a single situation where the White House has had special needs I could not accommodate," White said.
>
> How often does he have to go to the mat with the White House?
>
> "Every day," he says without missing a beat. But, with a nervous laugh, he adds, "I'm being facetious."
>
> White found out shortly after becoming a chairman that, "In this town, people try you on for size just for fun."
>
> Faced with a potential liberal revolt on the national committee, White quick-gaveled to acceptance some revisions of party procedure which had been cleared by Carter's political braintrust in the White House.
>
> At stake were rules for selecting delegates to the 1980 Democratic National Convention. Carter's White House operatives were interested in rules which would make it as easy as possible to renominate Carter. That's what was written, and that's what White pushed through over cries of "foul" from party liberals and reformers.

This was intended to keep the influence of anti-administration liberals to a minimum (New York *Times* 1977, 1978b). The Winograd Commission, which was established to set the rules for the 1980 convention, produced a generally pro-Carter report intended to discourage insurgencies, but most of its key provisions were compromised by the time the national committee made its final decision(*CQWR* 1978, p. 1217). On the key rules issue before the convention, the binding of delegates, the national committee prepared a legal memorandum stating that delegates who did not adhere to their commitments could be replaced by more loyal alternates (New York *Times* 1980b). Carter supporters also controlled the national committee's Compliance Review Commission, which forbade New York from automatically listing the uncommitted delegate option on the primary ballot, an option that could have helped the emerging Kennedy candidacy. The commission also sought to delay the date of the Massachusetts primary, in order to deprive Kennedy of an early victory, but the Carter people later dropped the matter (*CQWR* 1979b, p. 2006, and 1979c, p. 2660).

Time and Place

The decisions of when and where the convention is to meet are made by the national committee. A president can generally control those decisions, although other factors, notably the money and number of hotel rooms offered by the host city, can be influential as well. For example, the Democrats chose New York City for 1980 mainly because of the latter consideration. Jimmy Carter refrained from designating New York or Detroit for fear of offending the mayor of the city not chosen (*CQWR* 1979a, p. 1300; New York *Times* 1979). Moreover, there is no evidence that Dwight Eisenhower played a role in selecting Chicago for the Republicans in 1960.

The other four presidents were more instrumental in those decisions. John Kennedy selected Atlantic City and opted for a very late convention so that he could appear "presidential" all summer while the Republicans looked partisan (White 1970, p. 325; New York *Times* 1963). When Lyndon Johnson turned out to be that convention's nominee, it was noted that it coincided with his birthday, and that guided his planning for 1968: The 1968 Democratic National Convention was also held late in August, and the Democratic National Committee reserved Soldier's Field in Chicago all week for a birthday party that in Johnson's absence was never held (Humphrey 1976, p. 396n; Chester, Hodgson, and Page 1969, p. 519). Johnson chose Chicago as the convention site because it was in a state with a Democratic governor (in case the National Guard had to be called out), security seemed good, the location was central, the financial offer was

A site in Texas was rejected so that Johnson would not appear too heavy-handed, as well as to avoid the intraparty dispute between Governor John Connally and Senator Ralph Yarborough (White 1970, p. 325; *CQWR* 1967, p. 2074; New York *Times* 1967). In 1976 the Republicans selected Kansas City reportedly because of Gerald Ford's preference for the Midwest (New York *Times* 1975).

No site selection experience was more unusual than the Republican situation in 1972. Richard Nixon first chose San Diego because of its proximity to his San Clemente home and also because of California's electoral vote. Republican National Chairman Robert Dole had to exert firm pressure on the national committee's site selection committee to prevent it from opting for Miami Beach instead. Ironically, the party eventually did have to change to Miami Beach because of the ITT scandal; among the reasons given for the latter preference were the fewer protesters likely to converge on the city, its financial offer, hotel rooms, a favorable labor situation, and the convenience of the media that would be in Miami Beach for the Democratic convention (Magruder 1974, pp. 150-52, 199; New York *Times* 1972a; Lukas 1976, pp. 130-34, 182-85).

Convention Management

Each of the presidents in the period under study sent personal envoys to the convention, and most designated people to run the entire operation. In 1964 Johnson sent his key aide Walter Jenkins, his Texas ally Marvin Watson, and his national committee liaison Clifton Carter; working with them was a member of Clark Clifford's law firm, Tom Finney. Clifton Carter ran a telephone link to the White House and to all state delegations, and he approved all major decisions. Besides the decisions on the timing of the cinematic tribute to President Kennedy and the Mississippi delegation, Johnson made sure that Robert Kennedy would not appear in the film about his brother, that the keynoter would be someone who would help the ticket in the industrial Northeast (Rhode Island Senator John Pastore), and that Johnson would be nominated by the governors of the key states of California and Texas (Evans and Novak 1966, pp. 453, 456; Kessel 1968, p. 226; New York *Times* 1964b; O'Brien 1975, p. 178; White 1965, pp. 262-63). Watson, who was now postmaster general, was again dispatched to run the convention along with fellow Texan John Criswell, treasurer of the Democratic National Committee; they were assisted by Johnson staffers Joseph Califano and Jack Valenti. Not surprisingly, all of the featured speakers at the convention were staunch administration supporters (Chester, Hodgson, and Page 1969, pp. 540-42).

The famous script for the 1972 Republican National Convention was authored by White House staffer Dwight Chapin, who limited parliamentary matters to the daytime and reserved for prime time key speeches, demonstrations, and films. Security at the convention was managed by Nixon's congressional liaison, William Timmons, and press relations were handled by the White House communications aides, Herbert Klein and Kenneth Clawson. To insure that backers of the candidacy of Representative Paul McCloskey would not have access to air time, the convention's rules committee decreed that a candidate's name could be placed in nomination only if supported by a majority of at least three delegations (Magruder 1974, p. 262; New York *Times* 1972e; Schell 1976, p. 276). Four years later, Timmons's expertise was drawn on by Gerald Ford, who made the former Nixon aide his convention manager. Timmons was assisted by political consultant F. Clifton White and Commerce Department aide James Baker. They ran an elaborate network of coordinators and whips that easily outstripped the efforts of the Reaganites. Ford strategists vetoed national committee plans for the scheduling of speakers and tried to limit those speakers' references to the Watergate scandal. Reaganites were angered at the selection of Senators Robert Dole and Howard Baker as, respectively, temporary chairman and keynote speaker, and the only featured speaker who was a Reagan supporter was South Carolina Governor James Edwards (Arterton 1977-78, pp. 664-65; *CQWR* 1976a, p. 1737; Drew 1977, p. 358; New York *Times* 1976g; Witcover 1977, pp. 516-17).

For Jimmy Carter's staff, the 1978 Democratic midterm conference was a dry run for the 1980 convention, complete with a speech by Edward Kennedy attacking Carter's priorities. The Carter people's plans for the 1978 conference included a film extolling the president, nearly 150 administration staffers converging on Memphis with floor managers and walkie-talkies, and intense lobbying over the vote on the budget resolution. Democratic National Chairman Kenneth Curtis planned to have only administration speakers address the conference (although he subsequently had to yield to Kennedy on that point), and the president himself spoke on the opening night (*CQWR* 1977, p. 2616; New York *Times* 1978a, 1978c, 1978d, 1978e). In 1980 more than 300 members of the administration journeyed to New York, with Carter media adviser Gerald Rafshoon deeply involved in planning the program. Among the planning decisions were the appointment of Speaker Thomas P. O'Neill as permanent chairman and Representative Morris Udall as keynote speaker; these choices effectively neutralized those Kennedy backers. On the last night of the convention, the floor was packed to preclude unauthorized demonstrations (Drew 1977, pp. 229, 253-54, 257; New York *Times* 1980c, 1980d).

At a contested convention, campaign managers are keenly sensitive to favoritism about tickets, floor passes, and hotel accommodations. The candidate with the most tickets can pack the galleries with vocal supporters, and floor passes can enable one to mount a superior organization that can descend on delegates who need to be persuaded of the justice of one's cause. At each of the three divided conventions under consideration, backers of anti-administration candidates cried foul when the favors were distributed. In 1968 Eugene McCarthy's staff complained that Hubert Humphrey was given more telephones and more choice hotel rooms at the convention headquarters, when formally neutral but actually pro-Humphrey delegations were included in the count. The seating plan on the convention floor was initially kept from all delegations except the proadministration Illinois group, and it revealed that the worst locations were given to the antiadministration California and New York delegations (New York *Times* 1968a, 1968b, 1968c; White 1970, pp. 339-40).

Similar charges could be heard by the Reaganites at the 1976 Republican convention. Reagan aide Lyn Nofziger claimed that the Ford people had four times the hotel space that the Reagan supporters were given. While the Reagan staff was given 300 tickets to the Ford campaign's 200, the White House staff received 450. On the other hand, the number of floor passes and accommodations at the convention hall itself were equal (Moore and Fraser 1977, p. 53; New York *Times* 1976a). At the 1980 Democratic Convention, each candidate received 550 guest passes, but there were also 1,337 given to the national chairman (a Carter supporter, of course), 100 to the White House, 28 to the cabinet, 176 to the national committee's arrangements committee (Carter-controlled), 550 to New York City (headed by a pro-Carter mayor), and 1,104 to the delegates. Similarly, out of 5,409 floor passes, only 28 went to the candidates, which may help to explain why the Kennedy forces could field only 120 floor whips to more than 200 for Carter (New York *Times* 1980a, 1980e).

Writing the Platform

For an incumbent president, the platform is an opportunity to hear his policies praised and, if he is running, to see his campaign themes tested. Moreover, it is sometimes a battleground with those who would seek to repudiate his policies, and thus it may become a test of his leadership. Even Eisenhower took pains to insure that Nixon's platform would not imply criticism of the administration, and his aides Robert Merriam and Malcolm Moos drafted it. When a tug-of-war developed among Nixon, New York's Governor Nelson Rockefeller, and party conservatives, Eisenhower's representatives were instrumental in insuring that the outcome would reflect a liberal position on civil rights and no criticism of the administration on defense (David 1961, pp. 15-16; Kessel 1962, pp. 43, 47; Lamb 1962, p. 78; Tillett 1961, p. 37; White 1961, pp. 239-40, 246).

Having White House aides draft the platform has been standard practice in recent years, and this has raised questions about whether the incumbent's party speaks for interests other than the president's. According to most sources, State Department aide Frederick Dutton drafted the 1964 Democratic platform under the aegis of White House aide Bill Moyers, but Theodore White claims that Secretary of Labor W. Willard Wirtz wrote it (1965, p. 281; see also Evans and Novak, 1966, p. 457). According to Johnson's biographers Evans and Novak, Johnson overrode platform chairman Carl Albert's desire not to name "extremist" groups in the platform (but see New York *Times* 1964a), and persuaded Pennsylvania Senator Joseph Clark not to press for a disarmament plank (1966, p. 457). Johnson also saw to it that reapportionment was left out of the platform, but the platform committee overrode by one vote the administration's preference that congressional representation for the District of Columbia not be advocated (New York *Times* 1964c; *CQWR* 1964, p. 1962). The pattern in 1972, not surprisingly, was similar. The platform was initially drafted at the White House under the direction of domestic advisor John Ehrlichman, and sections were read to the platform committee. Committee members could not see or keep copies, and the draft was released to the press only the day before the convention opened. The platform committee chairman, Representative John Rhodes of Arizona, prevented dissident Congressman Donald Riegle from testifying before the committee. As in the Johnson case, however, this control did not prevent the committee from revising the platform, and the White House had to stifle a right-to-work proposal that would have hampered Nixon's efforts to appeal to labor. Ehrlichman and former presidential aide Bryce Harlow oversaw the process. On the convention floor, a balanced budget amendment was defeated and Indian rights added to the platform (Bain and Parris 1973, p. 341; Ripon Society and Brown 1974, p. 46; Schell 1976, pp. 273, 276; New York *Times* 1972b, 1972c, 1972d).

It was at the three contested conventions that the true test of presidential power occurred. Here the president's influence over the convention managers is pertinent, for in each case the platform committee was chaired by an administration loyalist—Louisiana Representative Hale Boggs in 1968, Iowa Governor Robert Ray in 1976, and Detroit Mayor Coleman Young in 1980. In 1968 Boggs insisted on clearing all references to Vietnam with Johnson, who was represented in the platform deliberations by Marvin Watson and Washington attorney Charles Murphy. They rejected the compromise that the Humphrey forces had worked out with antiwar delegates, and Humphrey gave in to Johnson and sacrificed an opportunity to unite the party. Here is an excellent example of a president's perceived self-interest taking precedence over the needs of his party (Chester, Hodgson, and Page 1969, pp. 524-37; O'Brien 1975, pp. 252-55; Humphrey 1976, pp. 388-90).

In 1976 Gerald Ford was more accommodating, perhaps because as the candidate he was more sensitive to the need for party unity. Moreover, because of equal representation of states on each convention committee, the Ford people controlled the platform committee by only a narrow edge. The 1976 Republican platform was initially drafted by about 50 people, many of them congressional staffers. The shadow of Watergate dictated not using administration staffers for this purpose, because the White House did not want to lay itself open to charges of violating the Hatch Act or repeating Nixon's practice of drafting the platform in the White House. The chief drafters were John Meagher of the House Ways and Means Committee staff and Stephen Hess of the Brookings Institution. There was an attempt to draft a document equally satisfactory to both Ford and Reagan, and for some time members of the Ford and Reagan staffs had been meeting secretly to iron out differences on foreign policy. However, all placatory gestures came to naught when Governor Ray sought to exert the same degree of control over the process that Nixon had, by keeping the draft secret until ten days before the meetings were to begin and by not allowing subcommittee chairpersons to keep copies. The ensuing outcry resulted in the abandonment of the drafts, the opening of meetings to the public, and subcommittees' electing their own members. This was not as much a defeat for Ford and Ray as it might first appear, for the subcommittees often found themselves using the drafts anyway, and the only subcommittee chair who was replaced was a congressman who had not been able to come to Detroit. The Ford managers who used walkie-talkies at the deliberations stopped using them, as another conciliatory gesture. Conservatives in the platform subcommittee voted not to endorse the Equal Rights Amendment, but the Ford forces overturned this decision in the full committee by a 51-to-47 vote. Only two minority planks received enough votes to go to the convention floor. One, on "morality in foreign policy," was advanced not by the Reaganites but by the followers of Senator Jesse Helms. Although it was implicitly critical of the Ford foreign policy, Ford's managers decided not to risk embarrassment by losing a fight over it. and they let it be passed by voice vote. When a North Carolina delegate tried to call for a roll-call vote on the measure, he was ignored by the convention chairman. The other dissident plank to delete all references to abortion, was rejected by voice vote. The result was a quite conservative platform in which Ford, in the words of one journalist, was "scarcely mentioned" (Weinberg 1977-78; Drew 1977, pp. 367-68; CQWR 1976b, p. 2262; New York *Times* 1976f).

Like Ford, Jimmy Carter wanted to compromise on the platform as much as necessary to unite his party. Unlike Ford, however, he fought the dissident planks with greater zeal. Elaine Kamarck, the executive director of the platform committee, worked with presidential aides David Rubenstein and David Aaron to work up the draft. This then went to a drafting subcommittee that represented the array of forces at the convention: nine Carter supporters, five Kennedy backers, and one neutral delegate, New York Senator D. P. Moynihan. It was chaired by a Carter backer, Governor Richard Riley of South Carolina. The subcommittee agreed to many planks offered by organized labor to which neither candidate objected. Carter staffers kept an eye on the deliberations, and in the full committee the president won most votes by about an 85-to-55 margin. Carter's closest calls came on votes on which some of his delegates put their issue positions — against the MX missile, against nuclear power, for homosexual rights — ahead of their support for the president. On the latter two planks, the Carterites compromised with the issue activists; nevertheless, there were 23 minority reports, 17 by Kennedy and 6 from others. As the convention neared, a procedural compromise was worked out between the two candidates. The result was that, as Carter wished, the rules issue was put on the convention agenda before the platform, and a limit was put on the number of roll-call votes; Kennedy in turn had six of his planks accepted, a speech on prime time, and Carter's agreement to respond to the platform in writing.

On the convention floor, Carter had to contend with not only the Kennedy forces but also a plethora of issue activists — for example, the AFL-CIO, the National Education Association, and the National Organization of Women, all of which had their own whip systems. Their efforts, as well as the impact of Kennedy's speech, led to several defeats for Carter on economic planks, and feminists won battles over abortion and whether to cut off party aid to anti-Equal Rights Amendment candidates, over Carter's wishes. The president did win a hard fight on the MX missile, with the unprecedented lobbying by the secretaries of state and defense and the president's national security adviser. All in all, the inclusion of several major platform planks that had been opposed by the incumbent was due in part to the presence of a sizable number of Kennedy delegates, in part to the role of issue activists at the convention, and in part to Carter's unwillingness to emulate Ford and simply roll over on most issues. It is unclear that any of these is a direct result of presidential *weakness* at the convention, but the first two are certainly related to the general devolution of power in the party. Like Ford, Carter did control the platform-writing process, but the delegate-selection process produced a convention without a comfortable margin of victory on issues (Malbin 1981, pp. 117-31; *CQWR* 1980a, pp. 1796-98; 1980d, pp. 2263-67; 1980f, pp. 2360-66).

Credentials and Rules

While the platform is largely of symbolic significance, the main reason to heed the credentials and rules is to affect the outcome of the convention. Like the platform committee, the committees governing credentials and rules can be controlled by the president's forces; but in the Ford and Carter cases, there were constraints on the president's influence that stemmed from rules governing representativeness on party bodies, and the strength of the challenges to both presidents' nominations.

No credentials or rules fights marred the 1960 Republican convention, while the only conflict at the 1964 Democratic convention involved the credentials of the Mississippi delegation. Here Johnson's desire for a placid convention ran headlong into the dramatic testimony of black Mississippians who had been brutally excluded from participation in party politics. The credentials committee chairman, former Pennsylvania Governor David Lawrence, was a Johnson staffer, and Johnson's men on the scene were aide Walter Jenkins and attorney Tom Finney, who helped Hubert Humphrey negotiate a compromise. That compromise provided for the seating of any member of the all-white Mississippi delegation who signed a loyalty oath, and the additional seating of two of the integrationists at large. For Johnson, the peaceful resolution of the dispute kept the convention harmonious and gave him greater confidence in his choice of Humphrey as vice-president (Evans and Novak 1965, pp. 451-56; Tillett 1966, pp. 31-33; White 1965, pp. 277-81). In 1972 the White House played little role in the dispute over delegate apportionment.

As with the platform, presidential power in rules and credentials fights is best tested at the divided conventions. At the 1968 Democratic

Convention, the respective committee chairs were two governors loyal
to Johnson: Samuel Shapiro of Illinois (rules) and Richard Hughes of
New Jersey (credentials). Aside from the designation of the chairs,
there is no evidence of involvement by Johnson in the credentials
fights, and certainly not to the extent that he influenced the platform
deliberations. At the 1976 GOP Convention, both committee chairs
were Midwestern party functionaries committed to Ford: Kent
McGough of Ohio (rules) and John McDonald of Iowa (credentials).
McDonald's job was easy because there were no credentials challenges
by either Ford or Reagan, but McGough's committee handled Reagan's
attempt to force Ford to name his vice-presidential choice before the
presidential voting. That the Reaganites chose to place their efforts on
a rules fight rather than the platform was to Ford's advantage, since
he maintained a larger majority on the rules committee; it ultimately
rejected Reagan's proposal by a 59-to-44 vote. The committee also
vetoed Reagan proposals to cut off debate by a two-thirds majority
(the vote was 51 to 47), to have candidates in 1980 name several vice-
presidential possibilities 20 days before the nomination (57 to 46), to
free delegates from primary commitments (50 to 47), and to use
Robert's Rules of Order. The only Reagan victory was the defeat of a
Ford proposal to give floor seats to elected officials in 1980 (48 to 36), a
victory that obviously could not help the Californian in 1976 (Witcover
1977, pp. 512-29; Drew 1977, p. 357; New York *Times* 1976d, 1976e).

Like Ford, Jimmy Carter had two friendly politicians, Hawaii
Senator Daniel Inouye (rules) and Connecticut Governor Ella Grasso
(credentials), in charge of the 1980 Democratic committees. As with the
Republicans, credentials were not the issue at the Democratic
Convention in 1980. Kennedy's challenge of six Virginia delegates was
dropped as part of a more general compromise with Carter, and this
was the only such conflict at that convention (*CQWR* 1980e, pp.
2356-57). Like Reagan four years earlier, Kennedy placed his hopes on
a rules fight, but an unfriendly convention rules committee put him at
a tactical disadvantage. That committee rejected his proposal to free
delegates of their commitments from the primaries by a vote of 87.25
to 65.5. It also raised the number of petition signatures required to
nominate candidates, in an attempt to dampen the move toward a dark-
horse candidate; limited the number of speakers on each side of each
debate to two; and required all nonnominating ballots to be conducted
by telephone. All these votes were defeats for the Kennedy forces, and
Kennedy also failed at attempts to increase debating time and require
the nominee to give a written response to the platform. Some of these
matters, and most notably the platform response, were later acceded
to by Carter in a series of compromises. The committee also rejected

proposals that would have provided for a mandatory 1982 midterm conference and would have required the Democratic National Committee leaders and staff to be neutral in presidential contests (*CQWR* 1980b, p. 1940; 1980c, pp. 2169-70).

Control of the Executive Branch

There is no question that incumbents have an enormous advantage throughout the nominating process because of their control of the administration. Above all, this provides them with a host of people on the public payroll who can draft platforms and attend conventions as political aides. Even Eisenhower used staffers for this purpose, and Jimmy Carter went so far as to use his top staffers in the national security area to lobby against minority platform planks. In recent years, presidents have brought vast entourages to conventions. Ford brought 59 staffers as well as his Secret Service contingent, communications team, military aide, and three aides from the National Security Council, while Carter brought nearly 150 of his aides to the 1978 midterm conference and more than 300 to the 1980 convention (New York *Times* 1976c, 1978d; Drew 1981, p. 229).

Beyond personnel, there are vast resources on tap for an enterprising president, as demonstrated by Carter's use of Navy Department film at the 1978 midterm conference (New York *Times* 1978a). But no president was more adept at using such resources for his own political purposes than Lyndon Johnson. In Atlantic City in 1964, more than 25 FBI agents compiled political intelligence for Johnson. Among other activities, they bugged and wiretapped facilities used by Dr. Martin Luther King, Jr. and other civil rights leaders, set up informers within pertinent groups, and posed as reporters. Under the direction of Assistant FBI Director Cartha DeLoach, they reported to Johnson aides Walter Jenkins and Bill Moyers. DeLoach was responsible for advising Johnson on such subjects as the Mississippi credentials fight, delegate seating, the vice-presidential nomination, Dr. King's political contracts, and Robert Kennedy's activities. In 1968 FBI Director J. Edgar Hoover set up a special squad at the Chicago convention that interfered with the antiwar demonstrators, and Army intelligence agents eavesdropped on radio communications at the convention and spied on political leaders (Wise 1978, pp. 287-94, 318, 406). While such illegal uses of intelligence agencies may or may not be the norm, they illustrate the great potential for presidential use of the executive branch at national conventions.

CONCLUSIONS

Clearly an incumbent president has powerful resources at his disposal with which to influence national party conventions. The most consistently useful resources have stemmed from his control of the national committee, which has given him tremendous sway over the following: the timing and location of the convention; the agenda and who gets to speak before the delegates; the allocation of tickets, hotel rooms, and seating on the convention floor; and who is designated to chair the gathering and its key committees. Moreover, control of committees leads in turn to a great tactical advantage in drafting the platform, settling on the rules, and resolving credentials disputes. In recent years, control of the Democratic National Committee has enabled a president to tip the scales of the vitally important reform commissions that have drafted the ground rules for future delegate selection.

Even with these tremendous resources, however, presidents today have far from unlimited control at national conventions. The two most recent conventions under consideration, the Republican parley in 1976 and the Democratic gathering in 1980, demonstrate the significant constraints even on presidents who are winning the nomination, and they are in bold contrast to the four earlier nominating contests. The early successes of the Reagan and Kennedy challenges led to two major problems for Ford and Carter. First, the insurgents' victories in primaries, caucuses, and conventions gave them representation on the convention committees, stemming from the Republican requirement that each state be represented on each committee and from Democratic proportional representation rules. Second, the appeal of the dissident candidate made the incumbent acutely aware of the need for compromise for the sake of party unity. Johnson in 1964 and Nixon in 1972 could afford to be as heavy-handed as they wished, for party unity had already been achieved with the collapse of the challenges to their nominations.

Assuming that the 1976 and 1980 experiences were not flukes, we must again confront the question of *why* presidents today and in the future may find it more difficult to win nomination. Certainly new rules have played a role, first in leading to the proliferation of primaries that enable challengers to go "over the heads" of party leaders in a direct appeal to "the people." A second pertinent effect of new rules has been the development of fairer procedures in the Democratic Party that prevent party leaders from exerting the necessary muscle to keep insurgents out of the convention hall.

At times, however, there has been an exaggeration of the causal significance of formal rules changes. The difficulty that presidents have had in willing the nomination antedated the reforms, In this light, it is worth remembering that the last incumbent before the McGovern-Fraser Commission met, Lyndon Johnson, dropped out of the race because of the New Hampshire primary. There are those who argue that Johnson could have won the nomination had he fought for it, but it is difficult to imagine any outcome in November other than an even greater debacle than the Democrats experienced that year. The Johnson case is important to bear in mind because it suggests that new rules have not been the only determinant of recent presidential weakness in seeking nomination. It is also significant because it is an ideal lesson in the follies of presidential heavy-handedness in the modern nominating process. A president who insists on every detail at a divided convention going his way could probably still achieve it, but it would leave the nomination worthless to the nominee. This is a lesson that future incumbents will ignore at their peril, or at least at the peril of their party.

So we end this chapter on a theme that is central to this book: To what extent do the interests of a president and the interests of his party diverge? It is too easy, and a violation of the concept of party government, to suggest that the president is the only rightful leader of his party. Putting the party under the thumb of the chief executive, and allowing him to run its convention as he so chooses, deprives the party of what it can uniquely provide in the political system: the organization and expression of long-standing political interests that go beyond those of one person or one discrete historical period. In certain respects, the changes that national conventions have undergone have reasserted the interests of the party. In particular, the Democratic Party's rules changes have routinized party processes in ways that make them less dependent on the whims of the leader of the moment. On the other hand, the party leaders' loss of power over nominations has introduced an element of chance into the nomination process that threatens to produce nominees like Jimmy Carter who may not be sensitive to the party's interests.

Calling for more independence of the party, and hence its national convention, from the president need not imply a weaker chief executive. To argue this point, it is useful to cite the distinction made by James MacGregor Burns between two kinds of strong presidents: the Hamiltonian president, who governs without collegial structures and uses "energy, resourcefulness, inventiveness, and a ruthless pragmatism in the executive office," and the Jeffersonian president, who relies on a vigorous party that can both help him to achieve his legitimate ends and serve as an often subtle rein on his ambition (Burns 1965, p. 29). Neither model results in a weak president, but the

Jeffersonian one is more likely to produce responsible, accountable leadership. It is apparent that most of the presidents under consideration here have aspired, usually with success, to behave in Hamiltonian fashion regarding their party's convention. Besides all of its other implications for the quality of presidential leadership, this stance has not helped to reverse the decline of American parties in recent decades.

We have seen that there are often profound divergences between the interests of the president and those of his party. The former probably wants either to be crowned by his party or else to see the party designate a successor who promises to continue each and every one of the president's policies. The party's interests include the accommodation of all major factions, the drafting of a platform that expresses something of what the party stands for beyond the current year, and the strongest possible ticket. The simultaneous satisfaction of both sets of needs is frequently impossible, and this tension is likely to be with us as long as we have national conventions and a vigorous presidency.

REFERENCES

Arterton, F. Christopher. 1977-78. "Strategies and Tactics of Candidate Organizations." *Political Science Quarterly* 92:663-71.

Bain, Richard C., and Judith H. Parris. 1973. *Convention Decisions and Voting Records*, 2d ed. Washington, D.C.: Brookings Institution.

Broder, David. 1971. *The Party's Over*. New York: Harper & Row.

Burns, James MacGregor. 1965. *Presidential Government*. Boston: Houghton Mifflin.

Chester, Lewis, Godfrey Hodgson, and Bruce Page. 1969. *An American Melodrama*. New York: Viking.

Congressional Quarterly. 1968. *The Presidential Nominating Conventions 1968.* Washington, D.C.: Congressional Quarterly.

Congressional Quarterly Weekly Report. 1964. "Credentials Fight Dominates Convention Opening." August 28:1958-62.

_____. 1967. "Democratic Developments." October 13: 2074-75.

_____. 1968. Transcript of Presidential news conference. September 6:2402-03.

_____. 1972. "Republican Convention: Almost Undisturbed Harmony." August 19:2043-49.

_____. 1976a. "Republicans." July 3:1737.

_____. 1976b. "A Conservative Blueprint for Government." August 21:2260-62.

_____. 1977. "Democrats Choose Memphis." December 17:2616.

_____. 1978. "Democrats Adopt New Rules for Picking Nominee in 1980." June 17:1571-72.

_____. 1979a. "New York City Will Host 1980 Democratic Convention." June 30:1300.

_____ . 1979b. "Democrats Struggle with Interpreting Rules." September 15:2006.

_____ . 1979c. "Democratic Review Panel Grants Massachusetts' Bid for Early Presidential Primary." November 24:2660-61.

_____ . 1980a. "Democratic Platform Reflects Carter Views." June 28:1796-98.

_____ . 1980b. "Carter Supporters Turn Back Kennedy Challenge on Rules." July 12:1940.

_____ . 1980c. "Open Convention Drive Targets Binding Rule." August 2:2168-70.

_____ . 1980d. "Kennedy Wins Few Platform Points." August 9:2263-67.

_____ . 1980e. "A Divided Democratic Party Renominates Jimmy Carter, Who Then Makes Unity Plea." August 16:2349-57.

_____ . 1980f. "Loser Kennedy Leaves Imprint on 1980 Democratic Platform." August 16:2360-66.

Crotty, William J., and Gary C. Jacobson. 1980. *American Parties in Decline.* Boston: Little, Brown.

Crouse, Timothy. 1973. *The Boys on the Bus.* New York: Random House.

David, Paul T. 1961. "The Presidential Nominations." In *The Presidential Election and Transition 1960-1961*, ed. Paul T. David, pp. 1-30. Washington, D.C.: Brookings Institution.

Drew, Elizabeth. 1977. *American Journal.* New York: Random House.

_____ . 1981. *Portrait of an Election.* New York: Simon & Schuster.

Evans, Rowland, and Robert Novak. 1966. *Lyndon B. Johnson.* New York: New American Library.

Hinderaker, Ivan. 1962. "The 1960 Republican Convention." In *Inside Politics*, ed. Paul Tillett, pp. 15-24. Dobbs Ferry, N.Y.: Oceana.

Humphrey, Hubert H. 1976. *The Education of a Public Man.* Garden City, N.Y.: Doubleday.

Kessel, John H. 1962. "Political Leadership: The Nixon Version." In *Inside Politics*, ed Paul Tillett, pp. 39-54. Dobbs Ferry, N.Y.: Oceana.

_____ . 1968. *The Goldwater Coalition.* Indianapolis: Bobbs-Merrill.

Key, V. O., Jr. 1964. *Politics, Parties, and Pressure Groups*, 5th ed. New York: Crowell.

Lamb, Karl A. 1962. "Civil Rights and the Republican Platform." In *Inside Politics*, ed Paul Tillett, pp. 55-84. Dobbs Ferry, N.Y.: Oceana.

Lukas, J. Anthony. 1976. *Nightmare.* New York: Viking.

Lyon, Peter. 1974. *Eisenhower: Portrait of the Hero.* Boston: Little, Brown

Magruder, Jeb Stuart. 1974. *An American Life.* New York: Atheneum.

Malbin, Michael J. 1981. "The Conventions, Platforms, and Issue Activists." In *The American Elections of 1980*, ed. Austin Ranney, pp. 99-141. Washington, D.C.: American Enterprise Institute.

Mandate for Reform. 1970. Washington, D.C.: Democratic National Committee.

May, Ernest R., and Janet Fraser, eds., 1973. *Campaign '72*. Cambridge, Mass.: Harvard University Press.

Moore, Jonathan. 1981. *The Campaign for President*. Cambridge, Mass.: Ballinger.

_____ , and Janet Fraser. 1977. *Campaign for President*. Cambridge, Mass.: Ballinger.

Nakamura, Robert T. 1977-78. "Impressions of Ford and Reagan." *Political Science Quarterly* 92:647-54.

New York *Times*. 1963. "Democrats Pick Atlantic City for 1964 National Convention." June 26:1, 26.

_____ . 1964a. "Johnson Seeking Extremism Plank." August 5:1, 14.

_____ . 1964b. "Convention Aides Borrow a Line From G.O.P. Telephonic System." August 22:8.

_____ . 1964c. "Democrats Begin Session Today, Pledge Foreign Policy Restraint." August 24:1, 16.

_____ . 1967. "Miami Beach Tops Nominating Sites." April 12:20.

_____ . 1968a. "Humphrey Given Chicago Phones." August 8:1.

_____ . 1968b. "Convention Biased Against McCarthy, Key Aide Charges." August 10:1, 14.

_____ . 1968c. "Democrats Have No Room for Public at Convention." August 15:1, 30.

_____ . 1972a. "G.O.P. Convention: A Switch in Time." May 7:IV:3.

_____ . 1972b. "White House Woos Unions in Plank." August 18:1.

_____ . 1972c. "Platform Hails G.O.P. Tax Record of 'Sound Reform.' " August 20:1, 50.

_____ . 1972d. "Power Conflicts in G.O.P. Unlikely to Disturb Parley." August 20:1, 50.

_____ . 1972e. "Vote for Brinkley a Welcome Script Change." August 24:46.

_____ . 1975. "G.O.P. Picks Kansas City For Its 1976 Convention." September 8:1.

_____ . 1976a. "Two Ford Backers Named To Key Convention Posts." June 25:A10.

_____ . 1976b. "Sears Seeks To Force Ford To Name Running Mate." August 10:14.

_____ . 1976c. "Ford, Breaking Tradition, to Go to Convention Early." August 12:17.

_____ . 1976d. "G.O.P. Rules Panel Delays Decisions on Key Issues." August 15:24.

_____ . 1976e. "G.O.P. Rules Panel Blocks Two Vice-Presidency Plans." August 16:18.

_____ . 1976f. "The Atmosphere Cools." August 16:19.

_____ . 1976g. "Convention Feels Watergate Toll." August 17:22.

_____ . 1977. "Carter Asks Democratic Leaders To Help Him on Panama Treaties." October 8:24.

_____ . 1978a. "One-Third of Footage In Film for Democrats Supplied by the Navy." December 8:A19.

_____ . 1978b. "Liberals Press Floor Fights Before Democratic Parley." December 8:A21.

_____ . 1978c. "Carter's Inflation Plan Draws Fire As Democrats Convene at Midterm." December 9:1.

_____ . 1978d. "Carter's Dual Role in Memphis." December 10:42.

_____ . 1978e. "Democrats, Under Pressure, Back Carter's Priorities." December 11:D10.

_____ . 1979. "Hotel Rooms Rather than Politics Main Factor in Democrat's [sic] Choice." June 29:B4.

_____ . 1980a. "Kennedy Camp Loses Bid to Raise Share of Tickets to the Convention." May 10:9.

_____ . 1980b. "Powers of Convention Delegates Weighed Amid Democratic Split." May 18:30.

_____ . 1980c. "O'Neill Urges Democrats To Rally Behind President." May 21:A26.

_____ . 1980d. "Udall Decides to Be Neutral in Carter-Kennedy Battle." August 8:A14.

_____ . 1980e. "On the Floor, Carter and Kennedy Camps Deploy Foot Soldiers to Follow Delegates." August 12:B10.

Nixon, Richard M. 1962. *Six Crises*. New York: Pocket Books.

O'Brien, Lawrence F. 1975. *No Final Victories*. New York: Ballantine.

Parmet, Herbert S. 1972. *Eisenhower and the American Crusades*. New York: Macmillan.

Polsby, Nelson W. 1981. "The Democratic Nomination." In *The American Election of 1980*, ed Austin Ranney, pp. 37-60. Washington, D.C.: American Enterprise Institute.

Pomper, Gerald. 1966. "The Nomination of Hubert Humphrey for Vice President." *Journal of Politics* 28:639-59.

_____ . 1977. "The Nominating Contests and Conventions." In *The Election of 1976*, ed Gerald M. Pomper, pp. 1-34. New York: David McKay.

_____ . 1981. "The Nominating Contests." In *The Election of 1980*, ed Gerald M. Pomper, pp. 1-37. Chatham, N.J.: Chatham House.

Ripon Society and Clifford W. Brown, Jr. 1974. *The Jaws of Victory*. Boston: Little, Brown.

Robinson, Donald Allen. 1974. "Presidents and Party Leadership." Paper read at the annual meeting of the American Political Science Association, August 29-September 2, Chicago.

Schell, Jonathan. 1976. *The Time of Illusion*. New York: Knopf.

Sullivan, Denis G. 1977-78. "Party Unity." *Political Science Quarterly* 92:635-45.

Tillett, Paul. 1961. "The National Conventions." In *The Presidential Election and Transition 1960-1961*, ed Paul T. David, pp. 31-56. Washington, D.C.: Brookings Institution.

_____. 1966. "The National Conventions." In *The National Election of 1964*, ed. Milton C. Cummings, Jr., pp. 15-41. Washington, D.C.: Brookings Institution.

Weinberg, Martha Wagner. 1977-78. "Writing the Republican Platform." *Political Science Quarterly* 92:655-62.

White, Theodore H. 1961. *The Making of the President, 1960*. New York: Pocket Books.

_____. 1965. *The Making of the President, 1964*. New York: Atheneum.

_____. 1970. *The Making of the President, 1968*. New York: Pocket Books.

Wise, David. 1978. *The American Police State*. New York: Vintage Books.

Witcover, Jules. 1977. *Marathon*. New York: Signet Books.

PART III

PRESIDENTS AND MIDTERM CAMPAIGNS

6

PRESIDENTS AS MIDTERM CAMPAIGNERS

Roger G. Brown

*O*ne of the few remaining instances of highly visible interaction between presidents and their parties is White House involvement in off-year congressional elections. Of all the potential opportunities for close cooperation between the president and his party's organizations, it is during the midterm races that he can, if he chooses, wear the hat of party leader most openly. For a period of several weeks before the November elections, the president is permitted, indeed expected by his party's leaders, to become a genuine party spokesman rather than the "leader of all the people."

However, presidents have used this opportunity most often not help secure support for the congressional party but to further administration goals—often at the expense of fellow partisans in Congress. From open attempts to punish uncooperative members of the party in the legislature to thinly veiled efforts to divert campaign funds away from congressional races, White House involvement with midterm elections often has been an occasion for intense intraparty rivalry rather than party leadership.

In 1964, V. O. Key wrote (p. 565): "An active role by the President in the midterm campaign is perhaps becoming a more accepted practice of our politics.... Yet the role that [he] should play ... has not become neatly crystallized." His statement is still true two decades later. All recent presidents have participated in midterm campaigns, but with widely divergent approaches and results. In the absence of an institutionalized role, the president's behavior is influenced by the existing political environment, including perceptions of his own popularity, the state of the nation's economy, the expectations of other members of his party, and his own predilections toward partisan campaigning.

Another set of influences may be termed the organizational environment, including White House interaction with the national party committee, with the congressional campaign committees, with candidate organizations, and with other organized fund-raising groups. These factors are summarized in Table 6.1. While all are part of a larger political "ecosystem," organizational and personal factors can be considered as subcategories with correspondingly less influence on a particular president's behavior at midterm.

TABLE 6.1: Factors in Presidential Midterm Involvement

Political Environment	Organizational Environment	
Presidential popularity	Relations with national party committee	President's personal attitudes toward partisan campaigning
National economic conditions	Relations with congressional campaign committees and independent candidate organizations	
Expectations of other actors: party leaders, congressional candidates of president's party		
President's existing legislative margin in Congress	Relations with other organized fund-raising groups	

Source: Compiled by the author.

Of course, the overall strategic goal of the president's campaigning at midterm is not spectacular gains for his party but the limitation of damage from the opposition party. This is true because in every off-year election since the Civil War, except for the one in 1934, the president's party has lost seats in the House of Representatives. The size of the losses has varied greatly in this century, from as many as 70 seats in 1938 to as few as five in 1962. So the obvious reason for committing White House resources to the party's campaign is to hold losses to the smallest number possible, thereby enhancing the president's chances for legislative success in the remainder of his term.

The president's endorsement and campaign assistance are sought by candidates from his congressional party in spite of the long-term trends in favor of national gains for the opposition. After all, each candidate sees his or her race as an individual one, fought out over local issues, rather than as a part of a national campaign. In this localized environment the prestige of the White House being used on behalf of a congressional hopeful may just provide the winning edge. The campaign help may come in the form of personal visits from the president or other members of the administration, written endorsements, White House letters to the candidate to be displayed at every opportunity, or smiling photographs of the candidate with his or her "old friend," the president. The increasing use of electronic technology in campaigns has added the use of live or taped television endorsements by the president, beamed to campaign rallies around the country. Perhaps most importantly, the president's help is needed for raising money, either for individual candidates or for his party's organizations.

It is ironic that presidential campaigning at midterm has become an integral part of the party-leader role in view of the troubled history of this enterprise. Woodrow Wilson began the practice in 1918 as an attempt to bolster congressional support for his conduct of the Great War. He appealed to the nation to strengthen his Democratic majorities in Congress in order to present a unified front to the rest of the world. Wilson's pleas went unheeded, except by those who were angered at the overtly partisan attack. Arthur Mullen, a Midwestern Democratic leader, called Wilson's statement "the most suicidal document ever sent out by the White House" (Key 1964, p. 565). The result was a resounding defeat for Democrats. Their party lost control of both houses of Congress — control they would not regain until 14 years later with the help of Franklin Roosevelt.

Failing to heed the lesson of this episode, FDR suffered his own midterm Waterloo in 1938 (see Milkis, Chapter 7 of this book). Attempting to quiet the growing criticism of his New Deal policies, Roosevelt campaigned against critics in his own party as well as against Republican candidates. Voters again took umbrage at the president's aggressive intrusion into local congressional races. This time, although Democrats did not lose control of Congress, their numbers in the House took a dizzying plummet from 331 to 261 (Hinckley 1981, pp. 144-45).

Midterm results have seldom been positive for either the president or his party. Wilson and Roosevelt felt the wrath of voters and party leaders for their heavy-handed tactics, while Lyndon Johnson was castigated by members of his party for avoiding the campaign of 1966. The criticism was exacerbated by the heavy loss of 48 Democratic House seats that year. In reality, of course, the

EDITOR'S PERSPECTIVE

Presidential Prerogatives and Midterm Campaigns

The following brief articles dramatically illustrate how presidents may use invaluable prerogatives of office—including free television time and costly government programs—to set the stage favorably for their parties' candidates in midterm races.

Reagan Tapes TV Speech
As Final Election Appeal

By a WALL STREET JOURNAL *Staff Reporter*

WASHINGTON—President Reagan will take to the airways one more time before next Tueday's elections to seek support for Republican candidates.

The White House said a five-minute videotape appeal from Mr. Reagan will be broadcast over the three major commercial televison networks Sunday and Monday evenings. The commercials and airtime will be paid for by the Republican National Committee.

• • •

Two weeks ago, Mr. Reagan requested and received free time from two of the networks for a longer economic and political speech. Republicans had first tried to buy time for that speech, but were turned down by the networks.

Wall Street Journal, October 26, 1982, p. 10.

Reaganites step up gestures of aid for voter groups as elections near.

The interest-rate ceiling on government-backed mortgages will likely drop again, probably to 13%. A grant and loan guarantee will go for job-created projects in the South Bronx, aiding unemployed minorities. Strategists hope to cope with "the fairness issue." EPA chief Gorsuch seeks to look beneficent by handing out money for hazardous-waste clean up.

The SBA postpones the end of special aid to 23 minority-owned firms found too large to qualify. Some sticky decisions will wait till after election. Included: a possible cut in Medicare payments for kidney-dialysis treatment. Interior Secretary Watt delays planned actions on offshore leasing, land sales, Western projects

Watt prepares for a flurry of action after Nov. 2. "If you think you've seen a lot of change so far," he tells aides, "you haven't seen anything yet."

Wall Street Journal, October 8, 1982, p. 1.

president's activity in off-year elections is a small piece in a complicated puzzle for those seeking explanations for the individual and aggregate outcomes.

The most widely used characterization of off-year elections has been that they are referenda on the success of the president and his administration. According to this view, the president and his policies are the central issues of the campaign, and the midterm election is a referendum on his performance thus far. However, scholars have identified a number of variables besides voter perceptions of administration performance that seem to help explain either individual or aggregate midterm outcomes. Their studies have not disproved the referendum thesis, but they have greatly enriched overall understanding of off-year electoral behavior.

Angus Campbell (1960) argued that off-year losses for the president's party could be understood in part as the product of a "surge and decline" in voter turnout from the presidential election to the succeeding off-year election. He reasoned that the drama and excitement of presidential races brought to the polls voters who would otherwise have been disinterested observers of the political process. These voters elect not only the successful candidate but many of the congressional candidates of the same party. In the succeeding congressional election, Campbell continued, many of these occasional voters stay home and thus deprive candidates from the president's party of a sizable bloc of votes. This paves the way for opposition gains. Hinckley (1967) refined Campbell's analysis by showing that the size of the president's winning margin is directly related to the size of his party's losses in the House at midterm.

However, Campbell's theory of aggregate outcomes had serious weaknesses when applied to individual election results. His explanation assumed that a different type of voter participated in presidential elections than went to the polls at midterm. Further study failed to find any meaningful differences in the voters who were surveyed over three elections, two midterm (1966 and 1970) and one presidential (1968) (Arsenau and Wolfinger 1973). Furthermore, the idea that presidential coattails carry a sizable number of House candidates into office has come under serious question. Several analysts have identified incumbency as a far more important variable than presidential vote in explaining individual results in congressional elections (on the coattail effect, see, for example, Moos 1952; Key 1964, pp. 556-71; Cummings 1966; on incumbency, see Mayhew 1974; Kritzer and Eubank 1979; Edwards 1979).

Even at the aggregate level, Campbell's explanation of midterm results has been shown to be overly simplistic. Kramer (1971) demonstrated that national economic conditions have influenced strongly the overall outcomes of congressional elections. By adding a measure of presidential popularity just before the election to an indicator of the country's economic health, Tufte (1975) generated a highly predictive model of aggregate results in off-year elections. Finally, Jacobson and Kernell (1981) argued that because political professionals have come to *expect* certain election outcomes based on their own readings of economic conditions and presidential popularity, they may alter those outcomes through a series of choices on candidate recruitment and the allocation of campaign resources.

Given this brief review of the many factors that can influence midterm results, the impact of presidential campaigning in such elections is problematic, to say the least. What is more important here is that regardless of the expected election results, presidents have continued to believe that they can better their political circumstances through active intervention in the off-year campaigns. Equally important is the expectation on the part of many party leaders and congressional candidates that the president will act as a prestigious symbol of party solidarity during the campaign. The expectation of the president's help in the off-year races is so pervasive, according to Koenig (1975), that the president "is expected to assist ... indiscriminately, including the campaigns of those whose election would injure his program more than their opponents' victories would." It is in the president's self-interest, then, that he make available to favored candidates of his party the prestige and resources of the White House in the hope that his generosity will be remembered in the midst of some future legislative battle over the administration's programs.

PRESIDENTIAL INVOLVEMENT IN MIDTERM CAMPAIGNS, 1962–82

Over the past two decades, six midterm congressional campaigns have formed an impressionistic jumble of political circumstances, candidate personalities, and degrees of presidential involvement. Six presidents, from Kennedy to Reagan, have surveyed the political battleground, and each has made a calculation of the most advantageous use of his time and resources balanced against the expected political benefits. The responses have ranged from Johnson's seeming desertion under fire of fellow Democrats in 1966 to Reagan's all-out effort to make himself and his economic policies the central issues in 1982. In the absence of clear evidence as to what effects the presidential activity actually had on mid-term voters, the focus of the following sections is on the political and organizational circumstances surrounding the president at the midpoint of his term.

The election results included in Table 6.2 provide a rather colorless summary of the six campaigns. They do not reveal the dramatic roles played by the chilling threat of a nuclear exchange in 1962, the pursuit of an increasingly unpopular war effort in 1966, the toppling of an administration under siege in 1974, or the euphoric accomplishment of a breakthrough in Middle East diplomacy in 1978. All of these events had some presumed but unmeasurable effect on presidential activity in the past six midterm campaigns and on voter judgments of the party in power at the time. The following sections describe the political and organizational circumstances that may shape the president's role in congressional campaigns.

TABLE 6.2:   Results of Midterm Congressional Elections, 1962–82

| Administration | Year | Changes in Seats for President's Party | |
		House	Senate
Kennedy	1962	-5	+ 2
Johnson	1966	-48	− 4
Nixon	1970	-12	− 3
Ford	1974	-48	− 5
Carter	1978	-16	− 3
Reagan	1982	-26	+ 1*

* Republicans gained one seat that had been listed previously as "independent."

Source: Barbara Hinckley, *Congressional Elections* (Washington, D.C.: Congressional Quarterly Press, 1981), pp. 124, 144-45. 1982 results from the New York *Times,* November 4, 1982.

The Political Environment

Low Presidential Popularity at Midterm: Johnson and Carter

Perceptions of how popular the president is with voters nationwide tend to influence both how involved the president wishes to be at midterm and how welcome his help is to congressional candidates of his party. As the campaigns of 1966 and 1978 approached, for example, both Presidents Johnson and Carter were having difficulties that translated into declines in their popular approval ratings. As a result, many candidates running on Democratic tickets were not anxious for presidential visits that might have called attention to even an indirect link between themselves and the president or his policies.

Despite his impressive legislative triumphs in 1965, Lyndon Johnson's popularity ratings had been steadily declining since 1964. They dropped an average of ten points per year from the end of 1963 to the end of 1967 (Kearns 1977). Although American commitments and casualties were increasing in Vietnam, conduct of the war did not appear to be the sole cause for erosion of support for the president. Mueller (1973) found, for example, that a majority of respondents in 1966 supported Johnson's decision to bomb Hanoi. The administration's domestic policies also were still supported by a majority of Americans, but what did show a marked decline were measures of the public's confidence in Johnson himself. Before the fall elections of 1966, Evans and Novak (1966) wrote that: "The Gallup Poll in June showed Johnson's popularity at only 46 percent, the lowest since Harry Truman. Never was there an unhappier warrior than the Commander-in-Chief in mid-1966."

Nevertheless, Johnson began a vigorous campaign effort that July, promising to do all he could to help Democratic members of the 89th Congress. He made 28 political stops between July and October, apparently ignoring advice from party leaders that the campaign might go badly for Democrats because of his eroding popularity. Then, abruptly, Johnson and his political advisers seemed to conclude that his involvement could hurt some embattled Democrats, particularly in the South where the president's push for the civil rights legislation was being used as a bludgeon against moderates of his party.

In the closing weeks of the campaign, Johnson was unavailable either for visits or for endorsements. He penciled into his schedule several meetings with foreign leaders, both in Washington and as part of an Asian tour. When he returned a few days before the election, Johnson remained aloof from his party's struggle for votes. Instead of resuming his campaign activity, he decided to undergo minor throat surgery. When prompted by reporters in a news conference just before election day, Johnson refused to endorse any Democratic candidate.

Even though his decision to stop campaigning was forced by public opinion and by the pleas of some candidates seeking to distance themselves from the White House, Johnson was criticized roundly. The returns showed crushing Democratic losses of 48 seats in the House and 4 seats in the Senate, while Republicans also gained 8 new governorships. *Congressional Quarterly* (November 1966, p. 2773) pronounced the GOP to be "in a position of new power and relevance on the national scene." The lesson for presidents in this episode seems to be that they have little to lose by campaigning vigorously at midterm. The party's leaders already expect some losses, and a president who remains above the fray is a convenient scapegoat on whom to lay the blame.

Jimmy Carter's experiences in 1978 illustrate the changes that can occur in the number of campaign invitations a president receives if his popularity suddenly improves. Early in his administration, Carter had created deep resentments among Democratic leaders by appearing to ignore the party throughout his first year in office. To make matters worse, his popularity ratings had gone into a steep decline following his impassioned defense of Office of Management and Budget Director Bert Lance, a close friend who stood accused of illegal banking transactions in Georgia. From July to October 1977, the Harris Poll tracked Carter's popularity as it nosedived from 59 percent to 48 percent (Glad 1980, p. 439).

Advisers to President Carter, including Vice-President Walter Mondale and political trouble-shooter Tim Kraft, warned him early in 1978 that Democratic fences were in serious need of mending. Taking the advice to heart, Carter scheduled a series of White House breakfasts for state party leaders, and he got an early jump on midterm campaigning. By the end of February he had already made campaign speeches on behalf of Democratic senators in three New England states: Claiborne Pell of Rhode Island, Thomas McIntyre of New Hampshire, and William Hathaway of Maine (Glad, p. 423). In spite of the show of party unity, however, many observers remained skeptical of Carter's intention or ability to help in the upcoming fall elections.

David Broder (1978) analyzed the situation in the Washington Post at midyear. He pointed out that it was fully "17 months after Carter took office [that] the White House finally got around to the basic courtesy of having the Democratic state chairmen and national committee members in for a drink and a chat." Broder warned that the efforts to reestablish party ties had come too late to "let Jimmy Carter and his agent make much of a positive contribution to the November campaigns." In the absence of presidential leadership, he wrote, the state parties and congressional hopefuls had gone ahead with their own fund-raising and organization plans and were "separating themselves from those Carter policies that are poison in their states and districts."

In spite of such warnings, Carter promised 15 to 20 days of campaign traveling by the November elections, in addition to numerous trips by Mondale, members of his cabinet, and family emissaries. But the campaign activity was not welcomed with grateful hearts by all. Open statements were made by both Democratic new-comers (such as senatorial nominee Bill Bradley of New Jersey) and incumbents (like Senator Floyd Haskell of Colorado) asking Carter not to appear in their states during the campaign, since they considered his help a liability. Disastrously low public approval ratings for Carter's job performance were the obvious reasons for such statements. By late July the situation had deteriorated to the point of provoking a response by Democratic National Chairman John White advising Democratic candidates to stop taking "cheap shots" at Carter. "The Democratic Party, White said, 'encourages dissent and disagreement' on issues, but considers personal attacks on the President out of bounds" (Peterson 1978).

For President Carter, though, the political world shifted dramatically in September 1978. A series of bold and risky initiatives had brought two ancient enemies, Israel and Egypt, together for serious peace negotiations at Camp David, Maryland. There, Carter badgered, cajoled, and sermonized until Egypt's Anwar Sadat and Israel's Menachem Begin agreed to an historic peace accord. Carter received international acclaim for his contribution to the Camp David settlement, and his approval ratings rebounded from 39 percent to 59 percent almost overnight (Glad, p. 443).

In the wake of the Camp David triumph, President Carter's campaign assistance was in sudden and universal demand. Carter spoke on behalf of both Bradley and Haskell, calling the latter "a national treasure." According to the *Congressional Quarterly* (November 1978, p. 3171),

> Democratic candidates decided *en masse* this fall that they wanted Carter to visit them—something many of them would not have predicted earlier in the year. . . . Even in Iowa and Kansas, where Carter administration farm policies appeared early in the year to threaten statewide Democratic candidates, the president has come and spoken and the Democratic nominees have been grateful for the attention and the fund-raising help.

It was, of course, unclear whether Carter's campaign help brought to individal candidates votes they would not have received otherwise. He was, however, able to improve briefly his relations with his party's organizations and no doubt garnered some feelings of indebtedness on the part of Democrats in Congress. Final results in November still showed a loss of 16 House seats and 3 Senate seats for the Democrats

(Table 6.2), and outcome that was not spectacularly successful but that was far better than the calamitous losses of 1966.

High Presidential Popularity: Kennedy

Unlike Presidents Johnson and Carter, Kennedy approached the off-year elections of 1962 with the solid backing of American public opinion. In September the Gallup Poll reported that 69 percent of respondents rated Kennedy positively. From the very beginning of White House preparations for the off-year contests, "the President planned a mid-term campaign more vigorous than that of any President in history" (Sorensen 1966, p. 396). His campaign help had begun as early as the fall of 1961, when he had stumped for New Jersey gubernatorial candidate Richard Hughes and for House candidate Henry Gonzalez in a Texas special election (Broder 1972, p. 34).

For President Kennedy, though, the 1962 elections presented an opportunity to alter the congressional balance that had stymied his major legislative initiatives for the first two years of his term. Elected by a thin margin in 1960 when he had run behind many Democratic congressional candidates in their districts, Kennedy had not been able to command a great deal of partisan loyalty on Capitol Hill. A conservative coalition of Republicans and southern Democrats had effectively bottled up his programs, often killing them in committee. Kennedy had realized the implications of the 1960 vote and was fond of quoting the Jeffersonian aphorism: "Great innovations should not be forced on slender majorities" (Schlesinger 1965, p. 708).

To enlarge those majorities in 1962, Kennedy hoped to convince voters that sending more Republicans to Congress would damage the public's interests as well as his own. From late July to November 1962, Kennedy and Vice-President Lyndon Johnson campaigned in over a dozen states each. Despite their efforts, many close observers predicted heavy Democratic losses in both House and Senate. However, the final results came as a pleasant surprise to the administration: The Democrats lost only five seats in the House, while the Republicans gained only three, because of redistricting. The net loss of two seats gave the Democrats the best showing for any party in power since 1934. In the Senate the Democrats actually increased their majority by four seats (Hinckley 1981, pp. 144-45). Despite his party's success, Kennedy made it clear that such campaigning was far from his favorite pastime. "One of the great myths in American life" he said, "is that those who are in politics love to campaign" (Sorensen 1966, p. 396).

It should be reemphasized that, like all midterm results, those of 1962 were influenced by a variety of factors besides the campaign involvement of President Kennedy. The small number of "coattail" congressmen in 1960, for example, meant that fewer Democrats were affected adversely by the absence of presidential voters in 1962. As Key explained (1966, p. 571):

> Democratic success in 1958 brought victory in a goodly number of marginal districts. In 1960, contrary to the usual results in presidential victories, Democrats lost many of these marginal seats and few Democratic representatives came into office on Kennedy's coattails. . . . Thus, in a sense, Democrats did not win in 1960 the seats they would have been expected to lose in 1962.

A more immediate influence on voters in 1962 was the Cuban missile crisis, a classic example of the "October surprise." By appearing to face down and embarrass Nikita Khrushchev, the Soviet navy, and Fidel Castro in one bold stroke, Kennedy turned a dangerous show of brinksmanship into a political boost. His apparently calm resolve in the face of the nation's most serious nuclear confrontation was hailed by many who thought President Kennedy had proven once and for all his presidential mettle. Although no one would suggest that Kennedy's handling of the Cuban missile crisis was undertaken deliberately for the benefit of midterm voters, the timing of that dramatic showdown may well help explain the relatively strong showing by Democratic candidates.

Polling As a Targeting Strategy

As the foregoing sections suggest, opinion polls have been institutionalized as part of political campaigns at all levels of the American system. They are used to monitor the president's popularity and that of his programs. They also have come to be used for targeting the allocation of party funding and presidential assistance on races where such help will be most advantageous. In 1982 the Republican Party, which enjoyed a huge edge over Democrats in campaign funds, used a sophisticated system of frequent "tracking polls." The polls, taken almost daily in key contests, were credited with alerting some senators to dangerous surges of electoral support for the opposition. According to the Washington *Post* (Broder 1982),

> this year the Republican Senatorial Campaign Committee headed by Sen. Bob Packwood (R-Ore.) invested more than a half-million dollars

in "tracking" 13 contests expected to be close. Nationally, it alerted Packwood and his staff in mid-October to the danger of lethargy and a disproportionely low turnout among Republican voters. As a result, they shifted $1.3 million into a direct-mail appeal to 7 million households for their voters to turn out to save President Reagan's majority.

The tracking polls were credited specifically with enabling Missouri Republican Senator John Danforth, a popular member of the Senate, to stave off a spirited challenge from Democratic state senator Harriet Woods. Assessing the damage done by the Republican polls, Woods's pollster complained, "we only had money for two polls all fall, so we were constantly looking back at data 10 days old and trying to guess where and how it might have changed. We just didn't have what they had."

The obvious utility of such polls for White House political strategists is their value in allowing more enlightened decisions on the best use of the president's campaign assistance. A decision might be taken to throw more resources into a tight electoral struggle, while races where the White House choice appears hopelessly behind may be written off as a waste of further effort.

Another twist on poll-based campaign strategy was illustrated during the 1982 races. The New York *Times* reported that President Reagan was attempting "reverse coattail riding" when he stumped for a North Carolina congressional candidate. William Cobey, a protégé of conservative Republican Senator Jesse Helms (R-N.C.) appearing to be a sure winner even before Reagan's visit. Other areas of the country, especially those where record high unemployment had crippled local economies, apparently were judged hostile territory and thus off-limits for his whistle stops. "So, North Carolina has emerged as a safe peripheral area for Mr. Reagan," the *Times* explained, "now that public opinion or political prudence has frozen him out of the main battlegrounds in the Middle West and the big states essential to Mr. Reagan's electoral base . . . ." (Raines 1982).

Partisanship As an Influence on Presidential Campaigning

Perceptions of the president's popularity, national economic barometers, and the expectations of members of the president's party may all be considered as facets of the external political environment surrounding the White House at midterm. Another influence on presidential campaigning is the internal constraint of the incumbent's own attitudes toward overt partisanship. Lyndon Johnson's apparent attitude that Democratic Party organizations were a hindrance to his broader "consensus" may help explain his sudden exit from the 1966 campaigns, for example (Kearns 1977, p. 256). On the other hand, Gerald Ford's energetic efforts on behalf of Republican candidates in 1974, despite the predictions of a post-Watergate drubbing for his party, were in part a reflection of his long-time commitment to party service. Again, in 1982, Ronald Reagan overlooked a disappointing 41 percent approval rating and a massive 10.1 unemployment rate as he mounted a highly partisan campaign. His goal appeared to be the elevation of local congressional races to the level of a national referendum on his economic policies. Far from striking a conciliatory tone, Reagan openly charged Democratic leaders with using demagoguery and lies. White House spokesman Larry Speakes added (Cannon 1982): "We feel the Democrats are waging a campaign of distortion. The whole Democratic campaign effort in the final days will be based on a campaign of fear."

Some presidents have left the most aggressively partisan midterm campaigning to other members of their administrations. Vice-Presidents Richard Nixon in 1958 and Spiro Agnew in 1970 played their surrogate party leader roles with particularly caustic enthusiasm. President Eisenhower's widely reported distaste for bare-knuckle politics meant that Nixon was dispatched with orders to say in campaign speeches what the president preferred not to say. According to Wills (1969, p. 128), "the Vice President was given the thankless task of campaigning for every Republican in America on off-years, when the ticket, without Eisenhower's magic name at the top, took woeful beatings."

Seizing his own opportunity to send the second-in-command into the thick of battle, Nixon called upon Spiro Agnew in the congressional campaign of 1970. Agnew "bombarded the Democrats with heavy rhetorical cannonade . . . against such liberal Democratic Senators as Albert Gore of Tennessee and Vance Hartke of Indiana" (Koenig 1975, p. 121). Vice-President Agnew appeared to revel in his position as partisan point man, and he seemed to take particular delight in baiting and then excoriating youthful anti-Vietnam war activists. As the campaign neared a frenzied conclusion, Agnew declared: "It's time to take my gloves off. No more of this Mr. Nice Guy." To prove he meant what he had said, Agnew then referred to a group of California protesters as "misfits . . . garbage. . . . It's time to sweep that kind of garbage out of our society" (Schell 1976, p. 130). Senator Gore (1972, p.

301) predictably bitter at having been defeated following a concentrated negative attack led by Agnew, later wrote that the 1970 campaign "was one of the shabbiest political episodes in American history." Such vitriolic surrogate campaigning serves, of course, to leave the president on the "high road" at the same time that a scathingly partisan attack is mounted by the administration.

The Organizational Environment

The National Committees and the Congressional Campaign Committees

As with the political environment, the organizational relationships that come into play during off-year elections are fragmented and greatly varied from one administration to another. The organizational components—the national party committees, Senate and House campaign committees, White House political advisers, and organized fund-raising groups—are standard elements of the campaign drama. The ways in which they interact are neither formalized nor predictable.

The history of White House relationships with the Senate and House campaign committees more closely resembles a blood feud than a bond of partisan kinship. The birth of the first Capitol Hill campaign committee has been traced to the bitter struggle between President Andrew Johnson and the House Republicans in 1866. "Lest the President use the national committee against it, the party in Congress formed an independent committee to campaign for the election of Republican Representatives in 1866" (Key 1964, p. 324). This epic battle between Johnson and the party that had chosen and elected him culminated, of course, in the great impeachment debate of 1867-68, with President Johnson narrowly avoiding removal from office. Although the intraparty competition fostered by the separation of powers has reached such a melodramatic pitch only rarely, the Hill committees have, until recently, continued to guard their independence jealously.

Understandably, the committees charged with promoting the election of fellow partisans to Congress are motivated much more by their own survival instinct than by concerns for White House political fortunes. This divergence of priorities surfaced dramatically during the 1982 congressional campaigns when the chairman of the Republican Senatorial Campaign Committee, Robert Packwood of Oregon, was openly critical of Reagan administration policies. Apparently fearful that his colleagues seeking reelection would be hurt seriously by the perception that the Republican leadership cared less about women, minorities, and blue-collar workers, Packwood publicly warned Reagan that he was turning the party into an "assemblage of white males over 40" (McGrory 1982). Reagan and his supporters in the Senate were so outraged by Packwood's break with the administration line that they voted to replace him with conservative Senator Richard Lugar (Ind.) shortly after the November elections. Mary McGrory reported in the Washington *Post* that "Lugar denied any White House complicity in the plot and minimized its ideological content ... Packwood's stewardship was not an issue; it was a question of discipline and loyalty to the Gipper [Reagan]."

Packwood's critics, including Reagan, appeared to forget that the traditional stance of campaign committee chairs has been independence from White House control and separation from unpopular administration policies. Senator Packwood was certainly not the first chairperson of the parties' campaign committees to advise candidates to stress local issues and their own records rather than binding themselves too closely to the president's record.

Presidents as Fund-Raisers

Aside from the desire of some congressional candidates to distance themselves from administration policies, the major source of friction between the White House and the national committee leadership on one side and the campaign committees on the other is the competition for funds. Often, the various party organizations solicit funds from the same group of identified donors, creating the possibility of animosity between the national committees and the Capitol Hill committees, among the four campaign committees in Congress, and among the party committees, independent candidate organizations, and political action committees. This is not to mention the likely dissatisfaction on the part of the donor who is approached by solicitors from all of the above.

White House intervention in the fund-raising process reached unprecedented levels in the early 1960s. Facing the large deficits left over from Adlai Stevenson's unsuccessful presidential campaigns in 1952 and 1956, the Democratic National Committee (DNC) had organized a series of coordinated fund-raising efforts in the late 1950s. They led eventually to establishment of the President's Club, a 1960 brainchild of the DNC's recently resurrected Finance Committee. This was apparently the first effort at centralized fund raising by the national committee and the campaign organizations in Congress (Cotter and Bibby 1979). The President's Club, made up of donors of

$1,000 each, reached a peak of 4,000 members in 1964. From 1961 through 1966, the President's Club raised over $6 million in contributions for Democratic candidates nationwide (Alexander 1972, pp. 96-98).

The unaccustomed integration of party fund-raising organs was short-lived, however. Congressional Democrats became disillusioned when they realized that nearly $1 million raised for Senate and House candidates had been spent by the DNC to help pay the 1964 presidential campaign debt. Questions about the sources of contributions for the President's Club and about the ways in which the funds were being allocated grew so numerous by 1966 that the White House was forced to abandon the device. According to Alexander (1976, pp. 131-68), the dubious legality of some President's Club practices, such as accepting contributions from government contractors, added to a growing chorus of demands for campaign finance reforms. Aside from questions of ethical practices, Kearns (1977, p. 256) argued that "Johnson's principal fund-raising device, the President's Club, diverted money and contributions from party organizations at all levels, concentrating control over party funds in the President's hands, and thus further contributing to the disintegration of the local party."

His fund-raising services are the most tangible support a president can provide for the party organizations' campaign activities. Of course, the level of enthusiasm for such work has varied widely among recent presidents. John Kennedy spoke at eight Democratic fund raisers in his first year alone (*Public Papers* 1962). In 1975, Gerald Ford spoke proudly of his success at raising money for Republican organizations at national, state, and local levels. Remarking that he had raised over $2 million at rallies and dinners, Ford explained that he felt an "obligation to try and strengthen and rebuild the Republican Party organization" (*Public Papers* 1976).

However, former presidential counselor and cabinet member Joseph Califano has written that the burden of raising money for party organizations is more often a source of annoyance and irritation for presidents. Recounting his experiences as a member of the Johnson White House, Califano (1975, p. 152) wrote:

> The Democratic Party was in debt when Johnson was re-elected in 1964 and, in order to defray that debt, he found it necessary to attend a series of dinners during the course of his presidency. He invariably found those dinners demeaning. Often he would say, "It is insulting to the presidency and wrong for a president to go hat in hand asking for money from the wealthy few."

EDITOR'S PERSPECTIVE

It's just "part of the territory" today that the president will be asked to serve as "chief fund raiser" (at least symbolically) for his party. This customarily involves addressing such gatherings as the party's Congressional Fund-Raising Dinner. President Johnson—though already quite unpopular with copartisans for neglecting the party organization—continued the custom in 1966. One can imagine that his opening remarks were carefully constructed to relieve anticipated tension, and that some in the audience found his description of the party to be far too accurate to be humorous.

REMARKS BY THE PRESIDENT
AT THE
DEMOCRATIC CONGRESSIONAL FUND-RAISING DINNER
MAY 12, 1966

It is a pleasure to be here tonight. I always enjoy seeing so many people who are concerned with the welfare of Democratic candidates. I have some slight interest in them, myself.

I am sure that some of you remember what Will Rogers used to say. "I'm not a member of any organized political party," he said, "I'm a Democrat."

I ran across that quotation just the other day in a magazine article. That article went on to say: "This week, any Democrat in the U.S. could borrow Will Rogers' words and describe his own status with as much accuracy as humor.... The Democratic party if disorganized, in debt and leaderless. ... Democrats are wondering where their next candidates... are coming from...."

Source: Lyndon Baines Johnson Library, WHCF Aides Files, Will Sparks file, dated 5/10/66 and labeled "Fund Raising Dinner-D.C.," p. 1.

One reason that presidents may find it unrewarding to spend valuable time in party fund-raising efforts is that the parties' share of total campaign spending has shrunk drastically. From 1972 to 1978, the party organization's share of spending in House campaigns declined from 17 percent to 7 percent (Huckshorn and Bibby 1982). This decline was the result, in large part, of legal limits on party spending enacted as part of a wave of campaign finance reforms in the 1970s, and the consequently increased use of independent candidate organizations and political action committees (PACs) as sources of campaign funds.

Under current guidelines of the Federal Election Commission, direct party contributions may not exceed $5,000 per House candidate in each election. This amount may be donated by the congressional campaign committee and by the national committee, so the total party contributions to a single House candidate must not exceed $20,000 for both the primary and the general elections. In addition, national party committees may spend a specified amount *on behalf* of candidates, which in 1980 brought the total legal expenditures by a party for any House candidate to $34,720 (Jacobson 1983, pp. 55-56). This amount appears almost trivial when campaigns for the House of Representatives cost as much as $1 million during the 1982 elections.

The legal limits for direct and coordinated party spending on behalf of Senate candidates are much higher, but even so, the amount of money spent by candidate organizations and PACs continues to dwarf the parties' share. In 1980, for example, political action committees accounted for 25 percent of all congressional campaign spending, and in 1982 more than 3,200 PACs picked up the tab for 30 percent of the most expensive congressional campaign in history (Taylor 1982). Such figures provide little incentive for presidents to work through party organizations for the purpose of raising congressional campaign funds. So presidents may be discouraged from assisting party fund-raising efforts at a time when that assistance is one of the parties' most urgent needs.

Two recent trends may offer a glimmer of encouragement to the parties in the competitive and conflictual environment of congressional campaigns. First, Republican national party committees have begun the practice of "agency agreements" with their state and local counterparts, which allows the national party to spend both its share and the state's share in congressional campaigns. Used mostly in Senate races, agency agreements made it possible for Republican Party national committees to raise their 1980 spending limit to nearly $1 million for a Senate race in California (Jacobson 1983, pp. 56-57). This amount is not overwhelming in an era when campaigns for the Senate may cost as much as $12-15 million, but it does make the party's contribution significant enough to help counter the growing electoral influence of PACs and single-issue groups. Of course, it must be added that some parties are more equal than others when it comes to raising and spending money. In 1979 and 1980, the national Republican committees raised a combined total of $111 million, while the DNC and Democratic campaign committees together raised only $19 million in contributions (Orren 1982, p. 38). So, according to recent results, agency agreements and other attempts to increase the level of party spending in campaigns may disproportionately favor the Republican Party organizations.

The second trend toward strengthening and coordinating the efforts of party organizations in campaigns was begun by President Reagan in the wake of substantial Republican losses in the 1982 election. To replace outgoing Republican National Chairman Richard Richards, Reagan chose his close friend and political ally, Senator Paul Laxalt (R-Nev.). Laxalt was offered a broad-ranging portfolio that was reminiscent of the strong party chairman of earlier eras. According to the Reagan plan, Laxalt would assume the new title of "general chairman" of the Republican Party, with authority to oversee not only the national committee but also the White House political operation and the congressional campaign committees. Under this arrangement, Laxalt would run the party from his position as Senator, while the day-to-day affairs of the national committee would be directed by another party leader to be named by Laxalt.

The arrangement proposed by Reagan presented the possibility of even more subordination of party affairs to the wishes of the White House. However, for proponents of stronger parties who have lamented the increasing institutional separation between the president and his party organizations, the plan appeared to offer better lines of communication and at least the chances of a closer working relationship. One of the benefits for party organizations could be less intraparty rivalry and less competition for funds during campaign periods. An integrated and coordinated party effort in off-year elections could help to rejuvenate party organizations and might lead to a better working relationship between the president and his party in Congress.

WOULD-BE PRESIDENTS AT MIDTERM

A final aspect of presidential involvement in midterm campaigns deserves mention. One of the most important off-year elections for recent presidents has been the one *before* each president's own election. While ostensibly campaigning for fellow party members, presidential hopefuls have been able to make nationwide contacts with state and local party leaders, with business and labor leaders, and, most importantly, with potential voters. The all-important goal of widespread name recognition has been furthered, and the initial framework for a national campaign organization has been built. Meanwhile, the prospective presidential candidates have accumulated political IOUs from congressional candidates who have profited from the campaign assistance.

Senator John Kennedy toured the country in the summer and fall of 1958, campaigning strenuously for fellow Democrats in spite of the fact that he was facing his own reelection challenge in Massachusetts. Even after his overwhelming victory, Kennedy continued to give pep talks to Democratic groups as far away as Washington State and Alaska, while his aides were busy gathering campaign intelligence and names of prospective cabinet members for 1960.

In 1966, while Democratic leaders criticized the lukewarm assistance of Lyndon Johnson in the congressional campaign, Richard Nixon worked feverishly on behalf of fellow Republicans. Although he had no need to increase his recognition by voters, Nixon was able to reassure party leaders and other potential backers he had the necessary desire and resilience to be a credible candidate for the 1968 Republican nomination. His efforts in 1966 won him praise from members of his party when they made substantial electoral gains.

Jimmy Carter made perhaps the best use of his preelection midterm experience of any would-be president. In early 1973 he actively sought the job as chairman of the Committee to Elect Democrats in 1974, to the surprise of DNC Chairman Robert Strauss (Witcover 1977, p. 117). Carter's young political advisors Hamilton Jordan and Jody Powell began traveling, meeting party leaders, conducting DNC polls, and holding candidate workshops—all in the name of helping congressional Democrats in 1974. According to Betty Glad (1980, p. 212).

> Carter himself "took off like he was being chased." . . . By August, 1973, as he wrote Senator Walter Mondale, he had met with Democratic leaders in thirty-nine states. . . . [He] met with the leaders of numerous groups normally affiliated with the Democratic Party—"labor unions, farmers, Spanish-Americans, teachers, environmentalists, women, local officials, retired persons, government workers, blacks, and the House and Senate campaign committees."

Carter parlayed his 1974 campaign experience into a nationwide network of party contacts and campaign volunteers that figured prominently in his successful bid for the presidency in 1976. Without that exposure, he might well have remained "Jimmy Who?"

The practice of using midterm campaigns as running starts for the next presidential campaign was continued by Republican Ronald Reagan in 1978 and Democrat Walter Mondale in 1982. Off-year elections have seemingly become institutionalized as the unofficial kick-offs to the now common two-year presidential races.

CONCLUSIONS AND RECOMMENDATIONS

Clearly, presidents as campaigners for their parties have been motivated by self-interest rather than altruistic urges to support and strengthen the party system. When they have been persuaded to shoulder part of the campaign burden, their efforts have been directed toward influencing the composition of the next Congress and fostering goodwill on the part of the congressional party. Sometimes, as in 1966 and 1982, presidents have used midterm campaigns as opportunities for concentrated defenses of unpopular administration policies. Off-year races have served as "time-outs" from stately nonpartisanship, while presidents have directed barrages toward the opposition party and toward critics in the presidential party.

Many congressional candidates and party organizations, though, still seek the president's help eagerly, even during periods of low presidential popularity. Presidents continue to be regarded as visible and powerful symbols of the parties they lead, in spite of the weakened organizational ties between the White House and the party. Also, the president and his policies serve as convenient scapegoats following the normal midterm losses for the presidential party.

Judging by the records of presidents as campaigners and fund raisers, there is much room for improvement. The following recommendations suggest actions on the part of both presidents and party organizations that could help to make congressional campaigns more cooperative and mutually beneficial occasions.

The president should continue to set aside as much time as possible for aiding his party at midterm. It is one of his best opportunities to fulfill the duties of party leadership without appearing to violate the unwritten restriction against excess partisanship. The White House has little to lose by providing this assistance since the party's losses will be blamed largely on the administration whether the president campaigns or not. Furthermore, there will be enough grateful members of the congressional party to provide a return on the president's investment in the midst of some future legislative struggle.

The president should resist the temptation to turn the off-year campaign into a national test of his popularity or of the rectitude of his programs. This strategy nearly always has been interpreted—correctly so—as self-serving and potentially damaging to the party's candidates. Abundant research has demonstrated that congressional candidates benefit most from such factors as incumbency and constituent recognition, not from a close association with the administration's record. Therefore, attempts to nationalize the midterm campaign take away from some candidates the localized advantages on which they depend for their electoral survival. Besides, such attempts have not been notably successful from either the president's or the party's point of view, witness the campaigns of 1938 and 1982, for example.

The president can be most useful to his party's campaign organizations by lending his name and, when possible, his presence to fund-raising activities. In order for parties to remain viable as institutional links between the government and the voters, they must be able to compete in the ultraexpensive, high-technology environment of PACs, single-interest groups, and independent campaign organizations. Besides the traditional dinners and rallies, presidents and party organizations must take more advantage of the new money-raising techniques, such as President Reagan's use of satellite broadcasts in 1982 to reach several Republican fund-raisers in a single evening without leaving the White House. Such technology, which has threatened the parties' very existence, may also be harnessed to speed their recovery.

The national party organizations should continue and intensify recent efforts to coordinate their candidate assistance programs, advertising campaigns, and spending targets during off-year races. Intraparty rivalry and competition for the same campaign contributions only add to the fragmentation and duplication of effort that place parties at a disadvantage in the "new politics." Agency agreements and other forms of party cooperation are small but significant steps toward the rebuilding of the American party system. In this regard, the proposed coordination of Republican organizations under one general chairperson appears promising. Even though the actual intent may be the consolidation of party control in the hands of a presidential lieutenant, this arrangement may reopen two-way communications between the White House and the party organizations—a prerequisite for a stronger party system.

From a broader perspective, presidents and parties have much to offer each other despite their estrangement in recent decades. Having its banner carried by the president is the most visible and effective symbol of a party's success. For the president, the dependable support of a nationwide party organization has become ever more desirable as the demands of his job and the expectations for his success have become more impossible to satisfy.

REFERENCES

Alexander, Herbert E. 1972. *Money in Politics*. Washington, D.C.: Public Affairs Press.

_____. 1976. *Financing Politics: Money, Elections and Political Reform*. Washington, D.C.: Congressional Quarterly Press.

Arsenau, Robert, and Raymond Wolfinger. 1973. "Voting Behavior in Congressional Elections." Paper presented at the annual meeting of the American Political Science Association, September.

Broder, David S. 1972. *The Party's Over: The Failure of Politics in America.* New York: Harper and Row.

_____. 1978. "A Neglected Democratic Party." Washington *Post*, June 14.

_____. 1982. "Tracking." Washington *Post*, November 7, p. A1.

Califano, Joseph A., Jr. 1975. *A Presidential Nation*. New York: W. W. Norton.

Campbell, Angus. 1960. "Surge and Decline: A Study of Electoral Change." *Public Opinion Quarterly* 24 (Fall): 397-418.

Cannon, Lou. 1982. "Reagan Stumping West . . . " Washington *Post*, October 29 p. A12.

Cotter, Cornelius P., and John F. Bibby, 1979. "The Impact of Reform on the National Party Organizations." Paper presented at the annual meeting of the American Political Science Association, September.

Cummings, Milton C., Jr. 1966. *Congressmen and the Electorate*. New York: The Free Press.

Edwards, George C. 1979. "The Impact of Presidential Coattails on Outcomes of Presidential Elections." *American Politics Quarterly*, January, pp. 94-108.

Evans, Rowland, and Robert Novak. 1966. *Lyndon Johnson: The Exercise of Power*. New York: New American Library.

Glad, Betty. 1980. *Jimmy Carter: In Search of the Great White House*. New York: W. W. Norton.

Gore, Albert. 1972. *Let the Glory Out: My South and its Politics*. New York: Viking.

Hinckley, Barbara. 1967. "Interpreting House Midterm Elections: Towards a Measurement of the In-Party's 'Expected' Loss of Seats." *American Political Science Review* 61 (September): 694-700.

_____. 1981. *Congressional Elections*. Washington, D.C.: Congressional Quarterly Press.

Huckshorn, Robert J., and John F. Bibby. 1982. "State Parties in an Era of Political Change." In *The Future of American Political Parties*, ed. Joel L. Fleishman, pp. 70-100. Englewood Cliffs, N.J.: Prentice-Hall.

Jacobson, Gary C. 1983. *The Politics of Congressional Campaigns*. Boston: Little, Brown.

————, and Samuel Kernell. 1981. *Strategy and Choice in Congressional Elections*. New Haven, Conn.: Yale University Press.

Kearns, Doris. 1977. *Lyndon Johnson and the American Dream*. New York: New American Library.

Key, V. O., Jr. 1964. *Politics, Parties, and Pressure Groups*, 5th ed. New York: Crowell.

Koenig, Louis W. 1975. *The Chief Executive*, 3rd ed. New York: Harcourt Brace.

Kramer, Gerald H. 1971. "Short-term Fluctuations in U.S. Voting Behavior." *American Political Science Review* 65 (March): 131-43.

Kritzer, Herbert, and Robert Eubank. 1979. "Presidential Coattails Revisited: Partisanship and Incumbency Effects." *American Journal of Political Science*, August, pp. 615-26.

Mayhew, David. 1974. "Congressional Elections: The Case of the Vanishing marginals." *Polity* 6 (Spring): 295-317.

McGrory, Mary. 1982. "More Mixed Signals." Washington *Post*, December 5, p. C1.

Moos, Malcolm. 1952. *Politics, Presidents, and Coattails*. Baltimore: Johns Hopkins University Press.

Mueller, John E. 1973. *War, Presidents, and Public Opinion*. New York: John Wiley.

Orren, Gary. 1982. "The Changing Styles of American Party Politics." In *The Future of American Political Parties*, ed. Joel L. Fleishman, pp. 4-41. Englewood Cliffs, N.J.: Prentice-Hall.

Peterson, Bill. 1978. "White Attacks Cheap Shots on President." Washington *Post*, July 28, p. A3.

Public Papers of the President: Gerald R. Ford, 1975. 1976. Washington, D.C.: U.S. Government Printing Office.

Public Papers of the President: John F. Kennedy, 1961. 1962. Washington, D.C.: U.S. Government Printing Office.

Raines, Howell. 1982. "President Alters Campaign Strategy..." New York *Times*, October 26, p. A25.

Schell, Jonathan. 1976. *The Time of Illusion*. New York: Knopf.

Schlesinger, Arthur M., Jr. 1965. *A Thousand Days: John F. Kennedy in the White House*. Boston: Houghton Mifflin.

Sorensen, Theodore C. 1966. *Kennedy*. New York: Harper and Row.

Taylor, Paul. 1982. "The PACs Are Spending More..." Washington *Post*, October 31, p. A11.

Tufte, Edward R. 1975. "Determinants of the Outcomes of Midterm Congressional Elections." *American Political Science Review* 69 (September): 812-26.

Wills, Gary. 1969. *Nixon Agonistes: The Crisis of the Self-Made Man.* Boston: Houghton Mifflin.

Witcover, Jules. 1977. *Marathon: The Pursuit of the Presidency, 1972-1976.* New York: Viking.

7

PRESIDENTS AND PARTY PURGES: WITH SPECIAL EMPHASIS ON THE LESSONS OF 1938

Sidney M. Milkis

PRESIDENTIAL LEADERSHIP AND PARTY RESPONSIBILITY

*T*he growing demand since the turn of the century for a strong national government has greatly strained the traditional party system that was established upon local and state interests. This demand, which was heightened by the depression and New Deal, has encouraged twentieth-century presidents, especially since Franklin D. Roosevelt, to act as levers of national purpose. One obvious way for presidents to strengthen the national resolve of their parties is to influence House and Senate primary election campaigns with a view to "purging" recalcitrant party members. The purpose of this chapter is to suggest that presidential efforts to impose discipline on political parties through purge campaigns are unlikely to work. In particular, Franklin D. Roosevelt's 1938 campaign to unseat several conservative Democrats in state primary elections demonstrates the probable futility of presidential purges and, thereby, one very important limitation on establishing party government in the United States.

The Extraordinary Isolation of the President

The use of presidential influence to "purify" party politics was first proposed by Woodrow Wilson, who is recognized as the first

The author thanks the Eleanor Roosevelt Institute for a grant in support of the research carried out to complete this chapter. A note of thanks is also owed to Erik Paesel who provided research assistance for the preparation of the manuscript.

American writer to advance the doctrine of responsible party government. This doctrine advocated a more "responsible" party system, comprised of national policy-oriented organizations capable of carrying out platforms or proposals presented to the people during the course of an election.[1]

Wilson recognized that the traditional party system in the United States was not well-suited to the formulation and adoption of a comprehensive national program. Parties developed in the United States in such a way that they reinforced the decentralization of power built into the Constitution. Although the system of checks and balances in the American political system has been modified to a degree by the development of national party organizations, more impressive is the degree to which the development of political parties have been shaped by federalism. National party organizations were built upon the loose cooperation of a multitude of state and local parties and, as such, were poor instruments for sustained progressive action on the part of the national government.

During the nineteenth century, when the primary national problem was fostering nationalism itself, the parties provided a sufficient remedy for what Wilson considered the excessive free play of territorial and economic self-interest within the political system. But the traditional party system, having, in a sense, built the nation, was incapable of engaging that nation in a new and more extensive expression of national purpose.

> Party organization is no longer needed for the mere rudimentary task of holding the machinery together or giving it the sustenance of some common object, some single cooperative motive. The time is at hand when we can with safety examine the network of party in its detail and change its structure without imperiling its strength. This thing that has served us so well might now master us if we left it irresponsible. We must see that it is made responsible (Wilson 1908, p. 220).

Wilson did not point out in a detailed way how the structure of the party was to be changed, but he did suggest that the modification of the party system would entail the strong assertion of the president as party leader (Wilson 1908, especially Chapter 3). He was impressed with the presidency as a potential catalyst of party government because it united the party and government leaders in one person. The partisan leadership of the chief executive had always been weakened somewhat by the adversary relationship between the president and the Congress built into the Constitution, a relationship that could be moderated, albeit not fundamentally changed, by a delicate process of give and take. Yet the political independence of the president from the Congress and his unique position within the political system as national representative make it very tempting for the chief executive to try to bring his party to heel by appeals to public opinion. For Wilson, this place of the executive within the political system imposed an "extraordinary isolation" on the president. This isolation, if used effectively enough, would enable the president to control programs within the party councils. Even should the president eschew to a degree his role as partisan leader and move a little outside his party, if he could become an effective enough leader of the nation, Wilson argued, his party could hardly resist him (Wilson 1908, p 69).

Franklin D. Roosevelt and the Imperative of Intervention

The temptation to attempt to dominate his party and Congress was especially strong for Franklin Roosevelt. The New Deal represented a fundamental departure from traditional politics in the United States and the Democratic Party. Up until the 1930s, the party of Jefferson was committed to individual autonomy, limited government, and states' rights. Even Woodrow Wilson's program of government regulation was in line with this tradition, insofar as the New Freedom was committed fundamentally to individualism, competitive capitalism, and decentralized government power. Under the leadership of Roosevelt, however, the New Deal came to represent the enlargement of power of the federal government over economic activity. Whereas previous great reform movements in the United States can be seen as reaffirmations of the American tradition of limited constitutional government, the New Deal, though not a direct rejection of this tradition, most seriously questioned the adequacy of fundamental American freedoms. Though Roosevelt was not fully committed to Wilson's theory of party government, the concern with implementing his extensive reform program led him to try to impose discipline on his party to a much greater degree than did Wilson.[2]

Even though Roosevelt thought he saw in the landslide victory of 1936 an impressive mandate to carry out reforms, his actions to turn that approving mandate into state action would be frustrated unless the desultory procedures of constitutional democracy were modified. He expressed hope in his 1934 annual message to Congress that the early political successes of his administration indicated that "a strong and permanent tie between the legislative and executive branches of government" was being constructed (Roosevelt 1938-50, Vol. 3, p. 14). Yet as soon as the economic emergency of the early 1930s eased somewhat, the more traditional adversary relationship between the president and the Congress reemerged. Roosevelt's "court packing" bill and his more consistent leftist orientation after 1935 contributed to the weakening of executive-legislative relations. By 1938 Roosevelt was ready to seek a more fundamental reorganization of the relationship between the president and Congress by instituting party discipline through direct influence on the off-year elections. When it became apparent that party unity within the traditional American party system would not outlast the feeling of panic in the country in the early 1930s, then Roosevelt attempted to influence the development of party politics that would allow for a more sustained period of coordinated party government. Without such a development, even the electoral mandate of 1936 would be insufficient to bring about a departure from traditional political practices in the United States.

Uncertain Precedent

Roosevelt's intervention in the campaign of 1938, though limited in certain respects, constituted the most dramatic aspect of the president's endeavor to stamp his policies upon the Democratic Party. In a dozen states, the president interceded in primary campaigns in an effort to unseat entrenched conservative incumbents within his party. Roosevelt's action stunned the nation. The degree to which this action was viewed as a shocking departure from precedents in American politics is indicated by the fact that the press soon labeled Roosevelt's partisan efforts as "the purge," a term that became notorious with Adolph Hitler's attempt to weed out dissension in the German Nazi Party and Josef Stalin's elimination of "disloyal" party members in the Soviet Communist Party. Yet, although FDR acted on an unprecedentedly large scale and with a vigor hitherto unsurpassed in an effort to create a more unified party, he was not acting totally without precedent. In particular, William Howard Taft and Woodrow Wilson had made limited efforts to cleanse their parties of recalcitrant members.

Taft attempted for a time to mediate between the badly divided factions within the Republican Party, but the resistance of the progressives to his legislative program of 1910 drove him to join conservatives in an effort to weaken insurgencey forces in the primary compaigns of that year. Although Taft did not take any public positions in these contests, patronage was distributed according to loyalty to the administration's program. Moreover, rumors spead throughout the nation that the president was cooperating with Speaker Joseph Cannon and Senate head Nelson Aldrich to raise money for the purpose of sending out to the prairie country "a group of standpat evangelists to wrestle with all the districts possessed of the progressive devil" (Mowry 1946, p. 98). Strong confirmation of this rumor came when the Republican congressional campaign committee began flooding progressive constituencies with sharp attacks on the house and senatorial representatives, advising that such men be defeated in the coming primaries.

Taft's aggressive, albeit surreptitious, partisan intervention was manifestly unsuccessful. Not only did almost all House and Senate incumbents opposed by the president win renomination, but progressives made important advances against conservative office holders in several primaries. In the wake of these primary reversals came the great disaster of the November elections. For the first time in 16 years the Democratic party controlled the House of Representatives, and although the Republicans kept their majority in the Senate, it was purely a nominal one. The insurgent Republicans, strengthened by the failed purge campaign, held the balance of power between the regular Republicans and Democratic forces (New York Times, November 10, 1910, p. 1; Mowry 1946, pp. 106, 130).

In effect, Taft's efforts backfired. His campaign mobilized progressives under the unassailable banners of local self-determination and congressional independence, resulting in a widened split as well as significant change in the balance of power between the contesting groups within the Republican Party. The results of the unhappy purge and the fact that the 1910 elections left Theodore Roosevelt deeply irritated at Taft set the stage for the disastrous party split that occurred during the 1912 presidential campaign (Mowry 1946, pp. 120ff; 1958, pp. 270-73).

Woodrow Wilson's party leadership, his long-standing belief in party government notwithstanding, was in some respects hardly more aggressive than that of the reticent Taft. Though a great partisan leader, Wilson in the last analysis reconciled himself to the sharp fissures within his party. In his use of patronage, particularly, Wilson pursued a strategy directed at controlling rather than reforming his party in order to get his programs passed; consequently, Wilson made little effort to strengthen the Democratic party's organization or its commitment to progressive principles (Link 1956). Although Wilson's partisan practice as president was generally accommodating to the disparate organizational structure and ideological commitment of traditional party politics, he did attempt a limited purge in the 1918 congressional primary contests. He actively sought the defeat of Democratic candidates in five southern states because they had opposed his policies. The president's intervention, like that of Taft, was for the most part characterized by quiet maneuvering rather than active campaigning; however, Wilson did write several public letters against congressmen and senators who adamantly opposed the war. He publicly opposed the renomination of Democratic Senators Hardwick of Georgia and Vardaman of Mississippi, for instance, because both of them voted against the declaration of war and virtually all measures carrying it on.

Wilson's intervention succeeded in defeating a few of his enemies within the Democratic Party. His public letter had an important effect on the Mississippi campaign, which sent Vardaman back to private life and brought Pat Harrison, who based his campaign on complete loyalty to the president, from the House to the Senate (New York *Times*, August 21, 1918, p. 5). The president's endorsement of William J. Harris helped the latter defeat Hardwick in Georgia (New York *Times*, September 12, 1918, p. 9). Southern Democrats suffered interference from Washington in these cases because of the powerful appeal of the loyalty issue during the conduct of war; both Harrison and Harris stressed patriotism in their campaigns.[3]

Nevertheless, Wilson's purge was limited and generally subordinated to preventing Republicans from taking control of Congress. For the most part, he was reluctant to discriminate between candidates of his own party and focused instead on a national appeal for a Democratic legislature (Baker 1939, p. 189). When such a plea was issued in a public letter, published on October 25, Wilson was loudly criticized for suggesting the Democrats had a monopoly on loyalty; such a partisan appeal was viewed as inappropriate during an international crisis. This negative response contributed to the Republicans making substantial gains in the November elections and taking control of both legislative chambers. The limited nature of the purge campaign and the failure of the appeal for a Democratic Congress left conservatives strongly entrenched within the party; the Democrats nominated conservative candidates for the presidency in 1920 as well as 1924.[4]

The Taft and Wilson efforts to purify their parties were very uncertain precedents since they were limited in scope, surreptitiously applied for the most part, and either manifestly unsuccessful, in Taft's case or only marginally successful, in Wilson's endeavor. These campaigns suggested that the extraordinary isolation Wilson saw in the presidency was a rather modest instrument for restructuring partisan politics in the United States. In fact, the authority of the presidency is extensively dependent on his eschewing, to a degree, partisan politics and being the leader of the whole body of the people. Unlike the British prime minister, the president is not elected directly by his party and indirectly by the people. Consequently, the authority of the president requires that partisan action be restrained. Although, after 1800, the president became party leader as well as leader of all the people, the broad commitment in the United States to separation of powers and federalism has disinclined the chief executive from connecting his ambition too centrally to his party in Congress.

Franklin Roosevelt was far from indifferent to this tradition. The traditional role of the presidency helps to explain his initial hesistancy to attempt to influence congressional contests. His primary campaign intervention, though far surpassing those of Taft and Wilson, demonstrated a limited commitment to restructuring partisan politics. Nevertheless, the purge campaign raised the issue of partisan unity in unprecedented fashion. The extensive policy reform envisioned by the New Dealers, combined with important modifications in the organization and style of campaigns during the first three decades of the twentieth century, encouraged Roosevelt to raise the issue of party government aggressively enough to undertake what E. E. Schattschneider (1942, p. 163) has called "one of the greatest experimental tests of the nature of the American party system ever made."

THE 1938 PURGE CAMPAIGN

Roosevelt considered the designation of his primary campaign as the "purge" by the press a slur on his actions as leader of the Democratic Party. Nevertheless, as Morton Frisch (1975, pp. 81-82) points out, since Roosevelt was attempting a "cleansing" of his party, by driving out those with conservative political orientations, this term was, in a sense, an appropriate description of his actions.

Although it was suggested in the press that the president and his close advisor and relief administrator, Harry Hopkins, had been talking about such a purging of the Democratic Party from the beginning of Roosevelt's term (Alsop and Kintner 1938, p. 91), for a long time Roosevelt made no substantial effort to modify party politics or to affect the outcome of primary contests. For example, when Senator Key Pittman, who up to this time had loyally supported the administration, asked Roosevelt for support in his 1934 Democratic primary fight, Roosevelt replied: "I wish to goodness I could speak out loud in meetings and tell Nevada that I am one thousand percent for you! An imposed silence in things like primaries is one of the many penalties of my job" (Roosevelt to Pittman, August 25, 1934, *Roosevelt Papers*, PPF 65).[5]

Roosevelt maintained this "imposed silence" until the summer of 1938 when he finally initiated the purge. In 1936 he had refused to fight the renomination of the Democratic incumbent Senator from Virginia, Carter Glass, who was the only congressional member of the majority party to oppose consistently the New Deal from the start. Even as late as January 1938, Roosevelt declared a "hands off" policy when liberal Democrats in Missouri asked for his help in the primary campaign against the conservative incumbent, Senator Bennet Clark (A. L. Meir to Roosevelt, January 12, 1938, *Roosevelt Papers*, PPF 4658).

Roosevelt did quietly intervene in a few primary contests prior to 1938. In July 1936, Eleanor Roosevelt wired the president that liberal Texas Congressman Maury Maverick was in danger of being defeated in the primary contest. Roosevelt wired back that he could not play any direct part in a primary compaign but assured Mrs. Roosevelt that the man in question was being helped (Eleanor Roosevelt to Franklin Roosevelt, July 17, 1936; Franklin Roosevelt to Eleanor Roosevelt, July 19, 1936, *Roosevelt Papers*, PPF 2). Partly as a result of the aid provided by Roosevelt's uncle Frederick Delano, Maverick was renominated against strong opposition. Roosevelt's confidential letter of congratulations to Maverick indicated that he considered it necessary, but somewhat frustrating, to proceed cautiously against conservatives within his party: "Highly private and extremely confidentially, I am told that I may send you my congratulations. (The etiquette arbiters who own Presidents would not let me publicly felicitate my own brother if he won a primary fight.)" (Roosevelt to Maverick, August 5, 1936, *Roosevelt Papers*, PPF 3446).

Roosevelt's hesitancy and cautiousness in undertaking aggressive partisan leadership was in part attributable to the administration's interest in awaiting a propitious time to begin working for a new Democratic Party. The question was not so much whether or not it was desirable to rebuild the Democratic party into a more unified liberal party. Rather, the great question was, when to start working for it (Alsop and Kintner 1938, p. 91).

Democratic Party Chairman James Farley felt Roosevelt had decided to undertake a purge well before the summer of 1938.[6] Roosevelt may, in fact, have always intended a purge, but his hesitancy in undertaking aggressive partisan leadership was not simply a matter of waiting for the right time to proceed. His cautiousness was partly connected to something more fundamental than such pragmatism. Given the ambiguity built into the historical role of the presidency, Roosevelt considered it neither desirable nor practical to immerse himself too extensively in party politics. In a radio address to Young Democratic Clubs of America on August 24, 1935, he expressed his understanding of the nonpartisan nature of the presidency:

Whatever his party affiliation might be, the President of the United States, in addressing the youth of the country—even when speaking to the young citizens of his own party—should speak as President of the whole people. It is true that the Presidency carries with it, for the time being, the leadership of the political party as well. But the Presidency carries with it a far higher obligation than this—the duty of analyzing and setting forth national needs and ideals which transcend and cut across all of party affiliation (Roosevelt 1938-50, Volume 4, p. 337).

It was really the conservatives within the Democratic Party who finally influenced Roosevelt to intensify his partisan activity, who struck the first blow, as it were, when they began to organize aggressively against the New Deal in 1937. In December a coalition of conservative Democratic and Republican senators issued a public statement proclaiming their opposition to any further government encroachment on "the American system of private enterprise and initiative" (New York *Times*, December 16, 1937, p. 10). This press release, which also called for an end to congressional weakness in the face of burgeoning presidential power, signaled the birth of the Conservative Coalition in Congress that to this day remains a thorn in the side of liberal Democrats. This group of conservative statesmen blocked several important New Deal measures during the 75th Congress of 1937-38, such as the Court Reform Bill, the Wages and Hours Bill, and the Government Reorganization Act. The struggle over this legislation soon developed into a conflict over control of the Democratic Party. Roosevelt's attorney general, Homer Cummings, wrote in his diary on August 1, 1937: "It is generally felt that back of all these various fights, including the Supreme Court fight, there lies the question of the nomination of 1940, and the incidental control of party destinies" (Diary, August 1, 1937, Box 235, Number 9, p. 119, *Cummings Papers*). Cummings, a long-time active participant in the Democratic organization and a close advisor to Roosevelt on party politics, was expressing the administration's view that the conservative opposition within the party had grown influential enough to impose a formidable roadblock to further reform.

Roosevelt's first action against recalcitrant members of his party came in July 1937, in the fight for Senate majority leader between

Alben Barkley of Kentucky, a supporter of the New Deal, and Pat Harrison, a conservative Democrat from Mississippi. The feeling in the Senate was that the election of Barkley would tend to strengthen the president's hand, and that the selection of Harrison would be hailed as still another rebuff of the president. Roosevelt, who expressed to Farley the fear that Harrison would not go along on liberal legislation, worked quietly behind the scenes to defeat the Mississippi senator. The president's support was crucial in Barkley's 38 to 37 vote victory.[7]

Roosevelt began to make the struggle for Democratic Party a public issue in August 1937. In a speech at Roanoke Island, North Carolina, he expressed the view that his oppenents were obstructing the will of the people as expressed in the 1936 election. After the speech, *Newsweek* (August 28, 1937, p. 9) reported: "Implicit in all this was a clear but unspoken threat: Mr. Roosevelt was asking the country to retire from Congress those Democrats who lately have opposed him — and hence, in his view, have obstructed popular rule."

Therefore, by the summer of 1937, the Roosevelt administration had begun seriously to apply both quiet and public pressure to advance party responsibiliy. More than any previous or subsequent president, Roosevelt was preparing to test the character of the American party system by seeking to hold the members of the Democratic Party accountable for a national party program. Because of his actions, the 1938 primary elections became a series of referendums on not only the New Deal but also traditional party politics in the United States.

It was the Wages and Hours Bill that actually triggered the purge campaign. The bill eventually passed at the very end of the 75th Congress, but several attenuating amendments substantially restricted the number of industries it covered. For a while it looked as though the bill would not pass at all. Then in May 1938, when the bill was tied up in the Rules Committee of the House of Representatives, Democratic Representative Mark Wilcox, an opponent of the measure and other major New Deal items, came out for the Florida Senate seat of "100 percent New Dealer" Claude Pepper, who voted for everything the administration proposed and announced to his constituents that he was willing to follow the president "to his death." After much anxious discussion at the White House, Roosevelt finally put the administration's prestige and patronage behind Pepper. Pepper won an overwhelming victory, receiving about 70 percent of the vote, and this New Deal triumph shook the Wages and Hours Bill loose from the House Rules Committee, whereupon it easily passed the Congress. This primary contest was watched closely, because it was thought that Pepper's fate was likely to affect all Southern elections, and after his victory many Southern Congressmen were "persuaded" to support the Wages and Hours legislation.[8]

After the Florida victory, the administration backed New Deal sympathizer Henry Hess's challenge of incumbent Democratic Governor Martin of Oregon. Interior Secretary Harold Ickes wrote a public letter attacking Martin, who had opposed Public Works Administration power projects, as "no Dealer at heart" (*Newsweek*, May 30, 1938, p. 9). When State Senator Hess defeated Martin in the Oregon primary, the Roosevelt administration concluded that this New Deal victory, coupled with the Florida triumph, indicated that the time was propitious for a realignment fight. An "elimination committee" comprised of close presidential advisors, which was organized by relief administrator Harry Hopkins during the winter of that year, now began to work in earnest against targeted conservative Democratic incumbents. On June 24, 1938, Roosevelt formally initiated the purge in a national radio address wherein he called for the selection of "liberal" candidates in the primary elections (Roosevelt 1938-50, Volume 7, pp. 391-400).

This effort undertaken on behalf of liberalism was not carried out with workmanlike precision. Not only did the Roosevelt administration enter the partisan fray reluctantly, but when the "elimination committee" finally became committed to the purge, its participation in the primary contests was hardly systematic. Although many members of the administration who supported participation by the president in the 1938 primaries wanted to make—with just a few exceptions—100 percent support of presidential measures the criterion for selecting targets for purging, FDR insisted on a selective campaign. He sought to make a few examples rather than totally overhaul the party organization (New York *Times*, June 29, 1938, p. 1).

Direct Versus Indirect Approach

Although there were some serious organizational efforts made during the campaign, the administration for the most part made no attempt to work through the regular Democratic Party. All of the members of the purge committee came from outside of the Democratic organization. Although Democratic Chairman James Farley, who had close relations with local and state party leaders, was bitterly opposed to the primary campaign, be became less influential once it was finally decided to seek a modification of partisan politics (Farley 1948, pp. 120-50). In fact, Roosevelt, in all but one of the primaries in which he personally participated, chose to make a direct appeal to the people rather than attempt to work through local party organizations. In retrospect this may have been an unfortunate strategy to follow. Edward Flynn, political boss of the Bronx, noted with interest that the most important victory Roosevelt obtained in the purge was the one that Flynn engineered in New York against House Rules Committee Chairman John J. O'Connor (Flynn 1947, p. 503).

Instead of seeking to overhaul party organization, Roosevelt sought to obtain party responsibility by transferring collective responsibility into executive responsibility. As Wilson prescribed, Roosevelt sought to obviate the recalcitrance of traditional party politics by exercising the extraordinary isolation of the presidency. In part he agreed with Wilson that the president, as the only popularly elected national statesman, could successfully appeal to public opinion in order to strengthen partisanship. Wilson's more limited policy goals did not encourage such an extensive appeal during his presidency; moreover, the Wilson administration felt it necessary to reach an accommodation with state and local party leaders in order to achieve the cooperation of the legislature; but the conditions seemed right for a national appeal to public opinion during Roosevelt's second term. In fact, Raymond Clapper (1938, p. 17) suggested after the 1938 primary campaigns that "interference on a large scale and with more vigor than Wilson exercised" was really inevitable. "It awaited only the appearance of a strong man in a highly controversial setting."

Importance of the Primary

The undertaking of a large-scale presidential purge was tempting because of the spread of the direct primary during the first three decades of the twentieth century, which provided an opportunity for a direct appeal to the electorate. This reform had begun to greatly weaken the grip of local party organizations on electors. For example, William H. Meier, Democratic County Chairman from Nebraska, wrote Farley in 1938 that his state's direct primary law had "created a situation that has made candidates too independent of the party" (Meier to Farley, December 23, 1938, *Roosevelt Papers*, OF 300, Democratic National Committee). But Roosevelt, following Wilson, supported the direct primary and the weakening of traditional party organizations. In his fireside chat initiating the purge campaign on June 24, 1938, Roosevelt said:

> Fifty years ago party nominations were generally made in conventions — a system typified in the public imagination by a little group in a smoke filled room who made out the party slates.
> The direct primary was invented to make the nominating process

a more democratic one—to give the party voters themselves a chance to pick their candidates (Roosevelt 1938-50, Volume 7, pp. 397-98).

The primary gave the president the opportunity to make a direct appeal to the people over the heads of congressional candidates and local party leaders; and radio broadcasting had made the opportunity to appeal directly to large audiences even more enticing. Of course this was bound to be particularly tempting to an extremely popular president with as fine a radio presence as Roosevelt.

The Democratic Party and the Campaign for a New South

Not surprisingly, Roosevelt considered the Southern bloc to be the greatest obstacle to the transformation of the Democratic Party into a purposeful liberal organization. Many of the Southern Congresssmen's aims and purposes paralleled more closely the views of conservative Republicans than those of Northern Democrats. As Thomas Stokes wrote after analyzing the important role played by Southern congressmen in scuttling the Wage-Hour Bill: "Southern Democracy was the ball and chain which hobbled the Party's forward march" (Stokes 1940, p. 503). For this reason, Roosevelt selected most of the individual targets of the purge from conservative Southern and border states. If the Democratic Party was eventually to become a national liberal party, conservative Southern democracy would have to be defeated.

Roosevelt did not confine his efforts to the South during the 1938 purge attempt, but his most outspoken and unequivocal opposition was directed against traditional Southern democracy. In particular he most actively sought to unseat incumbent Senators Walter George from Georgia, "Cotten Ed" Smith from South Carolina, and Millard Tydings of Maryland. Although Tydings represented a border state, his political values and practices identified him with the cause of his conservative colleagues from the South. Roosevelt made an especially determined appeal for administration candidates Lawrence Camp and David Lewis of Georgia and Maryland, respectively.

It has been suggested that Roosevelt erred in attempting to purge candidates from traditionally more conservative states. Charles M. Price and Joseph Boskin, after analyzing polls taken during the 1930s, argue that Roosevelt faced insurmountable odds because he attempted to oust senatorial incumbents in areas where he had weak local

EDITOR'S PERSPECTIVE

Please Purge "My Old Friend"

The following text of an address delivered by President Franklin D. Roosevelt on August 8, 1938, at Barnesville, Georgia, exemplifies his efforts to "purge" the Democratic Party of anti-New Dealers in the congressional primaries.

What I am about to say will be no news, to my old friend—and I say it with the utmost sincerity—Senator Walter George. It will be no surprise to him because I have recently had personal correspondence with him; and, as a result of it, he fully knows what my views are.

Let me make it clear that he is, and I hope always will be, my personal friend. He is beyond question, beyond any possible question, a gentleman and a scholar; but there are other gentlemen in the Senate and in the House for whom I have a real affectionate regard, but with whom I differ heartily and sincerely on the principles and policies of how the Government of the United States ought to be run.

For example, I have had an almost lifelong acquaintance and great personal friendship for people like Senator Hale from the State of Maine, for Representative James Wadsworth of New York and for the Minority Leader, Representative Snell. All of these lifelong conservative Republicans are gentlemen and scholars; but they and I learned long ago that our views on public questions were just as wide apart as the North Pole and the South.

Therefore, I repeat that I trust, and am confident, that Senator George and I shall always be good personal friends even though I am impelled to make it clear that on most public questions he and I do not speak the same language.

To carry out my responsibility as President, it is clear that if there is to be success in our Government there ought to be cooperation between members of my own party and myself—cooperation, in other words, within the majority party, between one branch of Government, the Legislative branch, and the head of the other branch, the Executive. That is one of the essentials of a party form of government. It has been going on in this country for nearly a century and a half. The test is not measured, in the case of an individual, by his every vote on every bill—of course not. The test lies rather in the answer to two questions: first, has the record of the candidate shown, while differing perhaps in details, a constant active fighting attitude in favor of the broad objectives of the party and of the Government as they are constituted today; and, secondly, does the candidate really, in his heart, deep down in his heart, believe in those objectives? I regret that in the case of my friend, Senator George, I cannot honestly answer either of these questions in the affirmative.

In the case of another candidate in the State of Georgia for the United States Senate—former Governor Talmadge—I have known him for many

EDITOR'S PERSPECTIVE (continued)

years. His attitude toward me and toward other members of the Government in 1935 and in 1936 concerns me not at all. But, in those years and in this year I have read so many of his proposals, so many of his promises, so many of his panaceas, that I am very certain in my own mind that his election would contribute very little to practical progress in government. That is all I can say about him.

The third candidate that I would speak of, United States Attorney Lawrence Camp, I have also known for many years. He has had experience in the State Legislature; he has served as Attorney General of Georgia and for four years; he has made a distinguished record in the United States District Court, his office ranking among the first two in the whole of the United States in the expedition of Federal cases in that Court. I regard him not only as a public servant with successful experience but as a man who honestly believes that many things must be done and done now to improve the economic and social conditions of the country, a man who is willing to fight for these objectives. Fighting ability is of the utmost importance.

Therefore, answering the requests that have come to me from many leading citizens of Georgia that I make my position clear, I have no hesitation in saying that if I were able to vote in the September primaries in this State, I most assuredly should cast my ballot for Lawrence Camp.

Source: Printed in Franklin D. Roosevelt, *Public Papers and Addresses*, Volume 7, (New York: Macmillan, 1941), pp. 463-71. The editor thanks Sidney Milkis for locating this material.

support. He might better have concentrated, they contend, on Northern industrial states where there was more support for his programs (Price and Boskin 1966).

This argument would seem to be supported by the fact that Roosevelt's one successful purge effort of an incumbent congressman was accomplished against conservative Rules Chairman John J. O'Connor from New York City—which was FDR's only effort in the urban North.[9] There were other factors that contributed to this victory besides the fact that it was carried out in a Northern metropolitan area. Since Roosevelt received the support of the local party organization in this contest and New York was his home state, the charge of outside interference that was lodged against him in other primary contests was not effective in this race. Nevertheless, Roosevelt's effort to transform the Democratic party into a liberal party might have garnered more support had it been directed more aggressively at some or the more recalcitrant Northern candidates. Successes in such an attempt might have sufficiently backed conservative Southern Democrats into a corner to the point where they either would have acquiesced to Roosevelt's liberal views or abandoned the Democratic Party.[10]

THE IMMEDIATE AFTERMATH OF THE PURGE

The purge campaign of 1938 was part of an attempt by Roosevelt to overcome the state and local orientation of the party system that was suited to congressional primacy and organized on the basis of self-interest, and to establish a national executive-oriented party, which would be organized on the basis of public issues. Roosevelt wrote in 1941 that he viewed intervention in the primary campaigns as a necessary action to "keep liberalism in the foreground" in the councils of the Democratic Party, "as well as in the legislative and executive branches of government itself." In the president's view there could be no realization of the campaign promises of 1936 without disciplining those Democratic candidates who acted in "repudiation of liberal and progressive government" (Roosevelt 1938-50, Vol. 7, p. xxxi). The toleration of conservative candidates under the banner of the Democratic Party would make the Democratic and Republican Parties "merely Tweedledum and Tweedledee," and elections would become "meaningless when the two major parties have no differences other than their labels" (Roosevelt 1938-50. Vol. 7, pp. xxviii, xxxii).

Like those efforts by Taft and Wilson, Roosevelt's 1938 campaign constituted an attempt to sustain a party form of government within a context where most political institutions and practices work to check party discipline on the national level. Roosevelt's purge represented and especially strong challenge to the localistic character of the American party system, and the strong reaction to his efforts indicates the great difficulty of seeking party unity through intervention in intraparty campaigns.

There has been a good deal of scholarly controversy regarding the effect of Roosevelt's purge attempt. To some, the 1938 campaign, for all its difficulties, was a success (Schattschneider 1942, pp. 163-69; Hopper 1966, pp. 220-21). Most immediately, the purge got wages and hours legislation enacted into law, along with other parts of Roosevelt's legislative program. It also freed the House Rules Committee from the conservative grasp of John J. O'Connor. In addition to these tangible results, the president's intervention revitalized party politics and laid the groundwork for the development of a significantly more liberal Democratic Party. To a degree, even in those cases where the drive failed, candidates had to make peace with the New Deal program. They thought twice about crossing Roosevelt after 1938, knowing that opposition from a popular president, even when ultimately frustrated at the polls, entailed long and costly campaigns, which otherwise might have foregone conclusions. It may very well be, as Schattschneider and others point out, that had Roosevelt not taken on conservatives within his party in such dramatic fashion, the Democratic Party would have remained rooted in its Jeffersonian traditions.

Notwithstanding these arguments, in the last analysis the purge was a failure, since it left the anti-New Deal coalition of Republicans and conservative Democrats in a powerful position in Congress. In the dozen states within which the president acted against entrenched incumbents, he was successful in only two of them—Oregon and New York. As Pendleton Herring noted in 1940 (p. 222), the success of the conservative Democrats in surviving the 1938 primary campaign indicated that "the purge failed both as a disciplinary measure and as a device for clarifying opinion." The divisions within the Democratic Party were too deeply rooted to be eliminated through a purge campaign; and, as James Farley (1948, p. 147) has argued, by violating "a cardinal political creed" of American politics "that the President keep out of local matters," Roosevelt widened and further entrenched the split within the Democratic Party between liberal and conservative factions.

In effect, the purge imbued the hitherto beleaguered conservative Democrats with a sense of unity and legitimacy that greatly strengthened their resistance to the New Deal. Consequently, the aborted purge campaign gave further impetus to the growth of a conservative coalition that came to dominate Congress sufficiently to block the extension of New Deal initiatives for the next two decades. Peter Gerry, a conservative Democratic Senator from Rhode Island, wrote North Carolina Senator Josiah Bailey in September 1938:

> The victories of Smith, Tydings and George have had even a greater effect than I had hoped for. They show that Roosevelt cannot control Senators for he does not have the weight with voters in his party that the New Dealers thought he possessed. They have also destroyed the picture of his being invulnerable. The Senate and the House will stiffen and the opposition to the New Deal has had a great stimulation to its morale (Folder: September to October 1938, *Bailey Papers*, Box 476).

Roosevelt never admitted the 1938 campaign was a failure, and he did not totally give up his attempt to "cleanse" the Democratic Party of its most dissident elements after this effort. In his 1939 Jackson Day speech he again declared that the Democratic Party must remain devoted to liberal principles—and he invited the discontented right wingers to move over to the other side (Roosevelt 1938-50, Volume 8, pp. 60-68). In fact, to some degree he envisioned and actively sought the formation of a more liberal party until his death. Apparently, Roosevelt made overtures to Wendell Wilkie, the liberal Republican who ran for president on the GOP ticket in 1940 and was rejected by conservatives in his own party in favor of Thomas Dewey in 1944, about the possibility of forming a new liberal party, leaving the conservatives in each party to join together as they saw fit. Wilkie was intensely interested in such a project but preferred to postpone such talk until after the 1944 election. The project was never pursued very far, however, since by election day Wilkie was dead, and five months after election day Roosevelt was dead also.[11] Roosevelt, then, never gave up his interest in making the Democratic Party the party of, as he put it, "militant liberalism" (Roosevelt 1938-50, Vol. 7, p. xxxi).

Nevertheless, the attempt to make the Democratic Party less ambiguously liberal was dealt a severe blow by the results of the purge campaign. The purge effort during the 1938 primaries demonstrated clearly enough to Roosevelt the great difficulty of establishing a responsible party system in the United States. What Schattschneider calls "one of the greatest experimental tests of the nature of the American party system ever made" seemed to indicate the recalcitrance of traditional party politics. Former Wisconsin Governor Philip La Follette (138, p. 587), wrote after the election of 1938: "The results of the so-called purge by President Roosevelt showed that the fight to make the Democratic party liberal is a hopeless one." The failure of the purge was further reinforced by the general election of 1938, in which the losses sustained by the Democratic Party were partly interpreted as a reaction to Roosevelt's participation in party battles.[12] Consequently, with the exception of the vague overtures directed at Wilkie in 1944, Roosevelt's aggressive partisan efforts were primarily rhetorical after 1938.[13] In fact, Roosevelt told Homer Cummings in December 1938 that his attitude toward recalcitrant Democrats, such as Pat Harrison and Burton Wheeler, has become "all milk and honey" (Diary, December 30, 1938, Number 8, p. 270, Box 235, *Cunnings Papers*).[14] Apparently, FDR reluctantly came to the conclusion that the decentralized character of American politics recommended conciliation and compromise rather than purges as a salve for intraparty struggles.

LONG-TERM CONSEQUENCES OF THE PURGE: THE LESSONS OF 1938

The congressional campaigns of 1938 represent the most significant attempt by a president to impose party discipline through intervention in House and Senate primary elections. Hence, the lessons of Roosevelt's purge deserve careful consideration by those who would consider undertaking such activity in the future, or who would recommend that presidents do so as a means of instilling some party discipline.

First, the probability of a successful purge might be enhanced by channeling intervention through state and local party organizations. Roosevelt's attempt to go over the heads of regular Democrats caused a good deal of resentment throughout the party, even among those members inclined to support the New Deal. In the states where the president made his most extensive efforts, Maryland and Georgia, his candidates polled the smallest proportion of votes. As an observer noted in 1939, "this suggests that a quiet campaign of 'pressure' upon party organization might have been more effective than a widespread appeal to 'public opinion' " (Shannon 1939, p. 279). A successful presidential purge depends on effective cooperation between local and national leadership. It was largely due to such cooperation that Roosevelt was able successfully to purge Rules Committee Chairman John J. O'Connor.

Moreover, the 1938 campaign indicates that purge drives might best be targeted on recalcitrant party members from areas of the country most sympathetic to the public philosophy and programs of the president. The defeat of O'Connor was also greatly aided by the fact he was a congressman from New York, allowing Roosevelt, in this campaign, to operate on friendly territory.

The most important lesson of the purge, however, is that a purge is very likely to be unsuccessful. In the last analysis, such presidential intervention will invariably be doomed to failure because of the prohibitive obstacles in the American political and party systems that stand in the way of establishing party government under dominant presidential leadership. Although the decentralized character of politics in the United States can be modified only by strong presidential leadership, a president determined to alter fundamentally the connection between the executive and his party will eventually shatter party unity. In this light, Herbert Croly criticized Wilson's concept of presidential party leadership. Party responsibility could never develop from such executive domination, because

> at the final test the responsibility is his rather than that of his party. The party that submits to such a dictatorship, however benevolent, cannot play its own proper part in a system of partisan government. It will either cease to have any independent life or its independence will eventually assume the form of a revolt (Croly 1914, p. 346).

Consequently, though purges might be successfully executed where overwhelming positive circumstances prevail, extensive purge efforts are likely to backfire on presidents, causing them to lose effectiveness as partisan leaders. More than anything else, the election of 1938 indicates that regardless of the particular strategy that is followed, a purge is likely to be self-defeating.

Apparently, later presidents learned this lesson well from the Roosevelt experience. In spite of resistance from conservative Democrats to their reform programs, neither John Kennedy nor Lyndon Johnson ever seriously considered a purge. New Deal scholar and John Kennedy advisor Arthur Schlesinger, Jr. warned Kennedy against involvement in the 1962 congressional nomination process, arguing that FDR's intervention in the congressional primaries of 1938 led only to disaster (Lord 1977, p. 125). The failed purge campaign also was well remembered by Lyndon Johnson, who began his career as a New Deal congressman in 1937; consequently, Johnson extensively avoided any attempt to influence intraparty politics in his pursuit of the Great Society (Greenfield 1966, p. 12).

Since Roosevelt's futile bid to unseat incumbents through the use of primary endorsements, only Richard Nixon seems to have seriously considered undertaking a purge of his party. During the 1970 senatorial election in New York he gave "tacit Presidential blessing" to Conservative Party candidate James L. Buckley in his campaign against incumbent Republican Charles E. Goodell. With White House approval, Vice-President Spiro Agnew referred publicly to Goodell, who was a strong critic of the administration's foreign policy, as a "radical liberal [who] has left his party" (New York *Times*, September 25, 1970, p. 47). Nixon made a special stop at Westchester County airport to speak kindly of Buckley, stating: "I appreciate the fact that he's for me" (New York *Times*, October 14, 1970, p. 35). Though Nixon stopped short of an open endorsement of Buckley, his tacit opposition to Goodell prompted the defeated incumbent senator to declare after the election that he hoped the Nixon administration "would back off from this temptation to purge" liberal senators with whom it disagreed (New York *Times*, November 13, 1970, p. 41).

The purging of Goodell hardly constitutes evidence that the enormity of Roosevelt's failure was now irrelevant or forgotten. Nixon's intervention stopped short of an open declaration of support or opposition; moreover, this incident was an exception to the laissez-faire political strategy of the administration. For example, the strategy of the Committee for the Re-election of the President in the 1972 campaign was to keep Nixon's efforts totally separated from congressional races (New York *Times*, March 27, 1973, p. 27). Apparently the White House was gearing up for a strong effort to revamp the Republican Party after the 1972 election, an effort that might have included intervention in primary campaigns, but Watergate made the intention and possible realization of these plans a matter of speculation (Ripon Society and Brown 1973, pp. 226-42).

One might suggest, however, that the Nixon administration could derive only limited encouragement for a large-scale purge from the successful elimination of Goodell. This action, as limited as it was, alienated several important Republican senators from the Nixon administration. Many conservative as well as liberal Republicans in the Senate criticized the president's purge campaign and actively supported Goodell's candidacy. During the primary, no less than 20 of his colleagues, including GOP leader Hugh Scott, came to the aid of

Goodell. Their gestures ranged from statements delivered on the Senate floor in praise of their beleaguered colleague to campaign tours in the Empire State (New York *Times*, October 14, 1970, p. 1; Reiter 1971, p. 72). It is questionable whether or not gaining James Buckley's support in the Senate outweighed the negative reaction among the Republican regulars caused by the martyrdom of Goodell.

In general, the "extraordinary isolation" of the presidency has been a limited weapon. Accordingly, presidents have been very reluctant to attempt major reform of their parties through purge campaigns. The experience of Franklin Roosevelt has served as a salient historical example of the improbability of presidents dominating party politics by intervening aggressively in primary campaigns.

Perhaps, given the present weakness of party organizations in the United States, presidents have reason to be bolder than before. As Richard Neustadt (1980, p. 207) has suggested recently, "so little else is real in party life, these days, that intervention now can scarcely hurt them." Yet, if there is less to lose by attempting a purge in an antiparty age, it would also seem that there is little to be gained by seeking to enforce party discipline by appealing to a public that has very little inclination to identify with partisan causes. If parties mean less today than they have in the past, appeals to public opinion for party unity will likely be less, and not more, successful than has been the case previously in American history.

NOTES

1. This view became more prominent in the late 1940s and early 1950s (Schattschneider 1942; Committee on Political Parties, 1950).

2. For a fuller discussion of Roosevelt's political values and political program as they relate to party politics, see Milkis (1981, Chapter 2; 1982).

3. On Wilson's outspoken attitudes in opposing the election of incumbent Democrats who fought his administration's policies in the conduct of war see the New York *Times*, August 12, 1918, and Holmes (1970, p. 353).

4. On Wilson and the 1918 congressional elections, see Adler (1937).

5. Roosevelt took some tentative steps toward encouraging a more fundamental party realignment when he gave tacit support to liberal Republicans against conservative Democrats in the states of California, Minnesota, Wisconsin, and New Mexico in the Senate election campaign of 1934. See Senate Campaign Committee Chairman James Hamilton Lewis's letter to Stephen Early, indicating the senator's intention to cooperate with the president in this endeavor (Lewis to Early, October 10, 1934, *Roosevelt Papers*, OF 300, Democratic National Committee).

6. Until Roosevelt decided to abandon his policy of noninterference in the summer of 1938, he responded to requests for help in local primary contests with a statement from Farley, which was released on January 27, 1938, indicating that the National Committee

would remain neutral in intraparty struggles. Roosevelt prevailed upon the chairman to weaken the original language of this statement, leaving the door open for intervention in a few contests. The president did so, according to Farley, because he had already decided to undertake a purge, and, therefore, did not want to foreclose future action by the administration and committee in certain cases (Farley 1948, p. 121).

7. It is interesting that Harrison, who, as noted above, was brought to the Senate by Woodrow Wilson to strengthen the progressive commitment of the Democratic Party, was viewed as a conservative obstacle to the New Deal. This is an example of the New Deal's fundamental policy departure from Wilson's Progressivism. For an account of the majority leader fight, see Farley (1948, pp. 91-92) and also Cummings's Diary (July 21, 1937, Box 273, Number 7, p. 97, *Cummings Papers*).

8. For a report on the importance of the Florida primary, see New York *Times*, May 3, 1938, Section 4, p. 2.

9. Roosevelt made the best of his lone primary triumph. He insisted that removing O'Connor from the important House Rules Committee chairmanship made the entire purge campaign worthwhile. He remarked: "Harvard lost the schedule but won the Yale game" (*Time*, October 3, 1938, p. 9).

10. This Northern strategy, however, might have relegated the Democratic Party to being a sectional organization. Roosevelt recognized that writing off the South would lead to the development of a doctrinaire liberal party in the North. This would cause a sectional split that Roosevelt wanted to avoid. The pre-Civil War party was based on a similar assumption, and it was designed to bury slavery as an issue precisely because it could not be managed. Roosevelt was willing to avoid a direct confrontation with the race issue, but he wanted to strengthen the national resolve of the Democratic Party on the basis of the issue of economics. Such a national Democratic Party could not leave the South alone; it had to be transformed.

11. For an account of the collaboration between Roosevelt and Wilkie, see Rosenman (1952, pp. 463-70); also see the letter from Roosevelt to Wilkie (July 13, 1944, *Roosevelt Papers*, PPF 7023).

12. James Farley wrote several party leaders throughout the country after the 1938 election, asking for an evaluation of Democratic losses. Many of those who responded, including many from non-Southern states, mentioned unfavorable reaction to the purge. For example, Illinois Congressman James A. Meeks wrote to Farley in February 1939: "The so-called effort to purge from the party certain Congressmen and Senators met with unfavorable reaction. You readily understand that" (Meeks to Farley, February 9, 1939, *Roosevelt Papers*, OF 300, Democratic National Committee).

13. The president's close advisor, Samuel Rosenman, notes in his memoirs that FDR "never forgot the lesson of 1938—and never tried again" (Rosenman 1952, p. 180).

14. No doubt Roosevelt's tentative partisan action after 1938 was also partly a result of the threatening foreign situation; see Ferkiss (1962). I would suggest, however, that, especially after the purge, Roosevelt considered aggressive partisanship to be as infelicitous a strategy in domestic politics as it was in managing foreign policy.

REFERENCES

Adler, Selig. 1937. "The Congressional Election of 1918." *South Alantic Quarterly* 36 (October): 447-65.

Alsop, Joseph, and Robert Kintner. 1938. "We Shall Make America Over." *Saturday Evening Post*, November, pp. 14, 15, 85-92.

Josiah William Bailey Papers. Senatorial Series, Political National Papers, Manuscript Department, William R. Perkins Library, Duke University. Durham, North Carolina.

Baker, Ray Stannard, ed. 1939. *Woodrow Wilson: Life and Letters, Armistice— March 1-November 11, 1918.* New York: Doubleday, Doran.

Clapper, Raymond. 1938. "Roosevelt Tries the Primaries." *Current History* 49 (October): 16-19.

Committee on Political Parties, American Political Science Association. 1950. *Toward a More Responsible Party System.* New York: Rinehart.

Croly, Herbert. 1914. *Progressive Democracy.* New York: Macmillan.

Homer Cummings Papers. (#9973) Manuscripts Department, University of Virginia Library, Charlottesville, Virginia.

Farley, James. 1948. *Jim Farley's Story.* New York: McGraw-Hill.

Ferkiss, Victor. 1962. "The Conservative Coalition." *Commonweal,* July 6, pp. 367-70.

Flynn, Edward J. 1947. *You're the Boss.* New York: Viking.

Frisch, Morton J. 1975. *Franklin D. Roosevelt: The Contribution of the New Deal to American Political Thought and Practice.* Boston: S. T. Wayne.

Greenfield, Meg. 1966. "LBJ and the Democrats." *The Reporter,* June 2, pp. 8-13.

Herring, Pendleton. 1940. *The Politics of Democracy.* New York: W. W. Norton.

Holmes, William F. 1970. *The White Chief: James Kimble Vardaman.* Baton Rouge: Louisiana State University Press.

Hopper, John Edward. 1966. "The Purge: Franklin D. Roosevelt and the 1938 Democratic Nominations." Ph.D. diss. University of Chicago.

La Follette, Philip F. et al. 1938. "Why We Lost." *The Nation,* December 3, pp. 586-90.

Link, A. S. 1956. "Woodrow Wilson and the Democratic Party" *Review of Politics* 8: 146-56.

Lord, Donald C. 1977. *John F. Kennedy—The Politics of Confrontation and Coalition.* New York: Barron's.

Milkis, Sidney M. 1981. "The New Deal, the Decline of Parties and the Administrative State." Ph.D. diss. University of Pennsylvania.

————. 1982. "Franklin D. Roosevelt and the Decline of Political Parties." Paper prepared for the Midwest Political Science Convention, April, Milwaukee.

Mowry, George E. 1946. *Theodore Roosevelt and the Progressive Movement.* Madison: The University of Wisconsin Press.

————. 1958. *The Era of Theodore Roosevelt.* New York: Harper and Brothers.

Neustadt, Richard E. 1980. *Presidential Power: The Politics of Leadership form FDR to Carter.* New York: John Wiley.

Price, Charles M, and Joseph Boskin. 1966. "The Roosevelt Purge: A Reappraisal." *Journal of Politics* 28 (August): 660-70.

Reiter, Howard L. 1971. "Purging the GOP." *Nation,* January 18, pp. 71-74.

The Ripon Society and Clifford W. Brown. 1973. *Jaws of Victory.* Boston: Little, Brown.

Franklin D. Roosevelt Papers. Franklin D. Roosevelt Library, Hyde Park, New York. (PPF = President's Personal File; OF = Official File; PSF = President's Secretary File.)

Roosevelt, Franklin D. 1938-50. *Public Papers and Addresses.* 13 Vols. New York: Random House.

Rosenman, Samuel. 1952. *Working with Roosevelt.* New York: Harper and Row.

Schattschneider, E. E. 1942. *Party Government.* New York: Holt, Rinehart and Winston.

Shannon, J. B. 1939. "Presidential Politics in the South — 1938, Part II." *Journal of Politics* 1 (August): 278-300.

Stokes, Thomas. 1940. *Chip off My Shoulder.* Princeton, N.J.: Princeton University Press.

Wilson, Woodrow. 1908. *Constitutional Government in the United States.* New York: Columbia University Press.

PART IV
PRESIDENTS AND THE PARTY-IN-GOVERNMENT

8

PRESIDENTIAL PARTY LEADERSHIP IN CONGRESS

George C. Edwards III

"What the Constitution separates our political parties do not combine" (Neustadt 1960, p. 33). Richard Neustadt wrote these words nearly a quarter of a century ago to help explain why presidents could not simply assume support from the members of their party in Congress. The challenge of presidential party leadership in Congress remains just as great and is just as important today as it was when Neustadt wrote his famous treatise on *Presidential Power*. In this chapter we examine both the potential for influence and the inevitability of frustration that party leadership provides the White House in its relationship with Congress.

First, it is important to make a distinction between the general support the president receives from his party in Congress and the support he receives as a result of active party leadership. Although the proclivity of party members to support a president of their party provides the basis for much of the potential of party leadership, most of the votes a president's program receives from his party members are not because of party leadership. Thus it is important to consider both party *support* and party *leadership* in some detail.

Since much of the support a president receives from his party in Congress is a result of the shared views of party members, the electoral aspect of party leadership is potentially even more significant than leadership focused directly on persuading party members once they are elected. Thus it is necessary to give attention to the possibilities of the president increasing the number of his party members in Congress through victories at the polls.

Finally, this chapter also focuses on the role of "bipartisanship" in partisan leadership. Since presidents usually cannot rely completely on support from their party members in Congress, either because they compose only a minority of either chamber or because they defect from the party coalition, the White House typically must solicit votes from the opposition party in order to pass its programs. Such a strategy provides additional challenges for party leadership.

PARTY SUPPORT OF THE PRESIDENT

Representatives and senators of the president's party are almost always the nucleus of coalitions supporting the president's programs. As one Nixon aide put it, "you turn to your party members first. If we couldn't move our own people, we felt the opportunities were pretty slim" (quoted in Light 1982, p. 135). No matter what other resources a president may have, without seats in Congress held by his party, he will usually find it very difficult to move his legislative program through Congress (on this see Light 1982, p. 31). Table 8.1 shows the annual average support given to the president by members of each party in the House and the Senate. The source for these figures is *Congressional Quarterly's* Presidential Support Scores, which measure the level of support of each member of Congress for votes on which the president has taken a stand. Table 8.2 shows the summary measures of partisan presidential support for the period 1953-81.

Two important points emerge from an examination of these tables. First, there is a great deal of slippage within the president's party in terms of loyalty, a point that will be developed further. Second, there is a substantial difference between the levels of presidential support by members of the two parties, with the gap generally exceeding 20 percent. Although four Republican and three Democratic presidents are covered by the tables, and although the presidents of each party varied considerably in their policies, personalities, and political environments, their fellow partisans in Congress gave them considerably more support than they gave presidents of the opposition party.

Although the president receives more support from members of his party than from the opposition, it does not follow that this is necessarily a result of their shared party affiliation. It is difficult to tell whether a member of the president's party votes for the president's policies because of shared party affiliation or because of basic

TABLE 8.1: Average Percentage Presidential Support by Party, 1953–81

Year	President's Party	House Democrats	House Republicans	Senate Democrats	Senate Republicans
1953	R*	49	74	47	67
1954	R	45	71	40	71
1955	R	53	60	56	72
1956	R	52	72	39	72
1957	R	50	54	52	69
1958	R	55	58	45	67
1959	R	40	68	38	72
1960	R	44	59	42	65
1961	D	73	37	65	37
1962	D	72	42	63	40
1963	D	73	32	63	44
1964	D	74	38	62	45
1965	D	74	42	65	48
1966	D	64	38	57	43
1967	D	69	46	61	53
1968	D	64	51	48	47
1969	R	48	57	47	66
1970	R	53	66	45	62
1971	R	47	72	41	65
1972	R	47	64	44	67
1973	R	36	61	37	61
1974	R	44	57	39	56
1975	R	38	63	47	68
1976	R	32	63	39	63
1977	D	63	42	70	52
1978	D	60	35	66	41
1979	D	65	34	68	45
1980	D	64	41	64	45
1981	R	42	65	49	80

* R = Republican; D = Democrat.

Source: Congressional Quarterly.

TABLE 8.2: Average Congressional Support for Presidents by Party, 1953–81

	Percent Support	
	Democratic Presidents	Republican Presidents
House Democrats	68	46
House Republicans	40	64
Senate Democrats	63	44
Senate Republicans	45	67

Source: *Congressional Quarterly.*

agreement with those policies. Undoubtedly, members of the same party share many policy preferences and have similar electoral coalitions supporting them. For example, much of the support that a liberal Democratic president receives from Northern Democrats for liberal policies is because of policy agreement. In this case there is little ground for attributing influence to the president's party affiliation, nor is there much need for influence. The president has simply taken stands that are in accord with the normal policy positions of this group of fellow party members.

In 1981 President Reagan won several crucial votes in Congress on his taxing and spending proposals. He was immediately credited with extraordinary party leadership because nearly 100 percent of the Republicans in Congress supported his programs. If we examine voting on budget resolutions under Democrat Jimmy Carter, however, we find nearly the same degree of Republican Party unity in the House (on this see LeLoup 1982). Thus we should not necessarily ascribe Reagan's success to party loyalty. Republican members of the House had been voting a conservative line well before Ronald Reagan came to Washington.

The most common way of examining the influence of the president's party affiliation on members of Congress is to see how a member's voting behavior differs under presidents of different parties. Of course, as discussed above, much of any change in presidential support will be because of agreement or disagreement with the president's policies. Some authors have examined changes in congressional voting on policy scales that are independent of the occupant of the White House. Issues are selected for study on which the policy stands of Democratic and Republican presidents are expected to be the same. Thus, changes in the voting of members of Congress can reasonably be attributed to the president's party affiliation (Kesselman 1961, 1965; Tidmarch and Sabatt 1972; Clausen

1973, Chapter 8; Clausen and Van Horn 1977, pp. 632, 635, 653; Asher and Weisberg 1978, pp. 409-16; Jewell 1962, pp. 31-33, 41-46).

The results of these studies show the greatest impact of party affiliation in the foreign policy area. Republicans have a tendency to be more supportive of internationalist foreign policies when there is a Republican president. They are also more likely to accept governmental economic activity under a Republican president. Democrats, on the other hand, have a tendency to move in the opposite direction when the opposition controls the White House.

The events of 1981 parallel these findings. With a conservative Republican in the White House, many Republicans in Congress shifted to support foreign aid and increasing the national debt ceiling. Supporting these policies was anathema to Republicans under the previous Democratic administration of Jimmy Carter.

It is not hard to understand the role of presidential party as a source of influence in foreign policy. Since most members of Congress are relatively free from constituency and interest group pressure in this area, they are less inhibited in following a president of their own party. Also, because the president has a greater personal responsibility for foreign affairs than domestic affairs, his prestige is more involved in votes on foreign policy. Thus his fellow party members in Congress have more reason to support him in these matters so as not to embarrass him.

In domestic policy areas two factors depress the influence of the president's party affiliation. One is constituency. The constituency of a member of Congress is more likely to have opinions on these issues than on foreign policies. When constituency opinion and the president's proposals conflict, as they often do for Southern Democrats on matters concerning civil rights, members of Congress are more likely to vote with their constituencies, to whom they must return for reelection.

The second important factor has already been mentioned: policy agreement between the president and his party members in Congress. As long as the new president sends proposals to Capitol Hill that are consistent with the policy stands taken by most of the members of his party under the previous president, there will be little need to influence these members. If the president's party has been divided, then there will be more need and more potential for party affiliation to be a source of influence.

Another way to see the influence of party affiliation in voting is to examine votes to override a presidential veto. In most cases many members of the president's party who voted for the bill when it was originally passed switch and vote against the bill after their party leader has vetoed it. For example, in June 1982 President Reagan vetoed a supplemental appropriations bill. After the veto 48

House Republicans changed their votes to bring them in line with the president's position. This was a change on the part of more than half the Republicans who had opposed the president originally. Only one Republican switched to vote against the president. The Democrats were quite a different story. Only nine switched to support the president and seven went in the opposite direction, from support for the president to voting to override his veto.

In conclusion, the president's party affiliation seems to be a source of influence in Congress, although a limited one. It is strongest in the area of foreign affairs in which members of Congress have fewer forces acting on them compared with domestic policy. In domestic matters, party affiliation plays its greatest role when the president's policies are contrary to the normal stances of his party and when constituency pressures are lax enough to allow members of Congress to respond to the pull of a copartisan in the White House. It remains a question whether a president can exploit this potential to increase his support among his party members. To answer this we must examine the president's active party leadership.

LEADING THE PARTY

Members of the president's party seem to have a proclivity for supporting him. This section begins with a discussion of why this is so. This is important for an understanding of presidential party leadership because it sets the context within which appeals for party unity are made. Then we focus on various means presidents use to attempt to lead their party in Congress.

The Appeal of Party Loyalty

That members of the president's own party are more open to his influence is clear. When John Kingdon asked members of the House in early 1969 who played a role in their decisionmaking, 42 percent of Republicans spontaneously mentioned the Nixon administration, a high figure for spontaneous mentions. Only 14 percent of the Northern Democrats and 12 percent of the Southern Democrats gave a similar response. Moreover, one-third of the Republicans replied that the administration played a major or determining role in their decision, about five times the figure for Democrats (Kingdon 1973, pp. 175-76).

Members of the president's party typically have personal loyalties or emotional commitments to their party and their party leader, which the president can often translate into votes when necessary. Thus, members of the president's party vote with him when they can, giving him the benefit of the doubt, especially if their own opinion on an issue is weak (Kingdon 1973, pp. 172, 175, 178, 180; see also Matthews 1973, p. 140). As speaker of the House "Tip" O'Neill said in 1977, "We loved to send Jerry Ford's vetoes back to him. But we have a Democratic President now, and who needs that?" (*Newsweek* 1977a, p. 15). One presidential aide described as "just amazing" how often members vote for the administration's proposals not on substance but on loyalty and desire to be helpful (Wayne 1978, p. 151; see also O'Brien 1969, p. 482).

These sentiments helped President Reagan, even with those Republicans most concerned about his policies. According to one close observer, they "did not drive as hard a bargain as their number would have allowed, for they were uneasy about abandoning the President. They could not play hardball with their leader and they settled for less than they could have gotten" (Schick 1982, p. 21). Moreover, this proclivity for supporting the president increases the effectiveness of other sources of party influence.

One of these is the desire of members of the presidential party not to embarrass "their" administration. This attitude stems from two motivations. The first is related to the sentiments discussed above, but the second is more utilitarian. Members of the president's party have an incentive to make him look good because his standing in the public may influence their own chances for reelection. The Reagan White House was quick to point this out to congressional Republicans. As one presidential aide commented, "We'll never ask a member to vote against his own political interest, but we sure will ... try to show them why it may be in their interest to support the President, whose strength and popularity will be a factor in their own election" (quoted in Kirschten 1982, p. 1057). The Republican congressional leaders were also persuasive in making this argument to their party colleagues (Smith 1981, p. 20),

A president may also find it easier to obtain party unity behind his program if his party regains control of one or both houses of Congress at the time of his election. Many new members may feel a sense of gratification for the president's coattails (see, for example, Smith 1981, p. 20). Moreover, the prospect of exercising the power to govern may provide a catalyst for party loyal while the loss of power may temporarily demoralize the opposition party. According to a leading student of Congress, "had the Republicans moved into majority status in Congress two or four years before Reagan's election, or had majority status been less novel to them, they probably would have displayed less party unity on key votes in 1981" (Ornstein 1982, p. 92).

But power was new to Republicans in 1981, not having had a majority in either house since 1953-54. Even before Reagan took office the renewed party spirit of the Republicans was a source of commentary by Washington insiders. There were many freshman and sophomore members of Congress who were anxious to make their mark on policy. They were also aware that there was power in unity. This enthusiasm was infectious and spread to their more senior Republican colleagues (Schick 1982, p. 16; Smith 1981, p. 20; *Congressional Quarterly Weekly Report* [hereafter *CQWR*], 1981a, p. 172).

All of the motivations to support the president are buttressed by basic distrust of the opposition party. There is a natural tendency for members of the president's party to view the opposition as eager to undercut the president (Kingdon 1973, pp. 172-73). This perception strengthens their proclivity to support him.

To effectively make use of the inclination of their fellow partisans to support the White House, presidents must become masters of role manipulation. On a tax question Lyndon Johnson might have emphasized budget balancing with Republicans and personal loyalty with Democrats (Bell 1965, pp. 93-94; Johnson 1971, pp. 85). Likewise, in appealing to Republican senators on the AWACs issue in 1981, Ronald Reagan stressed, among other things, party and personal loyalty and the necessity of Republican unity to preserve their ability to govern. To Democrats the president invoked the bipartisan tradition of American foreign policy (see, for example, Hunt 1981, pp. 1, 10).

Most such appeals are made by White House aides on behalf of the president. There are several reasons for this. Some presidents, Richard Nixon being the most notable, have found it difficult to press legislators for their votes on an individual basis. Some presidents have been less inclined toward and less interested in personally rounding up votes than others have been. Eisenhower, Kennedy, and Carter, for instance, were less likely to engage in personal appeals for votes than were Johnson, Ford, or Reagan (on the topic of personal appeals, see Edwards, 1980, pp. 124-28, 178).

Presidential aides are also concerned about conserving the president's time. Equally important, they wish to conserve the uniqueness of a presidential appeal. Calls from the president must be relatively rare to maintain their usefulness. If the president calls too often, his calls will have less impact. Moreover, members might begin to expect calls, for which the president has limited time, or they may resent high-level pressure being applied on them. On the other hand, they may exploit a call and say that they are uncertain about an issue in order to extract a favor from the president. In addition, the president does not want to commit his prestige to a bill by personal lobbying and then lose. Also, his staff's credibility when speaking for him will decrease the more he speaks for himself. Thus, presidents typically make personal appeals to individual legislators only after the long winnowing process of lining up votes is almost done and a last few votes are needed to win on an important issue.

Working with Congressional Leaders

Each party has a set of floor and committee leaders in the House and Senate, and in theory they should be a valuable resource for their party's leader in the White House. Because of their role perceptions and because they are susceptible to the same sentiments and pressures toward party loyalty as are other members of Congress, floor leaders of the president's party in Congress are usually very supportive of the White House. In the month before Ronald Reagan's inauguration, the new Senate majority leader, Howard Baker, declared: "I intend to try to help Ronald Reagan [carry out] the commitments he made during the campaign" (quoted in Sundquist 1981, p. 402; see also Schick 1982, p. 18; Destler 1982, p. 76; Wayne 1982, pp. 57, 63, 64).

Yet party floor leaders are not always dependable supporters. They certainly are not simple extensions of the White House. As one presidential aide said of Senate Majority Leader Byrd in 1977, "God, is he independent. He ain't our man — he's the Senate's man" (*Newsweek* 1977b, p. 27; see also Carter 1982, p. 69). President Eisenhower was opposed by many congressional party leaders on some of his more significant domestic and foreign policies, such as aid to education, foreign trade, and budgetary matters, and he was unable to influence Speaker and later Minority Leader Joseph Martin to involve more Republicans in party strategy and decisionmaking (see Edwards 1980, p. 80). Senate Majority Leader Mike Mansfield broke with President Johnson over the war in Vietnam and sustained his opposition for the rest of Johnson's term of office.

There is little the White House can do in such a situation. Presidents do not lobby for candidates for congressional party leadership positions and virtually always remain neutral during the selection process. Though they may occasionally express a preference for one of the candidates they are reluctant to do more (Eisenhower 1963, pp. 274, 363, 530 and 1965, p. 384; Donovan 1956, p. 112; Hughes 1975, pp. 128-29; Rather and Gates 1974, p. 303; for an exception see Humphrey 1976, p. 242). They have no desire to alienate important members of Congress whose support they will need.

Similarly, committee chairpersons and ranking minority members are usually determined by seniority. Furthermore, the chairpersons always come from the majority party in the chamber, which often is not the president's. The few exceptions to the seniority rule in recent years were not in any way inspired by the White House (which was controlled by Republicans while both houses of Congress were controlled by Democrats). For all practical purposes, the president plays no role at all in determining the holders of these important positions. Moreover, the norm of supporting a president of one's party is even weaker for committee leaders than for floor leaders.

One of President Carter's first proposals to Congress was a bill giving the president power to reorganize the executive branch. Representative Jack Brooks, chairman of the House Government Operations Committee, opposed the bill however, and the president could not convince any Democrat even to introduce it until the Republicans volunteered to do it themselves (Carter 1982, p. 71).

Presidents and their staff typically work closely with their party's legislative leaders, meeting regularly for breakfast when Congress is in session. Sometimes these meetings include the leaders of the opposition party as well. These gatherings provide opportunities for an exchange of views and for the president to keep communication channels open and maintain morale. The significance of these efforts has varied, however. On one extreme, Nixon's meetings were often pro forma, serving more as a symbolic ritual than a mechanism for leadership. On the other, Johnson used them as strategy sessions, integrating congressional leaders into the White House legislative liaison operation.

Although these and other sessions may be useful for coordinating party efforts, they take place within the context of an independent congressional leadership. According to then Senate Majority Leader Robert Byrd, at leadership meetings in the Carter White House the president

> urges certain actions and says he hopes he'll have our support. But he can't force it. The president is expected to make proposals, and we have a responsibility to him and the country to weigh them and act on them only if, in the judgment of the Senate, we should (*CQWR* 1980, p. 2700).

One reason that a president may not receive the level of support he desires from congressional party leaders is his and his aides' own lack of understanding of the role of these leaders. This seems to have been especially a problem in the Nixon administration. John Ehrlichman, Nixon's chief domestic advisor, complains in his memoirs of the president's troubles with "*his* own leaders" in Congress. Moreover, Ehrlichman was upset and surprised that Gerald Ford, then the Republican leader in the House, did not work for White House programs when he disagreed with them, and he termed Hugh Scott, the Senate Republican leader, a "hack" (Ehrlichman 1982, pp. 196-99).

Equally as important as the congressional party leaders' relations with the president are their relations with their party colleagues in Congress. Major changes have occurred in the past 15 years that have weakened the ability of party leaders to produce votes for the president. According to former President Gerald Ford,

> today a President really does not have the kind of clout with the Congress that he had 30 years ago, even in matters that affect national security. There is not the kind of teamwork that existed in the '50s, even if the President and a majority of the Congress belong to the same party.
>
> The main reason for this change is the erosion of the leadership in the Congress. Party leaders have lost the power to tell their troops that something is really significant and to get them to respond accordingly. The days of Sam Rayburn, Lyndon Johnson and Everett Dirksen are gone. That has adversely affected the Congress's ability to do things even in very difficult circumstances involving the national interest (Ford 1980, p. 30; also see Ford's comments quoted in Light 1982, p. 212, and Carter's similar views, 1982, p. 80).

One reason that party leaders have lost much of their power over their "followers" is the increased dispersion of power in Congress, especially the House. The face of Congress has changed over the past two decades. Seniority is no longer an automatic path to committee or subcommittee chairs, and chairpersons must be more responsive to the desires of committee members. In the words of Representative Thomas Foley, "If I as Agriculture Committee chairman say to a member, 'I don't like your bill and I'm not going to schedule it,' I'll walk into the committee room and find a meeting going on without me" (*Newsweek* 1978, p. 58).

There are also more subcommittee and more subcommittee chairpersons now, and these subcommittees have a more important role in handling legislation (see, for example, Haeberle 1978). While the power of subcommittees has increased, that of the Southern oligarchies has declined. Members of both parties have larger personal, committee, and subcommittee staffs at their disposal as well as new service adjuncts such as the Congressional Budget Office. This new freedom and these additional resources, combined with more opportunities to amend legislation, make it easier for members of Congress to challenge the White House and the congressional leadership and to provide alternatives to the president's policies.

Yet other reforms have increased the burden of leaders. In 1970 the House ended unrecorded teller votes (in which only the number of votes on each side is reported), and in 1973 it began electronic voting. Both changes led to an increase in the number of roll-call votes and thus an increase in the visibility of representatives' voting behavior. This has generated more pressure on House members to abandon party loyalty, making it more difficult for the president to gain passage of legislation. Reforms that have opened committee and subcommittee hearings to the public have had the same effect.

There has also been a heavy turnover in the personnel of Congress in recent years, and new members have brought with them new approaches to legislating. They are less likely to adopt the norms of apprenticeship and specialization than were their predecessors in their first terms. Instead, they have eagerly taken an active role in all legislation (see, for example, Ornstein, Peabody, and Rohde 1981, pp. 16-19; Foley 1980, Chapter 4). They place a heavy emphasis on individualism and much less on party regularity (see Sundquist 1981, Ch. 13; *CQWR* 1982b, p. 2175).

Thus congressional party leaders now have more decisionmakers to influence. They can no longer rely on dealing with the congressional aristocracy and expect the rest of the members to follow.

> Ten years ago [said a lobbyist for the Department of Transportation] if you wanted a highway bill, you went to see [former House Public Works Committee chairman John] Blatnik, the Speaker, and the chairman of the Rules Committee. There would be a small collegial discussion — and all the political decisions would be made. Now there's no one person to see. . . . You have to deal with everybody.

Andrew Manatos, a Commerce Department lobbyist, and his father Mike, a Johnson White House congressional liaison aide, recently wrote a report in which they concluded that the Ninety-fifth (1977-78) Congress was different from the Democratic Congresses President Johnson faced. "In the early 1960s," they wrote, "The 'Club' still controlled the congressional levers of power," but now leaders must persuade more people (Elder 1978, p. 1196; see also Lanouette 1978, p. 119; *CQWR* 1978, p. 3539). Tip O'Neill is just one of many who wistfully recalls the times when the party leadership could negotiate with a few other leaders and the latter would deliver the promised votes. Today things are different, he reflected, "You don't have the discipline out there" (*CQWR* 1980, p. 2696, see also Light 1982, p. 212).

The party leadership, at least in theory, possesses sanctions that it can exercise to enforce party discipline. These include exercising discretion on committee assignments, patronage, campaign funds, trips abroad, and aid with members' pet bills. In reality this discretion exist primarily on paper. Most rewards are considered a matter of right, and it is the leadership's job to see that they are distributed equitably (see, for example, Waldman 1980, p. 375). Party leaders do not dare to withhold benefits because they fear being overturned by the rank-and-file (see, for example, Sundquist 1981, pp. 398-401).

Threats of sanctions in such a situation are unconvincing and thus rarely occur. As the House Majority Whip commented in 1979: "When we say, 'vote with the party or else,' we don't have much on the 'or else' side of the equation." The House Majority Leader was in agreement when he stated: "You have a hunting license to persuade — that's about all" (quoted in Sundquist 1981, p. 398; see also p. 401). The next year the Senate Republican Whip added: "I've never even once threatened to punish a member. We probably don't even have the power to do so if we wanted to." Thus, as Speaker Tip O'Neill has publicly admitted, defectors from the party line have little to fear (*CQWR* 1980, pp. 2696, 2698).

The Carrot

The members of the president's party receive more attention from the White House than do the members of the opposition party. When a president seeks to build his winning coalition, he typically "writes off" a large part of the opposition party and he can generally depend upon a core of supporters from his own party. To obtain the additional votes he needs, a president usually begins with members of his party who fall into the "undecided" or the "movable" categories.

Since a member of Congress who is indebted to the president is easier to approach and ask for a vote, the White House provides many services and amenities for representatives and senators (for a more thorough treatment of this topic, see Edwards 1980, Chapter 6). Although these favors may be bestowed on any member of Congress, they actually go disproportionately to members of the president's party. Personal amenities used to create goodwill include social contact with the president, flattery, rides on Air Force One, visits to Camp David, birthday greetings, theatre tickets for the presidential box, invitations to bill-signing ceremonies, pictures with the president, briefings, and a plethora of others, the number and variety of which are limited only by the imagination of the president and his staff.

Also, the White House often helps members of Congress with their constituents. A wide range of services is offered, including greetings to elderly and other "worthy" constituents, signed presidential photographs, presidential tie clasps and other White House memorabilia, reprints of speeches, information about government programs, White House pressure on agencies in favor of constituents, passing the nominations of constituents on to agencies, influence on local editorial writers, ceremonial appointments to commissions, meetings with the president, and arguments to be used to explain votes to constituents. The president may also help members of Congress please constituents through patronage, "pork barrel" projects, and government contracts, and aid with legislation of special interest to particular constituencies. The principal reason that President Reagan kept the widely criticized Clinch River breeder reactor in the budget was that it is in Tennessee, represented by Senate Majority Leader Howard Baker.

Campaign aid is yet another service the White House can provide party members, and the president may dangle it before them to entice support (see, for example, Sorensen 1966, pp. 392, 395; Valenti 1975, p. 189). This aid may come in various forms, including campaign speeches by the president and executive officials for congressional candidates, funds and advice from the party national committees, presidential endorsements, pictures with the president, and letters of appreciation from the president. Some aid is more ingenious, as when Lawrence O'Brien, then postmaster general, held a stamp dedication ceremony, complete with parade and associated festivities, in Representative Stan Greigg's hometown in 1966 (O'Brien 1975, p. 185).

When it created a Political Affairs Office, the Reagan administration formalized an activity in which White House staff members have long engaged. Its main function is to secure support for the president in Congress, and it is closely tied to the Republican National Committee and the House and Senate Republican Campaign Committees. Officials from each unit meet weekly to coordinate their activities. No only is the office a liaison between the president and the campaign arena, but it is also a place where Republicans in Congress can come for favors (Kirschten 1982, pp. 1054-56).

All administrations are not equally active in providing services and amenities for members of Congress. The Johnson and Reagan White Houses fall on the "active" end of this spectrum, while the Nixon and Carter presidencies fall on the other end. Yet the important point is that any such differences are relatively small in comparison to the effects made by every recent administration to develop goodwill among its party members in Congress.

The Stick

In 1982 one of President Reagan's aides told of how he convinced two Republican members of the House to vote for the president's budget cuts. The representatives feared the political repercussions in their constituencies of supporting the president, so the aide promised them the maximum campaign aid the law allows a party to give a candidate and won their votes.[1] When asked what would have happened if the congressmen had not given in, the aide replied: "I would have nailed them to the wall" (*Wall Street Journal* 1982, p. 1).

Thus, just as the president can offer the carrot, he can also wield the stick. Moreover, the increased resources available to the White House in recent years provide increased opportunities to levy sanctions in the form of the withholding of favors. As the deputy chairman of the Republican National Committee said, there is more money than ever "to play hardball with. We're loaded for bear" (*Wall Street Journal* 1982, p. 1). The threats of such actions are effective primarily with members of the president's party, of course, because members of the opposition party do not expect to receive many favors from the president (Kingdon 1973, pp. 180-81, 184, 186).

Although sanctions or threats of sanctions are far from an everyday occurrence, they do occur. These may take the form of excluding a member from White House social events (see, for example, Light 1982, p. 138), denying routine requests for White House tour tickets, and shutting off access to see the president (see, for example, Farney 1981, p. 1). Each of these personal slights sends a signal of presidential displeasure.

Sometimes the arm-twisting is more severe and includes cutting projects in a district or state from the budget, cutting off patronage to a member, and refusing White House help in fund-raising and campaign activities (for a more thorough treatment of arm-twisting, see Edwards 1980, pp. 139-44, 176). The Reagan White House let it be known that campaign aid in the form of party funds and technical advice, appearances by top administration officials at fund-raisers and during campaigns, and the encouragement of Political Action Committee (PAC) contributions was contingent upon support for the president. The White House Political Affairs Office let junior Republicans in Congress know that it was watching their votes and public statements closely and warned them not to oppose the president. In the words of the office's director, "We will help our friends first" (*Wall Street Journal* 1982, p. 1; Hunt 1981, p. 1; *Newsweek* 1982, p. 26; Kirschten 1982, p. 1057).

Sheer psychological pressure also plays a role in presidential party leadership. One freshman congressman reported that when he told President Reagan he could not support his 1982 proposal to increase taxes, the president "got red-faced, pounded the table and yelled at me." Similarly, the director of the White House Political Affairs Office described the pressures of the White House put on Republican Senator Roger Jepsen on the issue of selling AWACs planes to Saudi Arabia: "We just beat his brains out. That's all. We just took Jepsen and beat his brains out" (*Wall Street Journal* 1982, p. 15).

Such heavy-handed arm-twisting is unusual, however. More typical is the orchestration of pressure by others (see Edwards 1980, pp. 169-73, 176-79). The Reagan White House has been especially effective in this regard. Operating through party channels, its Political Affairs Office, and its Office of Public Liaison, the administration has been able to generate pressure from party members' constituents, campaign contributors, political activists, business leaders, state officials, interest groups, party officials, and, of course, cabinet members. The Office of Legislative Affairs is also in regular communications with the president's party cohorts (see, for example, Hunt 1981, pp. 1, 10; Merry 1982, p. 19). Such efforts are by no means restricted to party members, of course, but they are the primary focus because of their general proclivity to support the president and the reverse situation among the opposition.

Despite the resources available to the president, if members of his party wish to oppose the White House, there is little the president can do to stop them. The primary reason is that the parties are highly decentralized; national party leaders do not control those aspects of politics that are of vital concern to members of Congress: nominations and elections. Members of Congress are largely self-recruited, gain their party's nominations by their own efforts and not the party's, and provide most of the money and organizational support needed for their elections. Presidents can do little to negatively influence the results of these activities, and usually they don't even try. As President Kennedy said in 1962, "party loyalty or responsibility means damn little. They've got take care of themselves first. They [House members] all have to run this year—I don't and I couldn't hurt most of them if I wanted to" (Sorensen 1966, p. 387).

Obstacles to Party Unity

The primary obstacle to party cohesion in support of the president is the lack of consensus among his party's members on policies, especially if the president happens to be a Democrat. This diversity of views often reflects the diversity of constituencies represented by party members. The frequent defection from support of Democratic presidents by the Southern Democrats or "boll weevils" is one of the most prominent features of American politics and requires no further elaboration here.

Republican presidents often lack stable coalitions as well. As we noted earlier, Ronald Reagan received nearly unanimous support from his party on his 1981 proposals to reduce taxes and expenditures. The next year, when he proposed legislation to increase taxes, to restrict abortions and forced busing for integration, and to allow school prayer, things were different. Republicans were in the forefront of the opposition to these policies.

The issues of the 1970s and 1980s, such as energy, welfare reform, social security financing, deregulation, containment of medical costs, and the social issues mentioned above lack either sizable constituencies, common underlying principles, or both. Yet these are necessary to provide the basis for consensus among party members (see Carter 1982, pp. 68-69).

A shift in the status of party members may present another obstacle to party unity. Just as regaining power may encourage party unity, having to share it may strain intraparty relations. When a party that has had a majority in Congress regains the White House, committee and floor leaders of that party typically will be less influential because they will be expected to take their lead on major issues from the president. This may cause tensions within the party and make party discipline more difficult (see Carter 1982, p. 71).

Yet other obstacles may confront a president trying to mobilize his party in Congress. If the president's party has just regained the presidency but remains a minority in Congress, its members need to adjust from their past stance as the opposition minority to one of a "governing" minority. This is not always easily done, however, as Richard Nixon found when he sought Republican votes for budget deficits (Safire 1975, p. 276; see also Martin 1960, p. 229).

Further difficulties may stem from the fact that the winning presidential candidate may not be the natural leader of his party. Indeed, as in the case of Jimmy Carter, he may have campaigned against the party establishment and not identified with whatever party program existed (see Light 1982, p. 51). Such a new president may arrive in Washington in an atmosphere of hostility and suspicion that is not conducive to intraparty harmony. Appeals for party loyalty under such conditions may fall on less than receptive ears.

EDITOR'S PERSPECTIVE

Ebbs and Flows in President-Congressional Party Relations

Presidents' relations with their parties' members in Congress are not always harmonious. Though "better times" for Ronald Reagan were captured in the title (below) of an article by Saul Friedman for the Knight-Ridder Newspapers in July 1981, less than a year later *Newsweek* ran two articles that described a more strained relationship in more troubled political times. Portions of the three articles follow.

From Friedman's article, which appeared in the Bryan (Texas) *Eagle* on July 25, 1981

REPUBLICANS UNITED: Together We Can Change the Course of History
By SAUL FRIEDMAN
Knight-Ridder Newspapers

WASHINGTON—It was the best of times Friday for Ronald Reagan as he journeyed to Capitol Hill to launch the final offensive for his tax-cut bill—the last piece of his vaunted economic program.

And if the happy, solidly united response of the House Republican Conference was any indication, the president appears to be headed toward another victory over the Democrats in Congress.

"The tax cut is the most crucial item left on our agenda for prosperity," the President told the cheering Republican members of the House. "The momentum is with us. . . . If we remain together we can change the course of history." . . .

From *Newsweek*, February 22, 1982

THE DEFICIT REBELLION

Refreshed by a two-day outing far from hothouse Washington, Ronald Reagan was in a sunny mood when his party's Congressional leaders came calling with grim tidings late last week. They were old and welcome friends—Senate Majority Leader Howard Baker, Sen. Paul Laxalt and House Minority Leader Robert Michel—and the President started to regale them with tales of his appearances in three Mid-western states, where he ripped into critics of his new, deficit-plagued budget. "You couldn't tell the Democrats from the Republicans with all the stomping and cheering," Reagan chortled. Suddenly, he noticed the stony expressions on the faces of his friends—and stopped. "I can see you're all overwhelmed with enthusiasm," he said.

They were distinctly underwhelmed, and for the next half-hour Reagan heard why. His impending deficits—$91.5 billion for fiscal 1983, by his own optimistic projections, no lower than $53 billion by fiscal 1987—had sparked a rebellion from Wall Street to Main Street to Capitol Hill. And despite

EDITOR'S PERSPECTIVE (continued)

Baker's assurances that it was normal for a budget to "come under fire" in its first week off the press, the fire this time was both widespread and withering. Even diehard Reaganites were reluctant to defend such lopsided imbalances in this fall's campaigns, and the alliance that joined mainstream conservatives with "boll weevil" Democrats and moderate Northern Republicans was rapidly unraveling (page 25). "Our people feel they've been pole-axed," Michel told the President. . . .

From *Newsweek*, March 15, 1982

THE GOP FAMILY FEUD

It was a week for Democrats to sit back and enjoy the fighting between Ronald Reagan and his fellow Republicans. First, the chairman of the Senate Republican Campaign Committee, Bob Packwood of Oregon, complained that the President's grasp of issues was dismayingly weak and that his "concept of America" was undercutting GOP efforts to broaden the party's appeal. No sooner had Packwood apologized for his remarks than the President himself was apologizing for a series of rhetorical attacks on "born-again budget balancers" that seemed to include key congressmen from his own party who are now working on an alternative to the Administration's deficit-ridden 1983 budget proposal. . . .

With many GOP congressmen worried about the damage Reagan's assaults could do in an election year, Senate Majority Leader Howard Baker complained to White House chief of staff James Baker and then by phone to the President. "I want to make sure there is no misunderstanding. I didn't mean our fellas," said Reagan, who excised from his next speech a reference to critics "on both sides of the aisle." All of which, of course, left Democrats still under fire and fuming. Rep. James R. Jones, chairman of the House Budget Committee, warned that unless Reagan signaled a willingness to compromise on taxes, bipartisan action on the budget could be stalemated.

MIDTERM ELECTION CAMPAIGNING

Members of Congress of the president's party are more likely to support him than are members of the opposition party, and presidents do their best to exploit the potential of partisan support. Nevertheless, such actions are inevitably at the margins of coalition building, because they take place within the confines of the partisan balance of the Congress. To fully exploit the benefits of party leadership, a president needs as many of his fellow partisans in Congress as possible. Once members of Congress are elected, however, they almost never change their party affiliation, and the rare instances when they do have not resulted from presidential persuasion. Thus, if presidents are to alter the party composition of Congress, they must help to elect additional members of their party. One way to accomplish this goal is to campaign for candidates in midterm congressional elections.

Campaign Efforts

President Eisenhower once stated: "Frankly, I don't care too much about the congressional elections." This was because of lack of support in the past from some Republicans in Congress and a personal liking for some Democratic candidates (Larson 1968, p. 35; see also Eisenhower 1963, pp. 519, 522-523, 1965, pp. 380-81). Still, in the 1954 campaign Eisenhower had a cabinet meeting televised. He also supported Vice-President Nixon's campaign activities, mobilized the cabinet to stump the country, made several trips to states with close senatorial contests, and broadcast a national appeal for a Republican Congress (Donovan 1956, p. 277; Eisenhower 1963, pp. 518-23; Adams 1962, pp. 167-68). In the 1958 campaign, Vice-President Nixon carried the brunt of the speaking chores, but the president made several speeches to promote a Republican Congress (Key 1964, pp. 566-67). Thus the "nonpolitical" Eisenhower became a more active presidential midterm campaigner than any of his predecessors. Eisenhower exemplifies the fact that modern presidents — whether they like it or not — are expected to lend a hand to their parties' midterm congressional candidates. Indeed, as Roger Brown has detailed in Chapter 6 of this volume, recent presidents have often taken an active role in midterm congressional elections.

In 1970, for instance, President Nixon was heavily involved in the congressional elections, though he chose Vice-President Agnew to carry the main burden of making speeches and offered him the services of several White House aides and speech writers. Nevertheless, behind the scenes Nixon was running the show, making strategic decisions such as selecting issues to raise and to avoid, labeling particular Democratic candidates as "radicals," encouraging people (mostly representatives) to run for the Senate, and deciding whom to support (Klein 1980, p. 177; Safire 1975, pp. 317-22; Evans and Novak 1972, pp. 318-22, 328-30, 336-45; also see Green et al. 1972, p. 101). He also made numerous campaign speeches. (The strident tenor of the White House campaign hurt Nixon's chances of having his welfare reform program passed in the remainder of the congressional session following the election. The Democrats viewed the president with bitterness and vindictiveness and were in no mood to go along) (Moynihan 1973, p. 531).

Sometimes presidents are so unpopular that the candidates of their party do not want their support. President Johnson, for example, adopted a low profile during the 1966 campaign because of his lack of public support (below 50 percent in the Gallup Poll). But midterm inactivity has been the clear exception rather than the rule. President Carter was an active campaigner in 1978, speaking on behalf of Democratic candidates all across the country. Ronald Reagan did the same in 1982, although some candidates asked him to stay away because of the recession with which many voters identified him.

Success of the President's Party in Midterm Elections

Presidential efforts in midterm elections have had quite limited success. As Table 8.3 shows, a recurring feature of American politics is the decrease in representation of the president's party in Congress in midterm congressional elections. Why the president's party usually loses seats in Congress in midterm elections is not clear. Certain events may contribute to such losses. For instance, President Nixon's taped 1970 election-eve speech was angry, hard-line, and heavily political. It also suffered from poor-quality film and a poor soundtrack. In contrast, Senator Edmund Muskie made a "cool" and generally well-received election-eve speech for the Democrats. But such events cannot account for the systematic losses over time, which are independent of the occupant of the presidency.

As Brown has noted in Chapter 6, recent research has yielded several explanations for the results in Table 8.3. Scholars have found, for instance, that the president's approval level correlates fairly strongly with the aggregate national vote received by candidates for the House of the president's party (Tufte 1978, Chapter 5; Kernell 1977). Studies have also found that voters who disapprove of the president's preformance are somewhat more likely to support a congressional candidate of the other party than are those who approve of the president

TABLE 8.3: Changes in Congressional Representation of the President's Party in Midterm Elections, 1954–82

Year	House		Senate	
	Losses	Gains	Losses	Gains
1954	18	0	1	0
1958	47	0	13	0
1962	4	0	0	4
1966	47	0	3	0
1970	12	0	0	2
1974	47	0	5	0
1978	11	0	3	0
1982	26	0	0	0

Source: Congressional Quarterly.

(Mann and Wolfinger 1980, p. 630; Kernell 1977; Arsenau and Wolfinger 1973; Nelson 1978-79). Conversely, scholars have found that evaluations of the president are less important in determining citizens' votes than the party identification, incumbency, and specific attributes of candidates for the House and Senate (Ragsdale 1980; see also Piereson 1975; Hinckley 1981, Chapter 7). This suggests a situation in which evaluations of the president are not a dominant cause of voters' decisions in congressional elections, though they may be important enough to affect the marginal change in the aggregate vote percentage for the candidates of the president's party in comparison with the most recent previous election.

That this vote shift is not an accurate reflection of the public's evaluation of the president's performance has been suggested by Samuel Kernell, who has carried the analysis further and suggested a reason why both Democrats and Republicans receive smaller percentages of the total congressional vote in midterm elections when the president is of their own party (even if the president is relatively popular, as he was in 1954, 1962, and 1970). He argues that negative opinions disproportionately influence political behavior and that the electorate votes *against* policies and incumbents more than it votes *for* new policies and candidates. The president is the only highly visible national actor and therefore is a prominent reference for choosing a candidate. Thus, a greater proportion of the voters who disapprove of the president are likely to vote than of those who approve, especially if the voters are Independents of the opposition party. Moreover, disapproval of the president is a stronger source of party defection than approval, and defectors from party voting occur disproportionately within the president's party, primarily among his detractors. Because voting turnout is low in midterm elections, a relatively small amount of negative voting may have significant consequences. About the only thing a president can do to counteract this effect is to be popular so that few voters will have negative opinions about him (Kernell 1977; but also see Hinkley 1981, pp. 118-21).

The seeming relationship between presidential approval and the vote for the president's party in midterm elections may also be influenced by another phenomenon. It is possible that national conditions, which also affect the president's public standing, influence the decisions of candidates to run for office, contributors to donate, and interest groups to become active in campaigns. If things are going well in the country and thus probably for the president, strong candidates should be representing his party, and they should be able to run effective campaigns. If things are going badly, the reverse should be true. In either case, it is national conditions influencing campaigns that affect the midterm elections rather than presidential approval (Jacobson and Kernell 1981).

PRESIDENTIAL COATTAILS

A second way in which the president may influence the partisan composition of Congress is through his coattails. Presidential coattails are part of the lore of American politics. Politicians project them in their calculations, journalists attribute them in their reporting, historians recount them, and political scientists analyze them. Yet we really know little about coattails. Most significantly, we have limited understanding of how they affect the outcomes in congressional elections. From the perspective of the president, this is *the* crucial question regarding coattails.

Our focus here is on the question of coattail victories for House seats (for a more complete discussion see Edwards 1983, pp. 83-93). A coattail victory is defined as a victory for a representative of the president's party in which presidential coattail votes provide the increment of the vote necessary to win the seat. A "coattail vote" is one where a person votes for a congressional and presidential candidate of the same party and votes for the former primarily on the basis of the personal appeal of the presidential candidate of the same party and not on the basis of party identification. Obviously, if coattail votes determine which candidate wins a seat, they will be more significant than if they only raise a winner's vote percentage a few points.

Coattail victories, whether they bring in new members or preserve the seats of incumbents, can have significant payoffs for the president in terms of support for the administration's programs. Moreover, it is possible that those members of the president's party who win close elections may provide him an extra increment of support out of a sense of gratitude for the votes they perceive they received as a result of presidential coattails or out of a sense of responsiveness to their constituents' support for the president.

To have influence on congressional election outcomes, presidential coattails have to be quite strong, that is, there has to be a large number of coattail votes in a district. Most House seats are safe for one party because of the balance of party affiliates in the district and the power of incumbency. The only way for a president's coattail vote to influence election outcomes in these districts is usually for a large number of Independents or affiliates of the other party to vote for both the president and a nonincumbent House candidate of the president's party based on their support for the president. This number must be large enough to win the district from the dominant party. A president's coattails may also save a seat for a representative of his party who previously won election in a district where the other party was dominant in terms of party identifiers. Finally, presidential coattails may make the difference in a highly competitive race in a district with a close balance between the parties. Since we should not expect these situations to occur very often, there should be relatively few presidential coattail victories.

Over the eight presidential elections from 1952 through 1980, there were 76 coattail victories or an average of 9.5 per election. These results are presented in Table 8.4. The largest number of coattail victories (17) occurred in the Johnson landslide of 1964, and the fewest (4) resulted from Jimmy Carter's narrow victory in 1976.

Presidential coattails are usually discussed in the context of picking up seats for the president's party. It is interesting to note that one of President Carter's four coattail victories in 1976 saved a seat for an incumbent. Maintaining a seat may be just as important as winning a new one, though it is not what the conventional wisdom leads us to expect. It is also important to note that in the other 75 coattail victories there was no incumbent in the race. Thus the potential for presidential coattails to affect the winners in House races is limited almost exclusively to open seats.

How one evaluates an average of 9.5 coattail victories in a presidential election depends somewhat on one's perspective—9.5 is

TABLE 8.4: Coattail Victories, 1952-80

Year	President	Number of Coattails
1952	Eisenhower	13
1956	Eisenhower	8
1960	Kennedy	7
1964	Johnson	17
1968	Nixon	10
1972	Nixon	12
1976	Carter	4
1980	Reagan	5

Source: G. C. Edwards III, *The Public Presidency* (New York: St. Martin's, 1983), p. 86.

about 2 percent of the total number of House seats up for election, not an impressive figure. On an absolute scale, presidential elections have little impact on the results of elections for the House. On the other hand, from the perspective of the president, some coattails are better than none, and the 13 coattail victories in the 1952 elections made the difference in giving President Eisenhower a majority in the House. Nevertheless, coattail victories are rather scarce, and the last two presidential elections produced only half of the average for the past eight elections.

Thus presidents cannot expect personally to carry like-minded running mates into office to provide additional support for their programs. To the contrary, rather than being amenable to voting for the president's policies because of shared convictions, representatives are free to focus on parochial matters and to respond to narrow constituency interests. Similarly, although we cannot know the extent to which representatives have felt gratitude to presidents for their coattails and thus given them additional legislative support in the past, we do know that any such gratitude is rarely warranted. The more representatives are aware of the independence of their elections from the president's, the less likely they are to feel that they must "thank" the president with an additional increment of support.

BIPARTISANSHIP

On July 27, 1981, President Reagan delivered an exceptionally important and effective televised address to the nation, seeking the public's support for his tax cut bill. In it he went to great lengths to present his plan as "bipartisan." It was crucial that he convince the public that this controversial legislation was supported by members of both parties and was therefore, by implication, fair. Thus he described it as "bipartisan" *eleven* times in the span of a few minutes! No one was to miss the point. The president required the votes of Democrats in the House to pass his bill, and he wanted their constituents to apply pressure on them to support it.

In October the president was hard at work attempting to obtain support in the Republican-controlled Senate for his decision to sell AWACs planes to Saudi Arabia. He gathered a bipartisan group of 16 high-ranking former national security officials at the White House to state their support of his policy. Reagan also received the backing of former President Jimmy Carter. (Carter had similarly obtained the public support of his Republican predecessor, Gerald Ford, and other high-ranking Republican officials for the Panama Canal treaties.)

In 1982 President Reagan's most important ally in obtaining passage of a bill to increase taxes was Democratic Speaker of the House Tip O'Neill. When the Democrats were given free time on television to respond to the president's nationwide speech on the tax package, House Democratic Whip Thomas Foley pleaded for support of the president's proposals. This was crucial because of the large number of Republican defections from the president's coalition.

These examples illustrate the fact that despite a president's advantage in dealing with members of his party in Congress, he is often forced to solicit bipartisan support. There are several reasons for this. First, the opposition party may control one or both houses of Congress. Even if the president received total support from all members of his party, he would still need support from some members of the opposition. For instance, since 1953 there have been 14 years (1955 through 1960 and 1969 through 1976) when the Republicans have controlled the executive branch with the Democrats in control of the legislative branch. In 1981 and 1982 Republicans had a majority in the Senate only.

A successful bipartisan approach depends upon restraining partisanship to avoid alienating the opposition. President Eisenhower, who faced a Democratic Congress in six of his eight years as president, and his staff consciously attempted to follow such an approach. (Eisenhower was also not inclined toward partisanship [Wayne 1978, p. 142; Holtzman 1970, p. 240; Larson 1968, pp. 34-36; Eisenhower 1963, p. 245].) He cultivated Democratic votes, especially on foreign policy (Ripley 1969, p. 125; see also Jewell 1962, p. 78). When he held fund-raisers to help build the Republican Party, he did so quietly so as not to contradict the impression of nonpartisanship he was trying to convey to the country (Greenstein 1979-80, p. 579).

Nixon and Ford also faced Democratic-controlled Congresses. They tried to steer a middle course between the Eisenhower soft sell and the more partisan approaches of Kennedy and Johnson. They wanted to maximize Republican strength while appealing to conservative Democrats by taking an issue-oriented, ideological line as well as a party line (Wayne 1978, p. 156). Ronald Reagan has followed a similar strategy. In his reelection campaign in 1972, Nixon did not adopt a heavily partisan line, hoping for a majority based on principles rather than just party. Moreover, he did little to help Republican candidates for Congress (Ehrlichman 1982, p. 204). Likewise, President Reagan traded promises of letters of thanks and an absention from personal campaign appearances in the districts of some conservative Democrats who supported him on important votes (see, for example, *CQWR* 1982, p. 2035; *Newsweek* 1981, p. 17).

A second reason for bipartisanship is that no matter how large the representation of the president's party in Congress, he cannot always depend upon it for support. Tables 8.1 and 8.2 showed clearly that members of the president's own party frequently oppose him. As Jimmy Carter wrote, "I learned the hard way that there was no party loyalty or discipline when a complicated or controversial issue was at stake—none" (Carter 1982, p. 80). Southern Democrats support Democratic presidents less consistently than do Northern Democrats. This is especially true regarding civil rights legislation, as Table 8.5 illustrates. Southern Democrats overwhelmingly opposed each piece of legislation listed in the table, and the president would have lost the vote each time without the support of some Republicans.

Civil rights is not the only policy area in which Democratic presidents have needed Republican support. When John Kennedy was elected president, an aide in the White House legislative liaison office made a detailed study of the prospects for his program in the House. He concluded that they were "very bleak" despite the clear Democratic majority there (Wayne 1978, p. 174, note 17). Lyndon Johnson concluded at the beginning of his presidency that as a progressive president, he would need help from the leaders of both parties to pass his domestic legislation (Califano 1975, p. 155). Thus he regularly consulted Republican congressional leaders and restrained evidence of partisanship in public forums.

Johnson worked very closely with Senate Republican leader Everett Dirksen. They had many intimate, one-to-one conferences, which Johnson regarded as essential for gaining the necessary

TABLE 8.5: Votes on Final Passage of Major Civil Rights Legislation Supported by Democratic Presidents

Legislation	House			Senate		
	Repub-licans	Northern Democrats	Southern Democrats	Repub-licans	Northern Democrats	Southern Democrats
24th Amendment (poll tax), 1962	132-15*	132- 1	31-70	30-1	39-1	8-14
1964 Civil Rights Act	138-34	141- 4	11-92	27-6	43-1	3-20
1965 Voting Rights Act	112-24	188- 1	33-60	30-2	42-0	5-17
1968 Open Housing Act	100-84	137-13	13-75	29-3	39-0	3-17

* Figures to left of dash are yes votes; those to right are no votes.
Source: Adapted from "GOP Played Key Role in Civil Rights Laws," *Congressional Quarterly Weekly Report*, April 29, 1978, p. 1050.

Republican support for controversial legislation. The president gave Dirksen the same preferential treatment given to Democratic Senate Majority Leader Mike Mansfield and spoke to Dirksen frequently, sometimes as often as ten times a day (Califano 1975, pp. 155-56; see also Goldman 1974, pp. 83-84, 385-87; Bell 1965, p. 40; MacNeil 1970, pp. 274, 276-81). Kennedy did not share the rapport with Dirksen that Johnson had but still had the senator to the White House monthly and talked to him on the phone slightly more often (MacNeil 1970, pp. 225, 281; see also Holtzman 1970, p. 241). In some instances the senator provided Kennedy with crucial support (see, for example, Bell 1965, pp. 38-39).

Republican presidents have also had trouble gaining support from members of their party in Congress, furthering their need for a bipartisan strategy. President Eisenhower was plagued in his first term by Senator Joseph McCarthy's irresponsible charges against his administration and by Senator John Bricker's attempts (nearly successful) to pass a constitutional amendment limiting the president's use of executive agreements. In the House, Representative John Taber, chairman of the House Appropriations Committee, fought him on mutual security (foreign aid) funds, and Representative Daniel Reed, chairman of the House Ways and Means Committee, did the same on income tax legislation. More generally, Eisenhower had trouble gaining support from the basically conservative congressional Republicans for his internationalist foreign policy and his moderate domestic policies (see, for example, Eisenhower 1963, p. 246; Reichard 1975, p. 121). President Nixon went to the highly unusual step of helping to defeat Republican Senator Charles Goodell of New York in the 1970 election because of the senator's politically liberal opposition to the president's policies.

Not only do partisan strategies often fail, but they also may provoke the other party into a more unified posture of opposition. "Where there is confrontation, there can be no consensus," and consensus is often required to legislate changes on important issues. Some observers believe President Reagan hurt his chances to reform and decrease spending on entitlement programs such as social security by his unwillingness to compromise with Democrats on his economic program (Schick 1982, p. 17; Ornstein 1982, p. 100).

The president is also inhibited in his partisanship by pressures to be "president of all the people" rather than a highly partisan figure. This role expectation of being somewhat above the political fray undoubtedly constrains presidents in their role as party leader.

Despite the frequent necessity of a bipartisan strategy, it is not without costs. Bipartisanship often creates a strain with the extremists within the president's party as a Republican president tries to appeal to the left for Democratic votes and a Democratic president to the right for Republican votes. Although it is true that the Republican right wing and Democratic left wing may find it difficult to forge a coalition in favor of alternatives to their own president's policies, it is not true that they must therefore support their president. Instead, they may complicate a president's strategy by joining those who oppose his policies.

It is not only in matters of ideology that a president following a bipartisan approach to coalition-building may irritate his fellow partisans. Providing discrete benefits to members of the opposition instead of to members of his own party may have the same effect. In late 1981 *Congressional Quarterly* reported: "To keep House Republicans in line behind his economic program, Reagan appealed to their party loyalty. But to assure the necessary Democratic votes, the president agreed to modify his programs according to the Conservative Democratic Forum members' desires" (1981b, p. 1950). This strategy angered some Republicans, especially the liberals and moderates who represented constituencies hit hardest by the president's proposed reductions in spending. They were less easily swayed by appeals to party loyalty alone in the following year.

Bipartisanship may also be hindered by the leaders of the president's party in Congress. Speaker Tip O'Neill and Senate Majority Leader Robert Byrd let Jimmy Carter know they would be upset if he dealt with Republicans in Congress very frequently. So Carter had fewer contacts with Republicans than he otherwise might have to avoid offending the Democratic party leaders (Mullen 1982, p. 525, Carter 1982, p. 67).

CONCLUSION

Presidential party leadership in Congress is a source of both influence and frustration for the president. Members of Congress from his party tend to give him more support than members of the opposition party. While much of this support is a result of shared policy preferences, on some issues the pull of party affiliation provides the president with additional support. Presidents typically work hard to exploit this potential through their appeals for party loyalty, working with congressional party leaders, and the provision and withholding of favors.

Sometimes this works very smoothly and when it does we may be inclined to share with James Sundquist (1981, p. 475) the view that "the bonds of party generate centripetal forces to counter the centrifugal forces inherent in the relations between the branches; they engender impulses toward harmony to offset the natural tendencies toward dissension."

Yet the president can do little to increase the number of his party's representatives in Congress, since midterm campaigning by the president and presidential coattails have little impact. Moreover, there are severe limitations on the responsiveness of members to appeals to party loyalty, the influence and reliability of party leaders, and the utility of favors and sanctions, and there are many obstacles to party unity. Thus the president cannot always depend on support from members of his party and must often resort to bipartisan appeals for votes, even when his party is in the majority in Congress.

Under such circumstances we must sympathize with Speaker Tip O'Neill's assertion that the Democratic party today is little more than an organizational convenience (*CQWR* 1980, p. 2696). Similarly, there is a great deal of truth in one scholar's argument that today congressional parties function to cooridinate the legislative process rather than to mobilize votes (Light 1982, p. 213).

As a result of the failure of presidential party leadership in Congress to produce reliable support from members of the president's party, promises made to the American people by winning presidential candidates have a lower probability of becoming law than if there were consistent party unity. This in turn makes majority rule less effective.

Moreover, it is more difficult for voters to know whom to hold accountable for public policy when party discipline is weak. Because it is not necessarily closely tied to the president, his party in Congress can avoid responsibility for governing and focus on parochial matters and constituency interests instead. As Tip O'Neill said, members of Congress no longer have to follow the national philosophy of the party. They can get reelected on their newsletter, or on how they serve their constituents (*CQWR* 1980, p. 2696). As Gerald Ford (1980. p. 30) lamented,

> Party responsibility does not have any real meaning any more, and that is tragic ... the parties provide a way for the public to see who is good and who is evil and who does a job and who does not do a job. The parties today are really more or less impotent, and if you do not have party responsibility, the system does not work.

Debate over public policy is obscured rather than clarified under such conditions, and programs needed now get passed later, if at all.

Despite the criticisms of party reformers, Americans seem content with the state of things. Voters evidently like to choose candidates independently of their votes for or opinions of the president; members of Congress value their freedom to act in whatever ways they choose and can actually enhance their prospects for reelection by ignoring party cues; and party leaders at the state and local level seem in no hurry to defer to centralized control. The big loser is the president, who can only do his best to exploit the limited potential of party in his continual efforts to persuade.

Any reforms aimed at strengthening the president's party leadership must come to terms with these attitudes. Structural reforms that would alter the ways in which candidates are nominated or congressional leaders chosen depend on the acquiescence of persons who have a stake in the status quo. So do internal congressional rules that would enforce party discipline. The probabilty of any such reforms occurring is very low. Once reforms are instituted, they require active support of these same people to ensure that the power they allocate is used on behalf of the president. But there is little incentive in our system for this to happen. The chances of changing voters' behavior are even slimmer than that of converting party elites. Thus, presidential party leadership in Congress is likely to remain as just one of the many tactics presidents employ in their ceaseless efforts to obtain congressional support.

NOTE

1. It should be noted that in the vast majority of cases the withdrawal of party campaign funds would not be seen as critical, since the average Republican Party contribution to a House candidate in 1982 was $10,420 (plus $8,350 in coordinated expenditures) and the average total campaign expenditure was $163,280 (including primary and general election campaigns). These figures are preliminary, based on the period through October 13, 1982, as reported in a press release from the Federal Election Commission entitled "1982 Congressional Races Set Record Spending," dated January 7, 1983.

REFERENCES

Adams, S. 1962. *Firsthand Report*. New York: Popular Library.

Anderson, J. 1974. "Kissinger Fears Assad Might 'Jump the Tracks.'" New Orleans *Times-Picayune*, April 12.

Arsenau, R. B., and R. E. Wolfinger. 1973. "Voting Behavior in Congressional Elections." Paper presented at the annual meeting of the American Political Science Association, New Orleans.

Asher, H. B. and H. F. Weisbert. 1978 "Voting Change in Congress: Some Dynamic Perspectives on an Evolutionary Process." *American Journal of Science* 22 (May): 391-425.

Bell, J. 1965. *The Johnson Treatment*. New York: Dell.

Califano, J. A., Jr. 1975. *A Presidential Nation*. New York: Norton.

Carter, J. 1982. *Keeping Faith: Memoirs of a President*. New York: Bantam.

Clausen, A. R. 1973. *How Congressmen Decide: A Policy Focus*. New York: St. Martin's.

_____ , and C. E. Van Horn. 1977. "The Congressional Response to a Decade of Change: 1963-1972." *Journal of Politics* 39 (August): 624-66.

Congressional Quarterly Weekly Report. 1978. "Organized Labor Found 1978 a Frustrating Year, Had Few Victories in Congress," December 30.

_____ . 1980. "House, Senate Chiefs Attempt to a Lead a Changed Congress," September 13.

_____ . 1981a. "Numerous Factors Favoring Good Relationships between Reagan and New Congress," January 24.

_____ . 1981b. " 'Gypsy Moths' Poised to Fly Against Reagan's New Cuts; Charge Pledges Were Broken," October 10.

_____ . 1982a. "Congress Clears $98.3 Billion Tax Increase," August 21.

_____ . 1982b. "In the Senate of the '80s, Team Spirit Has Given Way to the Rule of Individuals," September 4.

Destler, I. M. 1982. "Reagan, Congress, and Foreign Policy in 1981." In *President and Congress: Assessing Reagan's First Year*, ed. N. J. Ornstein. Washington, D.C.: American Enterprise Institute.

Donovan, R. 1956. *Eisenhower: The Inside Story*. New York: Harper and Row.

Edwards, G. C. III. 1980. *Presidential Influence in Congress*. San Francisco: W. H. Freeman.

_____ . 1983. *The Public Presidency*. New York: St. Martin's.

Ehrlichman, J. 1982. *Witness to Power: The Nixon Years*. New York: Simon and Schuster.

Eisenhower, D. D. 1963. *Mandate for Change: 1953-1956*. New York: Signet.

_____ . 1965. *Waging Peace: 1956-1961*. Garden City, N.Y.: Doubleday.

Elder, S. 1978. "The Cabinet's Ambassadors to Capitol Hill." *National Journal,* July 29.

Evans, R., Jr., and R. D. Novak. 1972. *Nixon in the White House: The Frustration of Power*. New York: Vintage.

Farney, D. 1981. " 'Gypsy Moths' Feel Reagan Is Up a Tree Without Their Vote." *Wall Street Journal*, October 1.

Foley, M. 1980. *The New Senate: Liberal Influence on a Conservative Institution, 1959-1972*. New Haven, Conn.: Yale University Press.

Ford, G. R. 1980. "Imperiled, Not Imperial." *Time*, November 10.

Goldman, E. 1974. *The Tragedy of Lyndon Johnson*. New York: Dell.

Green, M. J., J. M. Fallows, and D. R. Zwick. 1972. *Who Runs Congress?* New York: Bantam.

Greenstein, F. I. 1979-80. "Eisenhower as an Activist President: A Look at New Evidence." *Political Science Quarterly* 94 (Winter).

Haeberle, S. H. 1978. "The Institutionalization of the Subcommittee in the United States House of Representatives." *Journal of Politics* 40 (November): 1054-65.

Hinckley, B. 1981. *Congressional Elections.* Washington, D.C.: Congressional Quarterly Press.

Holtzman, A. 1970. *Legislative Liaison: Executive Leadership in Congress.* Chicago: Rand McNally.

Hughes, E. 1975. *The Ordeal of Power.* New York: Atheneum.

Humphrey, H. H. 1976. *The Education of a Public Man: My Life and Politics.* Garden City, N.Y.: Doubleday.

Hunt, A. R. 1981. "Out of the Fire." *Wall Street Journal,* October 29.

Jacobson, G. C., and S. Kernell. 1981. *Strategy and Choice in Congressional Elections.* New Haven, Conn.: Yale University Press.

Jewell, M. E. 1962. *Senatorial Politics and Foreign Policy.* Lexington: University of Kentucky Press.

Johnson, L. B. 1971. *The Vantage Point: Perspectives of the Presidency, 1963-1969.* New York: Popular Library.

Kernell, S. 1977. "Presidential Popularity and Negative Voting: An Alternative Explanation of the Midterm Decline of the President's Party." *American Political Science Review* 71 (March): 44-66.

Kesselman, M. 1961. "Presidential Leadership in Foreign Policy." *Midwest Journal of Political Science* 5 (August): 284-89.

————. 1965. "Presidential Leadership in Congress on Foreign Policy: A Replication of a Hypothesis." *Midwest Journal of Political Science* 9 (November): 401-06.

Key, V. O., Jr. 1964. *Politics, Parties and Pressure Groups*, 5th ed. New York: Crowell.

Kingdon, J. W. 1973. *Congressmen's Voting Decisions.* New York: Harper and Row.

Kirschten, D.1982. "Reagan's Political Chief Rollins: 'We Will Help Our Friends First.' " *National Journal,* June 12.

Klein, H. G. 1980. *Making It Perfectly Clear.* Garden City, N.Y.: Doubleday.

Lanouette, W. J. 1978. "Who's Setting Foreign Policy—Carter or Congress?" *National Journal,* July 15.

Larson, A. 1968. *Eisenhower: The President Nobody Knew.* New York: Scribner's.

LeLoup, L. 1982. "After the Blitz: Reagan and the U.S. Congressional Budget Process." *Legislative Studies Quarterly* 7 (August): 321-40.

Light, P. C. 1982. *The President's Agenda: Domestic Policy Choice from Kennedy to Carter.* Baltimore: Johns Hopkins University Press.

MacNeil, N. 1970. *Dirksen: Portrait of a Public Man.* New York: World.

Mann, T. E., and R. E. Wolfinger. 1980. "Candidates and Parties in Congressional Elections." *American Political Science Review* 74 (September): 617-32.

Martin, J. 1960. *My First Fifty Years in Politics.* New York: McGraw-Hill.

Matthews, D. R. 1973. *U.S. Senators and Their World.* New York: Norton.

Merry, R. W. 1982. "A New GOP Congressman Tries To Resolve His Dilemma over the President's Tax Bill" *Wall Street Journal,* August 19.

Miller, Warren E. 1955-56. "Presidential Coattails: A Study in Political Myth and Methodology." *Public Opinion Quarterly* 19 (Winter): 353-68.

Moynihan, D. P. 1973. *The Politics of a Guaranteed Income: The Nixon Administration and the Family Assistance Plan.* New York: Vintage.

Mullen, W. F. 1982. "Perceptions of Carter's Legislative Successes and Failures: Views from the Hill and the Liaison Staff." *Presidential Studies Quarterly* 12 (Fall): 522-44.

Nelson, C. J. 1978-79. "The Effects of Incumbency on Voting in Congressional Elections, 1964-74." *Political Science Quarterly* 93 (Winter): 665-78.

Neustadt, R. N. 1960; 1980. *Presidential Power: The Politics of Leadership* New York: John Wiley.

Newsweek 1977a. "Shadowboxing," June 6.

_____ . 1977b. "Jimmy's Oracle", October 3.

_____ . 1978. "Single-Issue Politics," November 16.

_____ . 1981. "The GOP and the 'Boll Weevils' " June 29.

_____ . 1982. "The Tax Battle Heats Up," August 23.

O'Brien, Lawrence F. 1969. "Larry O'Brien Discusses White House Contacts on Capitol Hill." In *The Presidency,* ed. A. Wildavsky. Boston: Little, Brown.

_____ . 1975. *No Final Victories.* New York: Ballantine

Ornstein, N. J. 1982. "Assessing Reagan's First Year." In *President and Congress: Assessing Reagan's First Year,* ed. N. J. Ornstein. Washington, D.C.: American Enterprise Institute.

_____ , R. L. Peabody, and D. W. Rohde. 1981. "The Contemporary Senate: Into the 1980's." In *Congress Reconsidered,* ed. L. C. Dodd and B. I. Oppenheimer. Washington, D.C.: Congressional Quarterly Press.

Piereson, J. E. 1975. "Presidential Popularity and Midterm Voting at Different Electoral Levels." *American Journal of Political Science* 19 (November): 683-94.

Ragsdale, L. 1980. "The Fiction of Congressional Elections as Presidential events." *American Politics Quarterly* 9 (October): 375-98.

Rather, D., and G. Gates. 1974. *The Palace Guard.* New York: Harper and Row.

Reichard, G. 1975. *The Reaffirmation of Republicanism: Eisenhower and the Eighty-Third Congress.* Knoxville: University of Tennessee Press.

Ripley, R. B. 1969. *Majority Party Leadership in Congress.* Boston: Little, Brown.

Safire, W. 1975. *Before the Fall: An Inside View of the Pre-Watergate White House.* New York: Doubleday.

Schick, A. 1982. "How the Budget Was Won and Lost." In *President and Congress: Assessing Reagan's First Year,* ed. N. J. Ornstein. Washington, D.C.: American Enterprise Institute.

Schlesinger, A. M., Jr. 1965. *A Thousand Days: John F. Kennedy in the White House.* Boston: Houghton Mifflin.

Smith, H. 1981. "Coping with Congress." New York *Times Magazine,* August 9.

Sorensen, T. 1966. *Kennedy.* New York: Bantam.

Sundquist, J. L. 1981. *The Decline and Resurgence of Congress.* Washington, D.C.: Brookings Institution.

Tidmarch, C. M., and C. M. Sabatt. 1972. "Presidential Leadership Change and Foreign Policy Roll-Call Voting in the U.S. Senate." *Western Political Quarterly* 25 (December): 613-25.

Tufte, E. R. 1978. *Political Control of the Economy.* Princeton, N.J.: Princeton University Press.

Valenti, J. 1975. *A Very Human President.* New York: Norton.

Waldman, L. 1980. "Majority Leadership in the House." *Political Science Quarterly* 95 (Fall): 373-94.

Wall Street Journal. 1982. "Playing Hardball," August 18.

Wayne, S. J. 1978. *The Legislative Presidency.* New York: Harper and Row.

_____. 1982. "Congressional Liaison in the Reagan White House: A Preliminary Assessment of the First Year." In *President and Congress: Assessing Reagan's First Year*, ed. N. J. Ornstein. Washington, D.C.: American Enterprise Institute.

9

PRESIDENTS, PARTIES, AND PLATFORMS: FROM CAMPAIGN PROMISE TO PRESIDENTIAL PERFORMANCE

Jeff Fishel

Expect Nothing!

A Sufi Proverb

*I*n time-honored fashion, various media commentators compete in ridiculing the idea that presidential campaigns or party platforms might have substantial policy content, or fundamental policy consequences. Listen to Howard K. Smith (1976), as he observed about a recent campaign: "Every election contains portions of fluff and nonsense, but this is the first presidential one since Al Smith was beaten for allegedly aiming to put the Pope in the White House that has been almost entirely fluff...." Or John Chancellor (1976), speaking to a group of editors, and complaining that in 20 years of covering national politics, he had never seen "a pettier campaign, an emptier campaign, a campaign so lacking in a discussion of the real issues than

This chapter is part of a larger project, *Presidents and Promises* (forthcoming). I have imposed on an unreasonable number of colleagues or critical advice, and I am particularly indebted to the following: Ellen Boneparth, Dom Bonafede, Thomas E. Cronin, Paul Halpern, Charles S. Hyneman, William R. Keech, John H. Kessel, Bernard S. Morris, James A. Nathan, Benjamin I. Page, Leroy N. Reiselback, Bernard S. Ross, Gloria Steinem, and Stephen J. Wayne. The Ford Foundation, the Lyndon Baines Johnson Foundation, and The Wilson Center have been generous in providing necessary financial support for various phases of the field work and writing.

this one." Neither of these condemnations exactly broke new ground: they are a perennial complaint about all elections, even those before Al and Howard K. Smith.

When one moves from commentary on campaigns to analysis of the agendas presidents actually pursue in office, public cynicism deepens further. Do presidents attempt to follow through on the promises of their campaigns or party platforms? "Only a political scientist," observed one of my Washington acquaintances, "would even think of formulating that as a question!"

Ronald Reagan, for example, is consistently accused of "sliding toward the center," of "making more reversals on his conservative principles than any Republican president of recent memory." Likewise Jimmy Carter was damned for "failing to adhere to the basic tenets of the Democratic Party's platform on which he ran in 1976," of "promising more and doing less than any President in modern history." Even Franklin D. Roosevelt, the architect of the most sweeping changes in public policy of this century, ran in 1932 on a platform promising a balanced budget and unremitting efforts to remove government from "America's free enterprise system."

Can this list—of platform promise and presidential (mis)behavior—be multiplied endlessly? Surprisingly, the answer is no; well, sometimes no, with a variety of large "maybes" scattered here and there, enough to keep the question and findings the subject of continuing dispute and debate. Linking campaign promise to presidential performance is a complex and little-examined task.[1] What is missing in most popular commentary is precisely what political science ought to provide: a perspective guided by recent (post-Eisenhower) historical and comparative example, quantitative and systematic where possible, and connected to larger questions of party and presidential accountability in an increasingly complex political system.

This chapter, which reports preliminary findings from a larger project focusing on elections and presidential agenda-building from 1960 to the present, is an assessment of the 1980 campaigns and their relationship to agenda development in the Carter and Reagan administrations. More generally, it considers the extent to which recent presidents' agendas in office reflect their parties' platforms and their own campaign pledges. Data on the presidencies of John F. Kennedy through and including Richard M. Nixon are presented in order to place the Carter and Reagan experiences in broader historical perspective. This report does not have much to say about foreign or defense policy. The emphasis here is on domestic policy.

ROLE OF PLEDGES IN PRESIDENTIAL CAMPAIGNS

Popular stereotypes about the irrelevance of elections for predicting what parties and candidates might do once they are in office create something of an indestructible hypothesis. It is "indestructible" precisely because there are so many disincentives, personal and institutional, to framing concrete and detailed future proposals of action during campaigns. (For a thorough discussion of the disincentives and how candidates, party activists, issue-oriented staff, interest group leaders, and media personnel cope with them, see Fishel forthcoming). Parties and presidential candidates who might otherwise construct very distinctive and ideologically consistent platforms are pulled by other forces to develop less controversial and more ambiguous campaign statements. Countervailing pressures stem from the specific demands of interest groups who are part of the party coalition (organized labor and the Democratic Party, for example), the policy commitments of party activists, and the historic identification of parties with broad orientation to enduring questions to public policy.[2] The campaign agenda that results is a *tradeoff between the electoral incentives to fudge and the coalitional incentives to deliver.*

Party platforms, somebody once observed, are one part apology, one part evasion, and large part bunkum. More empirically oriented students of these documents, most notably Gerald Pomper, might agree but would want to add two additional and contrary parts: From 1968 to 1976, slightly better than one-fourth of each party's platform carried fairly specific and testable policy pledges. In addition, the record of fulfillment was surprisingly higher than what one might expect. When testable pledges are allocated among the nine policy areas, the proportion fulfilled by the party controlling the presidency ranged from a high of 91 percent in Agriculture and Defense to a low of 54 percent in Labor. Paul David (1971, pp. 303-04) places these findings in appropriate perspective:

> The platforms involve a remarkable paradox of perception. [Many persons] have made it their business to denigrate the platforms as campaign trivia — ephemera to be forgotten as soon as the campaign is over. On the other hand, it is not possible to watch the amount of struggle that goes into any platform, thousands of hours of toil, sweat and strain that are devoted by people who value their time highly, without concluding that the platforms must be important to some people, for some purposes.

One consistent argument is that a large part of the "some" in platform purpose is residual and indirect. Platform building permits different factions to agree on the main programmatic conditions under which they will support and work for the presidential nominee. Platforms provide a reasonably precise reflection of the tradeoff between what the probable nominee's organization considers politically acceptable and the influence of group leaders who are interested in expanding or restricting the range of acceptability.

TABLE 9.1: The Parties Have Become Wordier: Growth in the Length of National Party Platforms, 1948–80

	Platform Length (in words)a	
Year	Democrats	Republicans
1948	2,800	2,000
1952	7,200	5,500
1956	10,800	8,000
1960	20,000	9,000
1964	5,500b	7,000
1968	14,000	11,200
1972	24,000	30,000
1976	20,200	23,700
1980	33,000	29,600

a Platform-length is rounded to the nearest 100th word.

b The Democrats produced a two-part platform in 1964, one of the regular variety (and which was distributed by the DNC as "the" platform), and a lengthy appendix, called "The Record," summarizing achievements since 1960. If one includes the second part, total length was 18,500 words.

Moreover, platforms have grown larger since 1948, now covering an astonishing number of policy areas. A glance at Table 9.1 easily confirms the expansion in length; a comparative reading of the 1948 and 1980 party platforms will just as easily confirm my assertion about policy variety. Platforms reflect the general growth in governmental activity since the New Deal. For those who want issue information, modern platforms are far superior now, covering more topics and covering them in greater detail, than they were even 25 years ago. Unfortunately, they are examined seriously by a minuscule number of the adult voting population. ("Thank God!" said one pro who helped write a number of them.)

The actual relationship between what platforms promise and what presidents *attempt* to do in office, as I will examine later in detail, is remarkably high. This holds for every president considered—Kennedy, Johnson, Nixon, Carter, and Reagan.

AT THE CONVENTIONS: BUILDING THE 1980 PLATFORMS

Platforms are normally accepted to be the party's major document for articulating a vision of the future. In practice, they can also be a useful tool for forging what is hoped to be a winning electoral coalition. The platform-building process in the 1980 Democratic and Republican conventions provides examples of the necessity to use the platform as a place to compromise the desires of various competing interests within the party—including, but not limited to, those of the winning presidential nominee.[3] To the extent that the resulting platforms really reflect the positions of the *parties*, rather than simply the *candidates*, they are useful as a standard by which to judge presidential conformance to party pledges.

The Outparty Convention: Building The Republican Platform

Republican political managers historically have prided themselves on being able to plan and run an efficient, well-organized national convention, one designed to maximize the advantages of television ("A family event where everyone ends up smiling") and minimize the disadvantages (Gerald R. Ford telling Walter Cronkite, much to the astonishment of Reagan's senior staff, that yes, he might consider the vice-presidency). Disdainfully referring to the "usual Democrat catastrophe" as a "model of how they run government," one RNC official predicted:

> You won't see any of that in July. Certainly we have some conflicts and disagreements but we've been pointing to this since 1977. Reagan's staff have been involved in all levels but they've allowed us to make the basic decisions. That includes the platform. The draft has emerged out of 3 years of careful study and consultation by our Advisory Councils, and we are more united this year than at any time since 1972. Oh, there may be a wild delegate here and there but most don't want to embarrass the candidate or the party, no matter how strong they may feel. *We know how to settle our differences in private!*

So concerned with negotiating out of the limelight were Republican officials that the platform chairman, Senator John Tower of Texas, through executive director Roger Semerad, decided to revert to pre-1976 Republican practice and close the committee and subcommittee deliberations to the public. The committee promptly overrode him, voting to open the sessions up as they had been in 1976. Semerad even refused to permit distribution of the platform draft to reporters and others not on the committee. Since Republicans on the committee always meet shortly before the convention, divide up into subcommittees, and then go over the staff draft line-by-line, this was tantamount to inviting 250 reporters to a press gathering and then refusing to talk. Delegates intent on modifying the document, however, were free to talk with whomever they pleased. Anti-Equal Rights Amendment (ERA) and antiabortion members of the Human Resources Subcommittee did so with abandon, as did their opponents, passing out copies of numerous amendments and proposed changes, in addition to the staff draft. As Michael Malbin (1981, p. 107) points out,

> the result was predictable...[since] the Human Resources Subcommittee was about the only place reporters could figure out what was happening.... Tower's decision ensured that the press could not cover anything [other than the struggle over the ERA and abortion] if it had wanted to. Thus, Tower's worst fears were realized; days of negative headlines about the big fights over two issues, with almost no coverage of the bulk of the document.

So much for settling one's differences in private!

The long struggle over the ERA and abortion planks, in which the Republican platform abandoned its 40-year support for the Equal Rights Amendment, ultimately approving language that neither opposed nor supported it, has been well told and will not be repeated here. From the viewpoint of using the platform to expand Reagan's coalitional support to include moderates, the committee's decision to abandon ERA, and the process that accompanied that abandonment, squandered a carefully worked out compromise, developed before the convention. Quite surprisingly, given the candidate's clear opposition to the amendment, the staff draft of the Republican platform included a back-handed endorsement of the ERA. The staff draft read: "We reaffirm our Party's historic commitment to equal rights and equal opportunity for women, a commitment which made us the first national party to endorse the Equal Rights Amendment. We are proud of our pioneering role and do not renounce our stand."

Equally surprising, this language was cleared by Martin Anderson, Reagan's primary lieutenant for domestic policy, before the convention. When asked whether the candidate might have to renounce this plank later in the campaign, one aide explained:

> Not really. His position is well known and he can say that "Of course, he supports equal rights for women, just not the amendment, but that many in his party are divided about the means for achieving equal rights and he respects their right to differ. The plank does not commit him to doing anything about it.

Perhaps; but it is unclear whether this position would have helped or hurt him any more than the final plank and the associated disharmony in the party did.

Malbin contends that the Reagan team came into the convention with three strategic goals: maintaining enthusiasm about his candidacy, reaching out to moderate Republicans who were considering Anderson, and building on his appeal to normally Democratic blue-collar workers. In effect, the *specific* commitments of the platform, as amended, permitted them to accomplish the goal of reinforcing conservative loyalty; the selection of George Bush along with extensive back-channel communication with dissatisfied moderates, particularly Republican women worried about the ERA and other matters, helped keep (most of) the moderates in line. The upbeat, progress-through-economic-growth rhetoric of the platform, plus the candidate's careful avoidance of anti-New sloganeering, was designed to break through blue-collar, Democratic resistance.

For the outparty, the temptation to emphasize attacks on the incumbent and to downplay creating an alternative program agenda is considerable. No matter how much this appealed to some of Reagan's managers, pressures mounting inside his own coalition prohibited it. Leading members of the "New" and "Old" Right did have an agenda and the platform gave them an opportunity to pursue it. The coalitional incentives to deliver on policy commitments, as Carter had learned in 1976, and Kennedy in 1980, were immense, particularly on social and foreign defense policy issues. The Jesse Helmses of the Republican party might concede here a point, there a sentence, but they were not going to be fobbed off by pleas for party unity, attacks on the Carter administration, and the rhetoric of supply-side economics.

Contrarily, moderates were unable to alter the changes pushed for by conservatives whether they involved the ERA, a constitutional amendment prohibiting abortion, a "pro-family" clause in support of Senator Paul Laxalt's "Family Protection Bill," or the celebrated judicial selection clause ("We will work for the appointment of judges at all levels of the judiciary who respect traditional family values and the sanctity of innocent human life"). The latter provoked intense consternation among some moderate Republican senators. Charles H. Percy of Illinois, in a bit of overstatement, labeled it "the worst plank I have ever seen in any platform by the Republican party." Mary Dent Crisp, former cochair of the RNC, delivered a well-televised and fiery speech denouncing the ERA and antiabortion clauses before the full platform committee actually adopted them. Still, all of this was of no avail; moderates did not even have sufficient votes to force a roll call on the floor, and the 1980 platform, as amended, was adopted by voice vote on July 15.

Combined with Reagan's long-standing commitments, the platform represented a substantial alternative to any Democratic administration. The GOP platform also mirrored Reagan's projected economic program: In terms of current policy, "supply-side" economics may be passing into one of many campaign has-beens, but in 1980 the dramatic promise of this untested theory became the foundation of the party's proposed economic programs.

William Greider, then of the Washington *Post*, neatly caught the shift when he wrote (1980, p. 37):

> The Republican party had played the national scold for 40 years, the permanent nay-sayer . . . counting pennies at the national treasury came before social security. . . . Now, they were the ones preaching growth and prosperity. They were the party of progress and hope and it was the Democrats, in the person of President Carter, who had become the scolds. Forget the caricature, elect Ronald Reagan and let the good times roll.

Supply-side theory bypassed the old GOP economic dilemma. Scrap the Phillips Curve, unemployment need not to be the "painful but necessary" cost of controlling inflation. Tighten credit, reduce the money supply? Unnecessary! Rather, push through a version of Kemp-Roth, lowering tax rates 30 percent in three years, cut out or eliminate "wasteful" domestic social programs (but retain that elusive "security net"), halt the permanent growth of government, and the American free market—through the resulting savings, investment, and growth—will create the jobs, lower interest rates, cure inflation, and permit a balanced federal budget—and provide the revenues for financing the large and expensive new weapon systems that Reagan promised as part of his plan to increase defense spending. Greider concluded that "Kemp's plan [now Reagan's] and the party's was called irresponsible, and many mainstream economists, including Republican economists, agreed" (p. 169).

However, no amount of criticism, inside or outside the Republican party, could undermine the basic *political* logic of the supply-side thrust. It was consistent with a postconvention strategy of expanding their coalitional base to include blue-collar workers and others threatened by increasing unemployment rates, trying to overcome in a spectacular way the long-standing public fears about the association of Republican presidents and economic hardship. Conversely, it did little damage, except among monetarists and other lonely figures in the GOP, to the older free-market "magic" that traditional leaders in the party had espoused so long. And it certainly jelled with the candidate's seemingly inexhaustible personal optimism and his managers' drive to present his and the Republican Party's economic promises in an upbeat, positive light. "Laffer lightens our load," observed one sardonic Republican.

With a brillant if illusory political sidestep, the Reagan coalition avoided dealing with painful tradeoffs between economic complexity and uncertainty, on the one hand, and the policy and electoral claims of the *anti*-New Deal coalition, on the other. Implied in the promise of a 30 percent cut in tax rates, and explicit in the promise of substantial capital gains and corporate tax cuts, was a considerable "redistribution" of resources back to the wealthy — to those in the top tax brackets, supply-side economics is a potential bonanza since a 30 percent rate reduction for families in the $100,000 and above brackets is both absolutely and relatively worth more than a comparable cut to families with annual incomes of $25,000 or less. When combined with reductions in government support for the poor and near-poor, Reagan's economic agenda promised a shift in the government's historic role of providing a moderate form of economic justice. Of course, they consciously and carefully avoided labeling it as "anti-New Deal."

There is no evidence that large proportions of the mass electorate understood or responded to the nuances of supply-side versus oldside Republican economics. Greg Markus (1982) demolishes the idea that issue-voting in the general election supported the Reagan administration's later contention that most voters cast their ballots in support of his future economic policies (the most generous estimate would be under 10 percent). The Reagan coalition used supply-side to circumvent internal party opposition and create harmony among the most active Republicans. They also employed it in a media campaign that sought to overcome traditional public fears about "Republican recessions," hoping to create a general mass belief, free of details, that Reagan and the GOP would do a "better job in handling the economy." In this they were partially successful: 21 percent of the American electorate thought Republicans would do better in dealing with inflation and unemployment compared to 10 percent who chose the Democrats. *Almost 70 percent reached another conclusion:* The GOP would do well in one area, the Democrats better in another, both would be disasters, and so on (Markus 1982).

How cynical was the original supply-side commitment? Two years later, after presiding over a $103 billion deficit for fiscal year 1982, President Reagan helped push through a $98 billion tax increase and the administration seemed discreetly to be abandoning many (not all) of the elements of supply-side economics. David Stockman's *Atlantic* "confessions" (Greider 1982) suggest that some around Reagan harbored serious doubts about the workability of his economic theory but held back in the belief that it could be fine-tuned if and when they won the election. The question is unanswerable when applied to Reagan's belief system or motivation; in fact, one need not be naive in reaching a generous conclusion because it is obvious that he has championed other ideas that also lack complexity. Additionally, the president and his party gambled considerably by actually trying to follow through on this economic package in their first year. Why assume he was acting in an uncharacteristically Nixonlike manner?

The In-Party Convention: Building the Democratic Platform

A careful observer of the last Democratic convention can be excused for agreeing with Nelson Polsby's wry comment that after the "open convention" rule vote on Monday the rest consisted mostly of waiting "to see whether Senator Kennedy would embrace the ticket, and how happily . . . " (Ranney 1981, p. 84).

Television commentary monotonously repeated the themes of "will he, or won't he" [hold the president's hand up in a show of unity — negative, he merely shook it], "will he, or won't he" [campaign for Carter in the fall — not much] in its usual preoccupation with the personally dramatic.

Of course these questions probed in their typically soap-opera way an important issue of party organizational maintenance. The extent to which postconvention unity could be achieved given the obvious divisiveness of the campaign and the numerous ways in which Kennedy declined to be gracious after losing at the convention was an important concern. On one measure, arguably the most important, the president benefited mightily from the convention, despite dire predictions to the contrary. Reagan's lead over Carter at the beginning of the August gathering, estimated by Gallup at 15 percentage points and by Harris at 23, dropped to 1 percent in Gallup's poll and 3 percent in Harris's after the convention ended. Malbin (1981, p. 107) stresses the irony when he notes:

> To almost every neutral observer in the New York's Madison Square Garden, the convention had caused Carter as many problems as it had solved . . . but the constant criticism of Reagan in every convention speech clearly had a cumulative impact that had little to do with the subtle tea-leaf variations observed by professional convention watchers.

Carter's relative electoral strength, despite the constant assaults on his administration and policies, rose substantially after his (as always) contentious party evacuated New York.

Underneath all this, however, an important chapter in agenda-building was being constructed. Kennedy's primary challenge had been a gamble on an untested hypothesis: *When the incumbent is faced with intense competition for renomination, agenda-development is a tradeoff between the electoral incentives to continue existing policies, and the coalitional incentives to shift toward the preference of the challenging faction.* Further, Kennedy's decision represented a gamble with both negative and positive dimensions; negative in that the obvious divisiveness and struggle would weaken *any* Democratic nominee against a Republican opponent in the fall and by implication, risk all Democratic policy alternatives; positive (for Kennedy and his partisans) because if he had won both the nomination and the general election, progressives would be free of the Carter "half-loaf" many had grown to hate. Kennedy's decisive loss to Carter had doomed the possibility of replacing the administration's agenda by replacing the incumbent. Altering the platform was the only channel left to those who supported more liberal policies.

Factional leaders in and around the liberal wing of the party negotiated, cajoled, pushed, threatened, and finally imposed an extraordinary number of revisions and then minority planks in the final version of the 1980 platform. It is important to emphasize that the original platform, carefully written under White House direction, was hardly a reactionary document. Still, groups as diverse as gays, feminists, antinuclear and environmental activists, and orthodox labor officials understandably wanted planks closer to their preferences, and they moved in various ways to change the administration's draft. While they may have lost the war in the nomination process, they most certainly won numerous important battles over the party's agenda as it is reflected in the national platform. Informal negotiations between the White House and factional leaders, first during the drafting state, then before the convention opened, led to significant changes, making the document more acceptable to liberals. The sometime emotional struggle at the convention, along with politically astute concessions by Carter officials, resulted in the adoption of more (14 of 23) minority planks than at any prior convention in the twentieth century. Among the most important changes, one would include:

- the first gay rights plank in the history of the American parties (compromise language was agreed to by the Drafting subcommittee with Carter's support);

- a commitment to "retire nuclear power plants in an orderly manner" (compromise reached between the administration and delegates supporting the Committee for Safe Energy's well-organized antinuclear campaign during the full platform committee's deliberations);
- the administration accepted six minority planks (numbers 5, 7, 8, 12, 16, 18) before the convention opened as part of a bargain with Kennedy involving scheduling and Kennedy's agreement to withdraw two (numbers 15 and 22). Kennedy forces also agreed to withdraw support from two others during the convention (numbers 14 and 23). The six accepted by the White House before the Convention opened included:

   (1) language pledging not to cut funding for welfare, education, and other programs directed at assisting "the most needy in our society" (5);
   (2) not to change the cost-of-living index in any way that would result in lower Social Security payments (7);
   (3) a commitment to have the federal government assume financial responsibility for state and local government welfare costs by the end of 1981 (8);
   (4) language denying the newly created Energy Mobilization Board "fast track" authority to override environmental, public health, and safety laws (12);
   (5) pledges to spend more on development of solar, wind, and other renewable energy sources than on synthetic fuels (16);
   (6) a commitment to give states and Indian tribes the power to veto sites they believed would be unsafe for disposal of nuclear wastes (18);

- under pressure from *Carter* delegates who nevertheless supported much of Kennedy's economic program, White House officials negotiated another bargain with Kennedy over his four economic minority proposals, plus a labor-backed jobs plank. The outcome permitted the White House to win in its opposition to wage-price controls (number 1) in exchange for losing three (numbers, 2, 3, 4). The pressure from both Carter and Kennedy delegates on an additional jobs plank led the administration to concede to labor on this issue (number 9). Altogether, the four included language committing the Democratic party to:

   (1) a $12 billion antirecession economic recovery plan (3);
   (2) take "no fiscal action, no monetary action no budgetary action" if it would cause "significantly" greater unemployment (2);
   (3) a statement of opposition to fighting inflation through a policy of high interest rates and unemployment (4);
   (4) pursuing a jobs policy that guarantees "a job for every American who is able to work as our single highest domestic priority."

All, including the Carter victory on wage controls, were gaveled through on voice vote by the Speaker of the House, Thomas P. O'Neill, Jr., with the prior support of both Kennedy and Carter operatives who had negotiated the package off the floor. Most neutral observers believe that, had they been put to roll-call vote, Carter would also have lost on the wage-price controls plank.

- feminists in the Democratic Party, generally supportive of the original document's commitment to women's rights, nevertheless challenged the administration in two areas — Medicaid support for abortions and a proposal mandating that the DNC deny support to candidates who opposed the ERA — and won both handily, the latter (10) by voice vote and the former (11) in a roll-call.

"Kennedy," observed one reporter, "lost the nomination and won the platform." Almost, but not quite. The White House was able to fend off Kennedy partisans in three important areas. One challenged the president's decision to move ahead on the MX missiles (minority plank 20 introduced, ironically, by a Carter delegate and defeated on a roll-call vote by almost 600 votes). The second substituted Kennedy's version of a national health insurance program (minority plank 6, defeated by slightly more than 200 votes) for Carter's, which supported the concept but sought slower implementation. The third minority plank won by Carter forces prohibited the federal government from using oil import fees or gas taxes to "artificially increase the price of gasoline" (14, bartered by Kennedy in exchange for Carter's support of the solar plank). In addition, the administration beat back a conservative effort to reverse the original document's commitment to freedom of choice on abortions, and two minority planks on which Kennedy abstained — a commitment to federally charter oil companies (minority plank 19) and a promise to "pursue an immediate nuclear freeze" (21).

Ironically, the defense-foreign policy language of the 1980 platform, considerably more strident in its argument for a defense buildup than it was in 1976, was never seriously challenged by Kennedy.[4] The platform does contain conciliatory language, particularly in its opening commitment to human rights and the use of "moral principle, rather than force in international conflicts," but the shift to a more confrontational posture vis-a-vis the Soviet Union, and the justification of 3 percent annual increases in defense spending during the Carter years, is in sharp contrast to the rhetoric and commitments of 1976. Indeed, Democrats even fault the Nixon-Ford administration for a "steady decline of 33 percent in real U.S. military spending between 1968 and 1976" as if the party and the president had never questioned the practicality or morality of large defense budgets.

In the end, however, Carter's formal statement to the convention made the essential point, reinforcing a feeling shared by most delegates: "There was . . . sometimes heated debate on the major domestic and foreign policy issues facing us. The end product is a strong and progressive platform . . . the differences within our party are small in comparison with the differences between the Republican and Democratic Party Platforms."

Does any of this now make a difference? After all, Carter and the Democrats were given exit visas from the White House shortly after they left Madison Square Garden. The obvious question, tantalizing the unanswerable, is whether the platform would have affected a potential second Carter term? Analyzing events that do not take place is like scoring a touchdown in your own end zone: it ignites considerable emotion and no points.

Since the fall campaign mandated that Carter turn to opposing Reagan, and mobilizing Democratic and independent support through rhetorical appeals, intraparty warfare among Democrats ended. Because my research and the supporting work of others demonstrates that both parties have implemented a major part of their platforms, one can assume that a second Carter term would not have abandoned it completely, despite Stuart Eisenstadt's comment that it was the "sum total of every group's maximum desires." The emphasis here should be on "parts"; we can never know precisely which parts Carter would have implemented, ignored, or scuttled. Precise as they are, platforms are still riddled with ambiguity. Carter's own response to the revised platform, imposed on him by an unprecedented rule change requiring candidates formally to declare their support of the platform, and to explain any specific disagreements, was masterly in its ambiguities. In those areas where he had reservations (for example, the $12 billion antirecession jobs plan), Carter wrote that he would "accept and support the intent" of the program, omitting a commitment to specific dollar figures. He neither rejected nor accepted the specifics of the plan, leaving precise federal responses to be determined if and when he returned to the White House. Like all presidents, Carter preferred to keep some options open.

The constitutional restriction of two terms dramatically reduces the political incentives to remain accountable to one's party or to any other group in the president's electoral coalition. The Constitution leaves us with only two constraints on presidential performance during their second term: how *they* perceive their "ultimate place in history," usually obscured by rhetoric about "serving the public interest" in some uncharted stratosphere "above politics," and their own conscience, beliefs, values, and goals. Whatever the intent of the amendment, it diminishes electoral and party accountability in the American presidency.

Of what impact on the Carter administration, then, was the Kennedy challenge? In Washington, Carter's fiscal year 1981 budget choices, analyzed in my larger study, suggest conflicting answers. Inflation blunted the piecemeal budgetary concessions made to liberals in Budget I, leading to a revision in the March 1980 Budget II, that ran counter to what most Kennedy partisans preferred. In New York, where party, not government decisions (except indirectly), were at stake, the challenge had a direct and substantial impact: the coalitional incentives to shift toward the preferences of the challenging faction were considerable, and the administration, with a feint here and an end run there, made the shift.

The rest, unhappily for my framework, is nonhistory. Losers have no one to be accountable to, the only advantage of not winning the presidency. Reagan, like Carter in 1976 and every successful presidential candidate before them, now had to face the issue of actually delivering on promises made. How do Carter and Reagan compare with their predecessors on this score?

PRESIDENTS IN OFFICE

In his first year in office, President Reagan and his administration moved forcefully and skillfully to redeem a substantial part of their campaign agenda on economic policy, including a massive 3-year tax cut and the imposition of dramatic reductions in government spending for social and other services.

In his second year in office, President Reagan "reluctantly" supported a tax "reform" bill that increased taxes in many sectors, seeking to recover about 25 percent of the revenue lost in the 3-year package supported in the first year.

In Jimmy Carter's first year in office, he issued an executive order granting pardons to all Vietnam War draft resisters and establishing procedures for case-by-case review of deserters. In a direct, visible, and unambiguous way, he redeemed a campaign pledge on one of the most bitterly disputed issues of the past decade.

In early 1979 the Carter administration submitted legislation as part of its second National Energy Plan, which would totally deregulate the price of crude oil, thereby reversing a frequently stated campaign promise to oppose the deregulation of prices for "old" crude.

Is this about all one can expect—acting consistently in some areas and inconsistently in others in predictably unpredictable fashion? Or

do each of these presidential responses to reasonably specific
campaign promises represent a pattern of compliance and/or reversal
that might be anticipated from what I have suggested about
presidential campaigns in general?

Answering this question requires a short detour. First, it
necessitates that one further examine claims about the lack of detailed
campaign promises made by candidates. Did the number and
specificity of Reagan and Carter campaign promises differ
substantially from Kennedy, Johnson, or Nixon? Data on this question
are presented in Table 9.2, using a modified version of Fred Grogan's
pioneering work (1977) on presidential fulfillment.[5]

Insofar as presidential campaign material meets standards of
reasonable specificity, these data suggest an intriguing finding about
these two presidents. First, and most dramatically, Reagan promised
far less (108) than Carter (186) who in turn far outdistanced Kennedy
(133), Johnson (63), and Nixon (153) in promise. (It should be noted that
these pledges do not meet Page's more elaborate criteria of specificity.
In these respects, Reagan, Carter, and earlier candidates framed
proposals that were remiss.) Still, the amount of specific information
provided in pledges of action and detailed pledges is surprising given
the normal tendency to dismiss most campaign issue information as
mere rhetoric. The data in Table 9.2 make it clear that the Carter
campaign was more ambitious than any of the earlier efforts in drafting program commitments that were fairly specific, and Reagan,
whose promises were more far-reaching in their impact, nevertheless
was much less ambitious in the number made.

Pledge Fulfillment: Quantitative Evidence

Two types of studies have been conducted that bring evidence to
bear on the conformance of presidential behavior to platform positions.
Pomper with Lederman (1980) has studied fulfillment of platform
pledges by the parties through 1978. Like Grogan, I will focus on the
fulfillment of presidential campaign promises, presenting data from
1960 through 1982.

Defining fulfillment of platform pledges as action (or inaction) by
the executive or legislative branches or both "in the promised
direction," Pomper has concluded that "pledges are indeed fulfilled"
(Pomper with Lederman, 1980, p. 161): "During the last decade
[1968-78] of government action, almost two-thirds of all promises were
fulfilled in some fashion, with 30 percent directly enacted through
congressional or executive initiations." Of particular interest for this
book, Pomper (with Lederman 1980, p. 167) also notes that "the power

TABLE 9.2: Number and Specificity of Presidential Campaign Promises, Kennedy to Reagan*

Type of Promise	Kennedy (1960) Percent	Number	Johnson (1964) Percent	Number	Nixon (1968) Percent	Number	Carter (1976) Percent	Number	Reagan (1980) Percent	Number
Pledge of continuity	10	(11)	10	(6)	4	(6)	3	(5)	20	(22)
Expression of goals and concerns	26	(34)	30	(19)	32	(49)	30	(56)	44	(47)
Pledges of action	43	(59)	44	(28)	44	(68)	41	(76)	25	(27)
Detailed pledges	21	(29)	16	(10)	20	(30)	26	(49)	11	(12)
Total	100	(133)	100	(63)	100	(153)	100	(186)	100	(108)

*For obvious reasons Ford was omitted and Nixon's second term was considered atypical. Data are from the general election period only. Coding roughly followed those categories used in Pomper (1968). The material for Johnson and Nixon was taken from Grogan (1977). Data for Kennedy, Carter, and Reagan are the author's.

of the Presidency is not needed to accomplish bland programs. It becomes valuable only when a party seeks to accomplish policies in dispute."

My own study focuses on presidential effort (rather than achievement) to fulfill campaign promises generally (that is, those contained in the party's platform and elsewhere). Because some of the data concern pledges made in other than party documents, my data are a reflection—rather than direct measure—of platform fulfillment. Still, they provide additional useful evidence on the extent to which presidential behavior in office reflects campaign promises, most of which *are* contained in the platform.

Three types of data have been collected. First, I have undertaken quantitative content analysis of presidential campaign speeches, position papers, platform presentations, building on and borrowing from the efforts of Grogan and Pomper. Similar analysis was done for all presidential legislative proposals and executive orders seeking to match these with campaign commitments. Although I modified Grogan's coding categories, I was able to utilize his data for the Johnson and Nixon administrations. Comparable data have been developed for Kennedy, Carter, and Reagan, omitting Nixon's aborted second term and Ford's brief stay in office. Thus I have crude but suggestive and fairly reliable "performance" data across the five major presidencies of the past 20 years.

Second, I have interviewed 136 key participants, selecting various people from the early Kennedy period through the Reagan administration. All interviews were structured but open-ended. In length they ranged from one lasting 12 minutes to one of three hours. The average was one hour.

Finally, I have "soaked and poked" through presidential libraries, DNC, RNC, and private files, countless published and unpublished campaign memoirs, new releases, hand-outs, and all the normal primary and secondary sources of presidential research.

What constitutes presidential fulfillment of campaign promises is a deceptively simple question (see Fishel forthcoming, for an elaboration). The inevitable political and personal definition of fulfillment, the flexible range of possible presidential responses, and the shift in priorities as reelection activity mounts—all impinge on any effort to assess performance. Such problems notwithstanding, I have developed some broad and crude performance measures for each president since Kennedy, relying heavily on Grogan's categories and prior research. Naturally, these categories involve considerable subjectivity in their application. The first is a measure of presidential office activity only, that is, executive orders and *proposed* legislation. I compare each campaign pledge that met my criteria of specificity with legislation proposals and executive orders, providing a rough measure of presidential *effort*, not achievement. The following categorization was used:

Fully Comparable. The president's proposal met the requirements of the pledge in a complete and comprehensive manner; for example the Reagan administration's 1981 three-year tax reduction measures, or the Carter administration's first welfare reform bill.

Partially Comparable. The president's proposal did not meet the full requirements of the pledge but still contained large and similar components, or represented action that was similar in purpose; for example, the Reagan administration's legislative package on tuition tax credits for private schools, or Carter's first set of amendments to the tax code in 1978.

Token Action. The president's proposal represents a gesture, and little more, to the pledge; for example, the Reagan administration's half-hearted support of a constitutional amendment mandating a "balanced budget," or the Carter administration's final support of the version of Humphrey-Hawkins that provided national economic planning measures but no specific unemployment remedies.

Contradictory Action. The president's proposal represented the opposite of what was suggested by the pledge; for example, the Reagan administration's support for continuing draft registration, or the administration's initial opposition to the deregulation of natural gas.

No Action. Neither legislation nor executive orders could be found that were consistent with the pledge.

Mixed Action. The president's proposal simultaneously met some requirements of the pledge but went in opposite directions on other parts, for example, the Reagan administration's "deregulation" package for natural gas, or aspects of the Carter administration's National Energy Plan.

Indeterminate. The nature of the pledge did not permit any classification.

The quantitative results of this classification, applied to the administrations of Kennedy, Johnson, Nixon, Carter, and Reagan are presented in Table 9.3.

It is important to reemphasize the very crude nature of my content analysis as well as to point out that this is not a comprehensive version of each president's policy record, particularly Reagan's, since the data are based only on his first two years in office. Further, every president has submitted more legislative proposals, and issued more executive orders, than are represented by my data. These proposals are restricted to those that relate to campaign pledges. (The ratio of

TABLE 9.3: Presidential Proposals in Relation to Campaign Promises about Domestic Policy, Kennedy to Reagan

Type of Proposal	Kennedy (1961-63)		Johnson (1965-68)		Nixon (1969-72)		Carter (1977-80)		Reagan (1981-82)	
	Percent	Number	Percent	Number	Percent	Number	Percent	Number	Percent	Number
Fully comparable	36	(49)	41	(26)	34	(52)	45	(84)	31	(33)
Partially comparable	31	(42)	22	(14)	26	(39)	20	(39)	12	(13)
Token action	6	(8)	8	(5)	5	(7)	11	(19)	8	(8)
Contradictory action	5	(6)	4	(3)	2	(3)	8	(15)	9	(10)
No action	6	(8)	5	(2)	27	(42)	10	(18)	20	(22)
Mixed action	12	(15)	13	(8)	4	(6)	2	(4)	10	(11)
Indeterminate	4	(5)	8	(5)	3	(4)	4	(7)	10	(11)
Totals	100	(133)	100	(63)	100	(153)	100	(186)	100	(108)

Sources: For Johnson and Nixon, Grogan (1977); for Kennedy, Carter, and Reagan, the author.

total presidential activity to proposals stemming from campaign pledges is about 3.5 to 1; the Kennedy administration, for example, submitted over 800 legislative proposals in the two-plus years of his presidency but only the 133 campaign pledges-to-presidential proposals are shown in the table.)

What conclusions can be drawn from scanning these data? Without question, each president has in fact submitted legislation, or signed executive orders, that are broadly consistent with about two-thirds of their campaign pledges (the reader should add the percentages for fully and partially comparable to reach this rough average). Reagan's first two years, of course, are characterized by less activity (43 percent of his proposals fall in this category) but this should increase before his first term is finished. If it does not, the Reagan administration will complete its first term with the lowest record of campaign-to-office fulfillment of any president in the past 24 years. The Carter administration, on the other hand, generated a far larger output of proposals-to-pledges than any of the three prior administrations. Adding proposals from the first two categories, fully comparable and partially comparable, which comprise the most consistent commitments, gives a total of 133 proposals from Carter in three years. By comparison, Kennedy took reasonably positive action on 91, Johnson on 40, and Nixon on 92. A large part of the difference stems from the point made earlier: Carter promised more of a specific nature during his 1976 campaign than the other four and his record of follow-through is thus higher in terms of aggregate performance.

Ironically, the president with the most far-reaching innovations in domestic policy during this period, Lyndon Johnson, conducted one of the most "promiseless" campaigns of the four. Perhaps this should not be so surprising. James L. Sundquist (1968) skillfully traces the origin and planning of the Great Society to the Kennedy administration and before. Johnson's major contribution was in helping to galvanize a large majority into action on what had developed as policy consensus in the Democratic Party. This was obviously a major achievement but one that was accomplished absent a large number of specific campaign proposals.

Also, of course, Johnson, like Nixon in 1972 and Carter in 1980, was an incumbent. The in-party does not have the incentives to develop the same type of comprehensive campaign agenda for the future that is characteristic of outparty candidates. Like Johnson, neither Nixon nor Carter in their bids for reelection came close to matching their earlier number of specific promises (data not shown). Incumbents stand, or fall, on their records and on the hope, or fear, that four more years will bring more of the same. Since Johnson was the only one during this period to stand as an incumbent and to complete a term after so standing, it is impossible to know whether his substantial achievements would have been matched by any of the others.

A predictable chasm always exists between presidential proposal and actual policy achievements, as every president in the twentieth century has learned (see Light 1982). The growing complications and challenge to the Reagan presidency by Congress are hardly unique. This president's stunning early successes inevitably have been followed by major setbacks, a fate shared by every president no matter how skillful they have seemed. A mythology about the relations of Johnson, and even Kennedy, with Congress has developed over the last decade that ignores the very real and significant defeats suffered by these presidents (see Edwards 1980; Manley 1978). Yet it is fair to assess the extent to which presidents have redeemed their campaign promises by also looking at their comparative legislative records. Despite the growth of executive power in the twentieth century, most of the specific commitments presidential candidates make are dependent on congressional approval. Clearly, the president is not responsible for Congress (even when both institutions are controlled by the same party) but since presidential achievement is so dependent on the national legislature, it behooves one to examine aspects of their interaction, particularly as this bears on the questions here. Two broad performance measures are presented in Tables 9.4 and 9.5. The first is an assessment of presidential achievement relative to how many of their pledges are dependent on congressional approval; the second is *Congressional Quarterly*'s "Presidential Legislative Success Score," where data are presented for the same period.

The findings in Table 9.4 quickly underscore the obvious: Much of the problem of the last two presidents is really a problem of how their agendas have fared in Congress. First, consider Carter. More of his promises were dependent on congressional action (labeled as "P/CD" or Presidential/Congressional-Dependent) than any of his predecessors and his administration was considerably less successful than either Kennedy or Johnson, and somewhat less successful than Reagan, in obtaining favorable action on those promises. His record of legislative success is better than Nixon's, who of course faced a Congress controlled by the opposition party. Of P/CD-proposed legislation that was submitted, and that represented full or partial action on their proposals, Kennedy was successful in 81 percent of his requests, Johnson 89 percent, Carter 71 percent, Reagan 77 percent. The difference is even more dramatic if the reader examines the last line of the table, P/CD promises passed (the ratio of successful legislative struggles to total promises dependent on congressional

TABLE 9.4: From Presidential Promise to Congressional Legislation, Kennedy to Reagan

Legislative Flow	Kennedy (1961-63)	Johnson (1965-68)	Nixon (1969-72)	Carter (1977-80)	Reagan (1981-82)
P/CD promises[a]	59/91 = 61%	28/40 = 70%	64/115 = 56%	90/158 = 56%	40/70 = 60%
P/CD proposed legislation passed[b]	48/59 = 81%	25/28 = 89%	39/64 = 61%	64/90 = 71%	31/40 = 77%
P/CD promises passed[c]	48/91 = 53%	25/40 = 62%	39/115 = 34%	64/158 = 41%	31/70 = 44%

[a] Presidential/Congressional-Dependent. The figures here mean that the Carter administration submitted 90 pieces of legislation that met the criteria of "full" or "partial" action on promises made. The figure of 158 represents all promises requiring congressional action, that is, it excludes executive orders and the "indeterminate" category.

[b] Percent passed of that submitted.

[c] Percent passed of *total* requiring congressional action.

Source and coding convention: Grogan (1977) for Johnson and Nixon; the author's for Kennedy, Carter, and Reagan.

TABLE 9.5: Presidential Legislative Success Scores, Kennedy to Reagan (in percents)

Kennedy		Nixon-Ford	
1961	81	1974	59
1962	85		
1963	87		
Kennedy-Johnson		Ford	
1964	88	1975	61
		1976	54
Johnson		Carter	
1965	93	1977	75
1966	79	1978	78
1967	79	1979	77
1968	75	1980	78
Nixon		Reagan	
1969	74	1981	82
1970	77	1982	72
1971	75		
1972	66		
1973	51		

Source: *Congressional Quarterly*, January 12, 1980, p. 91, October 11, 1980, January 1ᴠ, 1983, p. 94.

approval). Here Carter's record (41 percent) is only slightly higher than Nixon's (34 percent), considerably less successful than either Johnson's (62 percent) or Kennedy's (53 percent), and slightly lower than Reagan's (44 percent).

The Carter administration's legislative record looks better if one uses *CQ*'s box-score, although it is still problematic when compared with the two earlier Democratic presidents. The contrast, reflecting the fact that *CQ* scores most bills on which the president took a position, and mine represents only those bills related to his campaign pledges, proved particularly troublesome for the administration's reelection campaign: Carter was unable to deliver on many (not all, of course) of those promises made in 1976, even though he framed thoughtful proposals and placed them before Congress. The *perception* that he actually had reneged on most of his promises was widespread, and largely erroneous. This is particularly ironic because, measured against their interest in making good on much of the 1976 campaign, at least until late 1978, when they began a series of selective reversals, the record of the Carter White House was every bit as strong as that of Kennedy or Johnson.

The Reagan administration, on the other hand, was remarkably successful in its first year—reaching a *CQ* legislative success score that matches Kennedy and is close to Johnson's even though they faced a Congress that was divided in party control. They began to lose on a growing number of its legislative struggles during 1982. The midterm election further weakened the Reagan presidency in Congress; Democrats picked up a net gain of 26 seats in the House; and moderate Republicans in the Senate, chastised by a number of near defeats, were openly challenging Reagan's agenda in economic, social, and defense policy.

Pressures to modify or fundamentally alter their earlier campaign-related agendas grew substantially in both administrations as they neared, then came out of the midterm elections. Why?

SELECTIVE REVERSALS IN CAMPAIGN AGENDAS

I suggested earlier that every president during this period except Kennedy reversed himself on major domestic policy commitments stemming from his first campaign—and significantly for this book, many of those commitments were found in the party platforms—partially in response to unanticipated events, partially because of the different political demands of governing rather than campaigning, and partially as a response to the upcoming reelection struggle. As of January 1980, for example, the Carter administration was moving in two fronts in a manner diametrically opposed to what was promised in the 1976 campaign, or what was proposed in his first 18 months: fiscal and monetary policy, and defense spending (perhaps generally in foreign policy but a thorough discussion of that dimension is beyond the focus of this research).

The Carter experience reflects common tensions in Democratic *campaign* agendas: for 20 years, perhaps longer, tradeoffs between environmental uncertainty, issue complexity, and the economic claims of the New Deal coalition have been resolved in favor of quasi-New Deal or comparable solutions. Democratic presidential campaigns encourage policy commitments of relatively high federal spending, low interest rates, and bountiful money supplies. Recession, not inflation, has been the major economic problem faced by Democratic presidents.

Both Kennedy and Johnson, at least until the economic squeeze of the Vietnam War, carried the same emphasis into office. The Carter administration moved in precisely the same direction during the first 18 months (except for the decision to reverse on the "50-cent tax credit"); what changed, obviously, was the uncertainty associated with 7, then 13, then 18 percent annual inflation. No Democratic president of the past 20 years has faced comparable rates of inflation.

Little consensus exists among economists typically associated with the Democrats or "liberal" members of Congress about appropriate remedies, remedies that would be economically *and* politically feasible. Despite Edward Kennedy's claims, wage and price controls were not advocated by most liberal economists in the period of 1979-80. Although what follows is clumsy, I assert that *unpredictability in Democratic presidential agendas increases dramatically when uncertainty about causes and effects (in this case involving inflation) undercut the legitimacy of "New Deal" solutions.* William R. Keech has made an astute observation: Jimmy Carter was sand-bagged by the irresponsible economic policies of Lyndon Johnson and Richard Nixon, particularly Nixon.

The problem of unpredictability in agenda action becomes more intense when not even a general consensus exists among the elements of the "old" Democratic Party coalition. Energy politics and environmental regulation, as in the struggle over deregulation or clean air emission standards, are good examples. To expect the Carter administration to have formulated a "comprehensive and consistent" agenda in the absense of a supporting coalition inside the Democratic Party is to have expected the impossible.

Further, Norman Furniss and Timothy Tilton (1977) have argued persuasively that every Democratic president since and including FDR has encouraged or been forced to conduct a war, sometimes "hot," sometimes "cold," and that the consequences have been devastating on their domestic agendas. Raising defense expenditures, as Carter proposed and as Reagan is doing aggressively, will always affect domestic social programs in a negative fashion.

A pattern of early attempts to redeem much in the campaign agenda, followed by *selective* reversals, drift, and displacement, as mentioned earlier, was also characteristic of the Johnson and Nixon administrations. Only Kennedy avoided this, partially because of his assassination, but more importantly because the agenda Kennedy was seeking, later incorporated into the "Great Society," was perceived by Kennedy staffers as politically viable, in fact central to his reelection.

Selective reversal occurs usually around the midterm elections, when incumbent presidents and their advisors come to believe that the *tradeoffs between pursuing the policy commitments of the last campaign and the next one substantially favor a shift in the priorities and direction of the old agenda.*

This proposition applies even more strongly to the Reagan presidency. The extravagant claims made about the beneficial consequences of his first year budget policies were confronted shortly thereafter by the harsh reality of: the highest unemployment rates in the past 30 years; the failure of business investment and savings to increase in the way predicted by supply-side economics; an alarming increase in both the number and rate of business bankruptcies; and a mushrooming federal deficit for fiscal years 1982, 1983, and 1984—deficits that were economically and politically unacceptable to many Republicans. Moreover, the enormous increases in defense spending sought and won by the administration, and its belligerent anti-Soviet rhetoric, were clearly boomeranging by late 1982; even conservative Republicans and Democrats were looking for ways to alter the administration's defense increases and budget cutbacks in domestic social and economic programs. One White House staffer put it bluntly: "Everyone around here knew our [fiscal year 1984] budget would be dead in the water before it got to Congress."

What has been well documented concerning members of Congress—that ties to party positions weaken as the next campaign approaches—appears to be true of presidents as well. Uncertainty in the environments presidents face undermines accountability to commitments made during the *last* campaign because all presidents face many unanticipated policy questions. Parties and presidents are making policy from platforms designed for the environment of the last campaign; as circumstances change, presidents naturally begin departing from the "old" platform. Such departures, however, must be carefully defended. Otherwise, they are likely to confront bitter opposition from members of their own party coalition.

CONCLUSION

One political scientist has observed that many people complain bitterly that Carter did not live up to his party platform promises and, "at the same time, actively hope Reagan won't live up to his ... what is seen as a vice in Carter is rendered a virtue in Reagan" (Cronin, 1980).

Can we have it both ways? Of course! As in *Alice in Wonderland*, and only at the expense of securing greater policy accountability in presidential elections. Certainly opponents of Reagan's programs can work actively in Congress and other institutions to prevent him from implementing those parts of his agenda with which they disagree, praise the president for "coming to his senses" when he does compromise, and so forth. Organized and sophisticated opposition, using every nonviolent tool that is available in democratic politics, is as essential to policy accountability as presidential follow-through. All this is desirable and need not lead to the potentially destructive belief that, when one is opposed to presidents, it is desirable that they function in office in a manner that runs completely contrary to what they promised in their campaigns.

The key problem is how different presidents (or presidential candidates) *should* be on major issues to satisfy a norm of accountability *within a shared policy consensus*. Since the New Deal, both major American parties have typically nominated presidential candidates who have reflected a broad consensus on certain issues and differed vigorously on others. Enormous latitude is possible within this usual consensus in American politics. Presidential accountability — to the party and to the country — is undermined if those campaign promises, offered as different solutions within a spirit of shared values, are systematically broken or ignored.

I am decidedly *not* suggesting one can mechanically add up a platform's pledges and the candidate's other campaign promises, check off the number of programs proposed or enacted, and vote or judge accordingly. Incumbent presidents face new issues, new problems and new contingencies that cannot be anticipated from the last campaign. They must be willing to change, to compromise, to be flexible about some of their campaign promises; otherwise, if they are unwilling to alter their course, and unable to persuade voters that it is essential to do so, they will doom their party and themselves at the next election. This is a sticky problem, an inherent tradeoff, in any conception of presidential accountability. Evaluating an incumbent president or party seeking reelection involves retrospective and prospective judgments, as well as some ordering principle, no matter how rough, that permits observers to filter the important from the inconsequential, the old from the new, the controllable from the uncontrollable.

Platforms and candidate issue papers, ambiguous as they frequently are, provide useful information about the broad countours of future presidential policy — even if they are ignored by a vast majority of the voting population. Presidential behavior suggests that platforms are not irrelevant to performance in office, though the correspondence does significantly decline from the early to the later years in office. Moreover, presidential conformance to party platform directives are not ignored by their potential competitors for leadership of the party. Although their fates differed, Johnson, Ford, and Carter all learned that reversing directions in their agendas, or, as in Ford's case, not paying sufficient attention to the aspirations of conservative Republicans, can have devastating consequences on their desire to be reelected. Each paid the price—in primary challenges to their incumbency—of failing to sustain the unity of the party coalitions that put them in power. Again, Ford's case is somewhat different but he too failed because the task of party leadership also involves policy leadership in a manner that is broadly acceptable to the party coalition. The goal of party leaders, organizational activists, and journalists who believe that platforms and policy commitments are essential in judging candidates, and their performance in office, is to translate and filter this policy-relevant information in such fashion that voters can use it. Otherwise, elections will always verge toward being little more than exercises in "hiring and firing" one's leaders, leaving to fate and the manipulative capabilities of modern advertising the political responsibility of presidents for their programs.

If citizens are misled into believing they do not bear some responsibility for making presidents accountable for what they promise as candidates, then elections and parties are truly meaningless as institutions for the representation of policy alternatives.

NOTES

1. The most important are Pomper with Lederman (1980), David (1971), Kessel (1977, 1980), and Grogan (1977). Others have investigated the broad effects of party, leadership, or governmental change on public policy: Ginsberg (1982), Bunce (1981), Rose (1980), Wayne (1981), Tufte (1978), Hibbs (1977), and Keech (1968). The most comprehensive and detailed study of such relationships in the American presidential context is Sundquist (1968).

2. Sophisticated recent work on these themes will be found in Page (1978), Aldrich (1980), and Kessel (1980).

3. The 1980 elections and presidential campaigns are covered in Harwood (1980), Germond and Witcover (1981), Wayne (1981), Ranney (1981), Ferguson and Rogers (1981), and Pomper (1981).

4. Partly because Kennedy strategists believed that it would open a division between them and other anti-Carter Democrats like Henry Jackson who were more "Hawkish" than Kennedy.

5. See Grogan (1977) and Pomper (1968, pp. 274-79) for an elaboration. Treating my data as comparable to Grogan's poses some tough methodological problems: no tests of intercoder reliability were possible and we may, therefore, be using different standards; and, more importantly, the written record of the Reagan, Carter, and Kennedy general election campaigns, particularly issue-relevant information, may be more complete. The findings reported comparing the five presidents could be an artifact of this potential disparity, although I doubt it. For Kennedy, the source was two volumes published by the U.S. Senate, Committee on Commerce, Subcommittee on Freedom of Communication (1961); for Carter, my collection of issue papers and campaign speeches, plus U.S. House of Representatives, Committee on House Administration (1978). The Carter organization

released a total of 184 "Issue Papers" during the entire campaign, December 1975 to November 1976. These ranged in length from a single-page, three-paragraph statement on abortion to a 14-page document on the economy. Of the total, 94 Issue Papers were released before the convention, 90 after. Many of the latter, however, were rewrites of preconvention versions. The Ford volumes also were prepared by the House Administration Committee and published in 1979. For Reagan, the primary source is a series of press releases, issued between the New Hampshire primary and election day, supplemented by major speeches. The Reagan organization released 91 press releases in the "Reagan on the Issues" series. I am indebted to Michael Baroody, then Public Affairs Director of the RNC, for making them available to me. Further details are covered in Fishel (forthcoming).

REFERENCES

Aldrich, John H. 1980. *Before the Convetion: Strategies and Choices in Presidential Nomination Campaigns.* Chicago: University of Chicago Press.

Bunce, Valerie. 1981. *Do New Leaders Make a Difference?* Princeton, N.J.: Princeton University Press.

Chancellor, John. 1976. Reported by Charles Serb in the Washington *Post,* October 23.

Cronin, Thomas E. 1980. "Why Carter?" Washington *Star,* November 2, p. E4.

David, Paul. 1971. "Party Platforms as National Plans." *Public Administration Review* 31 (May): 303-15.

Edwards, George C. III. 1980. *Presidential Influence in Congress.* San Francisco: Freeman.

Ferguson, Thomas, and Joel Rogers, eds. 1981. *The Hadden Election.* New York: Random House.

Fishel, Jeff. Forthcoming. *Presidents and Promises.* Washington, D.C.: Congressional Quarterly Books.

Furniss, Norman, and Timothy Tilton. 1977. *The Case for the Welfare State: From Social Security to Social Equity.* Bloomington: Indiana University Press.

Germond, Jack W., and Jules Witcover. 1981. *Blue Smoke and Mirrors: How Reagan Won and Why Carter Lost the Election of 1980.* New York: Viking.

Ginsberg, Benjamin. 1982. *Consequences of Consent: Elections, Citizen Control and Popular Acquiesence.* Reading, Mass.: Addison-Wesley.

Grieder, William. 1980. "The Republicans." In *The Pursuit of the Presidency 1980,* ed. Richard Harwood. New York: Putnam.

_____ . 1982. *The Education of David Stockman and Other Americans.* New York: E.P. Dutton.

Grogan, Fred. 1977. *"Candidate Promise and Presidential Performance: 1964-1972."* Paper delivered at the Annual Meeting of the Midwest Political Science Association.

Harwood, Richard, ed. 1980. *The Pursuit of the Presidency 1980.* New York: Putnam.

Hibbs, Douglas A., Jr. 1977. "Political Parties and Macroeconomic Policy." *American Political Science Review* 71 (December): 1467-87.

Keech, William R. 1968. *The Impact of Negro Voting: The Role of the Vote in the Quest for Equality.* Chicago: Rand McNally.

Kessel, John H. 1977. "The Seasons of Presidential Politics." *Social Science Quarterly* 58 (December): 418-35.

————.1980. *Presidential Campaign Politics: Coalition Strategies and Citizen Response.* Homewood, Ill.: Dorsey.

Light, Paul. 1982. *The President's Agenda.* Baltimore: Johns Hopkins University Press.

Malbin, Michael J. 1981. "The Conventions, Platforms, and Issue Activists." In *The American Election of 1980*, ed. Austin Ranney. Washington, D.C.: American Enterprise Institute.

Manley, John F. 1978. "Presidential Power and White House Lobbying." *Political Science Quarterly* 93 (Summer): 255-75.

Markus, Gregory. 1982. "Political Attitudes During an Election Year: A Report on the 1980 NES Panel Study." *American Political Science Review* (September): 538-60.

Page, Benjamin I. 1978. *Choices and Echoes in Presidential Elections.* Chicago: University of Chicago Press.

Pomper, Gerald M. 1968. *Elections in America.* New York: Dodd, Mead.

Pomper, Gerald M., with Susan S. Lederman. 1980. *Elections in America*, 2d ed. New York: Longman.

Pomper, Gerald M. 1981. *The Election of 1980.* Chatham, N.J.: Chatham House.

Ranney, Austin, ed. 1981. *The American Elections of 1980.* Washington, D.C.: American Enterprise Institute.

Rose, Richard. 1980. *Do Parties Make a Difference?* Chatham, N.J.: Chatham House.

Smith, Howard K. 1976. ABC News, October 11.

Sundquist, James L. 1968. *Politics and Policy: The Eisenhower, Kennedy and Johnson Years.* Washington D.C.: Brookings Institution.

Tufte, Edward R. 1978. *Political Control of the Economy.* Princeton, N.J.: Princeton University Press.

Wayne, Stephen J. 1981. *The Road to the White House: Politics of Presidential Elections.* New York: St. Martin's.

West, Darrell M. 1982. "Rehetoric and Agenda-Setting in the 1980 Presidential Campaign." *Congress and the Presidency* 9 (Autumn): 1-21.

PART V
CONCLUSION

10

PRESIDENT-PARTY RELATIONS IN THE MODERN ERA: PAST, PROBLEMS, AND PROGNOSIS

Robert Harmel

THE RECORD

*A*lthough American presidents have never been as vigorous and effective in party leadership as their counterparts in parliamentary systems, and understandably so, the record of the more recent presidents suggests that the situation has actually deteriorated over time. From the evidence presented in the preceding chapters and elsewhere, the current recipe for presidential relations with their parties seems to call for one pound of dominance and another of neglect for every ounce of genuine leadership.

After analyzing the party relationships of the four presidents from Eisenhower to Nixon, Robinson (1974, p. 5) concluded that all four "for one reason or another . . . have left their respective parties in a shambles. From this record, one is tempted to conclude that presidents, far from being Party Leaders, are their party's worst enemies." Although Gerald Ford's brief appearance in the White House brought party relations that were "considerably less overbearing" (Bass 1978, p. 212) than his predecessors', this may have been due in part to the very special circumstances that brought him to the office and that make his case difficult to compare with the others. According to Bass (1978, pp. 215-16), the first year of Jimmy Carter's presidency saw "the establishment of White House control over and simultaneous neglect of the national party organization," a description that would prove appropriate throughout most of Carter's presidency. Even though

Ronald Reagan may break the recent pattern of leaving his party "in shambles," the credit belongs to former party chairman William Brock—who rebuilt the party while a Democrat was in the White House (See Bibby 1980)—rather than to Reagan himself. As Steven Roberts argued in the New York *Times Magazine* in 1983:

> Institutionally, the Republican Party is in good shape despite Ronald Reagan, not because of him. The President came to partisan politics late in life, and he has always been a lone wolf, more devoted to promoting his own ideas and ambitions than the interests of the party. Accordingly, Mr. Reagan has played down the role of President as party leader, and has shown little concern for the inner workings of the complex organism that is the modern mass political party (p. 33).

Reviewing the record of the recent presidents provides ample evidence to support Cronin's (1980b, p. 191) assertion that "we really have not had a president in recent decades who has gone the extra mile and tried to be a party leader."

In Chapter 1 we indicated that the context of presidential politics provides few incentives for presidents to lead their party organizations, and most recent presidents have acted accordingly. While none has totally abandoned his party, it can be said without exaggeration that the record has been one of neglect more than active party leadership. Recent presidents have largely ignored their party organizations when choosing administration personnel, when formulating policy (especially in the later years of an administration), even when planning for the reelection campaign (except to *use* the party apparatus to gain renomination). It is indeed true, as Broder (1972, p. xxiii) has asserted, that the parties have suffered from presidential "neglect" and, as Seligman (1978, p. 300) put it, from the presidents not giving them anything to do.

When the presidents have had reason to concern themselves with party organization—most notably when planning strategies for the midterm campaign and for their own renominations—they have tended to dominate rather than lead the party. In the pages of this book, Bass, Brown, Reiter, and Milkis have all argued that it has been self-interest, rather than an altrustic concern to support and strengthen the party system, that has often motivated presidential involvement with the party organization. It is when the self-interests are not consistent with those of the party that real and lasting harm may be done. When presidents use midterm election campaigning to promote their own unpopular programs, the party may reasonably be expected to suffer. When presidents successfully "rig" the party's nomination procedures so as to assure renomination in the face of strong opposition, it is at least doubtful that the best interest of the party—and, for that matter, the nation—have been served. When a president subordinates the national committee and its chairman to "his people" at the party headquarters, he is serving his own interests, often to the detriment of his party's.

Some scholars have gone beyond the suggestion that presidents are merely self-centered and uncaring, and have argued that presidents at times have intentionally sought to reduce the effectiveness of their party organizations. Bass (1978, p. 15) has referred to "recurring and systematic presidential efforts to undermine the development and maintenance of a strong national party organization." Milkis (1981) has probably taken this theme the farthest in his carefully substantiated argument that Franklin Roosevelt, often recognized as one of the stronger party leaders in American history, actually "recognized the inevitability of party decline and acted to adapt to, *and accentuate*, this development" (p. 53; emphasis added). According to Milkis, behavior that people usually identify as stemming from Roosevelt's concern with revitalizing the Democratic Party was in large part "Roosevelt acting to enchance the *partisan* influence of the Executive in the short run so as to increase the *independence* of the president in the long run" (pp. 56-57; emphasis added), to "lessen the importance of traditional party politics and make party government unnecessary" (p. 5). As Milkis has stated in Chapter 7 of this volume, "Instead of seeking to overhaul party organization, Roosevelt sought to obtain party responsibility by transferring collective responsibility into executive responsibility." According to Milkis, then, Roosevelt was actually pursuing a strategy of making the Democratic Party "the party to *end* all parties" (1981, p. 5; emphasis added) in order to lessen constraints on the presidency.

Of course, presidents do not *always* see parties as negative elements that can be or need to be overcome. This is especially true for the party in Congress, which even the recent presidents have called upon for support when the legislative going has gotten rough. But Congress also has undergone withdrawal from party resources, such that presidents are increasingly unlikely to find a substantial "followership" that will readily respond to the party battle cry. What Cronin has said of Jimmy Carter's legislative problems generally—that his "difficulties with the Congress arose in no small measure from his desire to offer leadership to a nation that has turned inward, introspective, and self-centered" (1980a, p. 230)—is especially true of his more limited offers of leadership to the *party* in Congress. When presidents have planned midterm campaign strategy to help strengthen congressional party ties, they have often been publicly embarrassed by candidates' requests that the president "stay out" of their campaigns. Johnson, Nixon, Carter, and Reagan have all had such experiences. Faced with congressional party resistance to leadership, the recent presidents have increasingly turned to bipartisan strategy and ad hoc coalition-building in attempting to accomplish their legislative goals. As Edwards concluded in Chapter 8 of this book, presidents cannot rely single mindedly on party leadership as a source of congressional influence—far from it, they must view it "as just one of the many tactics" that must be employed to gain congressional support.

In a system where presidents find it relatively easy to alternately ignore and dominate their party organizations, and where their attempts to lead the congressional party are often openly and effectively resisted, it should probably come as little surprise that presidents tend to avoid the potentially difficult and politically costly role of party *leadership*. Leadership requires listening to and often compromising with the would-be followers. It would naturally seem more inviting simply to dictate to the party or ignore it altogether when that is possible, especially when the rewards seem so uncertain.

The record of party leadership in America has been inauspicious at best, and the record of president-party relations generally has been one of a mutual lack of respect and trust. Cronin (1980b, p. 177) has noted that "both often become frustrated and even annoyed with each other," and Bass (1978, p. 3) commented that "one need only make a cursory review of recent American political history to discover recurring and rather disconcerting instances of mutual reservations, discontents, and even antagonisms between representatives of these two linked institutions." Neither institution trusts the other to watch out for its interests, so the president tries to "go it alone" and the party becomes wary of attempts to "plant" White House operatives in the national headquarters. Neither institution has *seen* much in the other that would make the cost of leading or following worthwhile.

Therein lies the real irony of the recent period of president-party relations. Neither president nor party has been sufficiently motivated to work together to prevent a precipitous decline in the relationship. Yet the most immediate consequence of that decline may be to point up the very real benefits that effective presidential party leadership could provide for the presidency, for the parties, and for the system in general.

THE CONSEQUENCES

The deterioration of presidential party leadership has a number of important ramifications. It contributes to further weakening of the

EDITOR'S PERSPECTIVE

Dear Mr. President, Stay Home!

Imaginary question to a presidential aide: What would be worse than being hounded to have the president campaign for candidates in midterm campaigns? Obvious answer: Having him asked not to! Johnson, Nixon, Carter, Reagan—all have been asked by their own party's candidates to stay out of at least some congressional campaigns. One can only imagine the White House's acute embarrassment, if not terror, at reading a headline like the following.

The Houston Post/Sun., Feb. 19, 1978

Washington notes

Candidates may not ask Carter aid

Post Washington Bureau

WASHINGTON—President Carter probably would be ready, willing and able to stump Texas next fall for various statewide and congresional candidates, White House sources say.

The question is whether Democrats will be anxious for his help.

The new Democratic national chairman, Texan John C. White, says party polls show Carter would win the state today by an even bigger margin than his fairly narrow 52 percent victory in 1976. But other Democrats are skeptical about that—some have openly said Carter couldn't carry Texas now.

The administration's energy policy has inflamed the state's oil and gas industry and deeply embarrassed Democratic officeholders like Gov. Dolph Briscoe (not to mention his re-election challenger, Atty. Gen. John Hill) who pulled out all the stops to elect a supposedly pro-deregulation Carter two years ago.

The Panama Canal treaties also are hugely unpopular in the state, with Democratic Sen. Lloyd Bentsen saying two-thirds of the voters oppose them.

On the record, it's hard to find a Democratic candidate who says he wouldn't "welcome" a campaign appearance by the president in September or October. Off the record, it's hard to find one—at least one with a strong Republican opponent—who will be requesting that kind of assistance, at least not yet.

Carter still may make such a trip, however. By next autumn, his political stock in Texas could be on the rise again. The Panama Canal treaties probably will have been ratified by then and the energy impasse may have been broken.

White repeatedly predicts that the president will be in much stronger shape by year's end. He sees "significant successes" for the administration that will begin rolling in by spring.

already feeble political parties. It makes the passage of legislative programs even more complex and difficult for the presidents themselves. It strips the citizenry of an important tool for maintaining presidential accountability, thereby furthering the personalization and isolation of the presidency. The consequences cut to the heart of American democracy, and they are already having a profound impact on the way the system works.

Although it is impossible to say with any certainty which came first—the decline of the parties or the decline of presidential interest in them—it is clear that each has had ample opportunity to contribute to the other. It is just as clear that presidents have been in a far better position to end the downward cycle—indeed, even to reverse it—than have been the parties themselves.

The decline of American parties since the 1950s has been well documented (for example, see Sorauf 1980; Crotty and Jacobson 1980; Ladd and Hadley 1978; Harmel and Janda 1982). While the American parties have never been the focus of great affection, dramatically falling percentages of party identifiers and rising numbers of split-ticket voters signaled significant new rejection. Several explanations have been offered, including the lack of party response to important new issues and the assumption of several party roles by special interest groups, mass media, and candidate-oriented campaign organizations (see Harmel and Janda 1982, Chapter 8). If those explanations are correct, then party rejuvenation would seem to require vigorous *party* attention to the controversial and especially difficult issues of postindustrial America, and the development of a competitive edge in performing the functions and providing the services that have been taken over by the "new" institutions of American politics. Accomplishing either of these tasks would be no simple matter and would require committed and effective party leadership. Therein lies the special importance of presidential party leadership—or rather, the lack of it—for the future of the parties themselves.

At a time when parties have been in desperate need of help and guidance from their leaders, the presidents have generally shown disinterest or, worse, have shown contempt. When recent presidents have neglected their parties, and especially when they have *used* them for personal gain without regard for the interests of the party, they have actually furthered the process of party demise.

If the parties have suffered from the decline of presidential leadership, so has the presidency suffered from the decline in party followership. The "automatic" base of party support that presidents could once depend upon in the electorate has diminished with the decline of the parties. Although party discipline has never been easy to achieve in Congress, it has been even more difficult for presidents to effect in the past few decades.

We noted in the first chapter of this book that past presidents may have justifiably felt that they had few benefits to gain from actively leading their parties. But the lessons of recent years may serve to convince future presidents that the few benefits that have existed were very important ones. Although the American parties of old may have never afforded the president the kind of party loyalty that is assured to prime ministers, neither did they require as much of him as their leader. The American parties did *aid* their presidents in ways that we may only now—in the age of a relatively nonpartisan presidency—begin to fully appreciate. Hodgson (1980, pp. 165-66) recently recounted some of those benefits:

> They acted as two-way channels of communication, letting the president know what was on the voters' minds and allowing him to educate and lead them in return. . . . [They mediated conflicts and] left the president, as party leader, with only the most important decisions to make—those that could not be brokered or compromised at some lower level. . . . They provided the ready made coalitions that could deliver the votes in Congress [and thereby] spared the President the need for him to put together a separate coalition in Congress, at some political cost to himself, on every vote.

In sum, the parties "bound together the President and Congress, separated powers in constitutional theory, just enough to allow the President to emerge as the effective leader of the government and to respond, in the persons of the two Roosevelts, Wilson, and Truman, to the great new challenges of the first half of the twentieth century."

The second half of the twentieth century has brought its own "great new challenges," and there is reason to doubt that they can be handled as effectively without the parties' influence. Koenig (1981, p. 122), for one, has argued that "the presidency is handicapped in struggling with conundrums like inflation and energy by the diminished state of party organizations and their declining capacity to weave regional and local differences into the complex mosaic of a national consensus." Jimmy Carter, whose job it was to wrestle with such conundrums, had been elected with little dependence on or concern for his party's organization, but later he came to lament his party's declining influence over its members in Congress.

> I learned the hard way that there was no party loyalty or discipline when a complicated or controversial issue was at stake—none. Each legislator had to be wooed and won individually. . . . Well-intentioned

reforms in the organization of congress and of the Democratic party had undermined the power of party leaders. This situation was completely different from the time of Lydon Johnson's Presidency, when he, the Speaker of the House, and the Chairman of the House Ways and Means Committee could agree on a tax or welfare proposal and be certain the House of Representatives would ratify their decision (Carter 1982, p. 80).

Great new issues have arisen in the 1970s and 1980s, but the parties without committed leadership have proven incapable of addressing them forcefully, and the presidents without party followership have found it significantly more difficult to forge the programs with which to solve them.

Presidents may have sometimes felt that they would be better off in a nonparty environment—without the need to resort to or play down partisan ties, but they now find themselves in the much more complicated world of interest group politics—and without the buffer that parties once provided. Interest groups who once sought to channel influence through the party organizations have not been blind to their decline, and so have largely abandoned them in favor of direct dealings with the office-holders. For the office-holders, the cure for the maladies of party has proven more troublesome than the sickness. "Presidents, like congressmen, arrive [in Washington] to find that they have exchanged the encumbering and sometimes embarrassing alliances of party for the loneliness of the traveler who must defend himself against the marauding interest groups" (Hodgson 1980, p. 182).

The decline of the parties and presidents' growing disinterest in them has had profound effects on both institutions, and indeed on the entire system. Parties have served to link not only the president to Congress but also the people to their president. Brown and Welborn (1982, p. 302) have noted that "parties can be a major means for reflecting popular impulses in ways that inform and channel uses of presidential power," and Cronin (1980b, p. 180) has argued that "having a president constrained and informed by party platforms and party leaders is what was intended when our party system developed."

Not only have parties provided for presidents a source of contact with the reality outside of Washington; they have also served democracy as a tool for "checking" and "balancing" (Cronin 1980b, pp. 191-92) the powers of the presidency. When presidents depended on the party's acceptance for nomination and its support for their programs in office, the party's demands to be taken seriously had some credibility. Presidents would *lead* their parties by pursuing not only their personal wishes but also their parties' goals, or they would risk losing support that would be essential for their political survival. President-party politics involved some communication and compromise, rather than simply domination. Parties, in this sense, could help keep presidents "responsible" to their electorate. "A president who divorces himself from his party does so at the risk of becoming a prisoner of his own whims, [such that] a partyless presidency is potentially an arbitrary one, one which may be too much in the business of self-promotion at the expense of party and public interests" (Cronin, 1980b, p. 179). Parties *can* act as a restraint on presidential behavior, "checking" and "confining" it, and therein may lie part of the reason why recent presidents have preferred to go it alone. It is also one of the reasons why Americans might wish to care about the condition of their parties.

The foregoing comparisons of parties "then and now" are not meant to idealize the American parties of yore, which also fell far short of most party "models," but rather to suggest that an already weak and flawed party system has grown substantially weaker over time. We do not mean to suggest that presidents were ever slaves to their parties, but rather that parties today have substantially less reason to expect presidential respect.

Nor do we mean to suggest that *only* parties are capable of organizing support for presidents, or of informing and restraining them, but rather that parties do these things differently and in some ways better than interest groups, the media, opinion polls, and presidential staffs.[1] Stronger parties could act as a constant and relatively stable source of cues from a large and varied clientele outside of the White House, and could provide (or withdraw) a substantial and stable base of electoral and congressional support. Presidential politics without parties is more difficult, more complex, and more uncertain—both for the presidents and for the citizens who would hold them accountable.

SOME PROPOSALS AND THEIR PROSPECTS

Proposals for strengthening the relationship of president and party have taken many forms, including recommendations that would require changes through constitutional amendment, statutory revision, and procedural reform. What these proposals share is an emphasis on creating a stronger bond—greater interdependence between the president and his party in Congress, and greater reliance of both on their party organization.

The most ambitious proposal—often considered but seldom made—would involve adapting the Constitution to include a cabinet government of the British variety, which would *force* the effective head of government to work with the party, and vice versa. The 1950 *Report* of the American Political Science Association (APSA) Committee on Political Parties states the usual argument:

> *A responsible cabinet system makes the leaders of the majority party* in the legislature the heads of the executive departments, *collectively accountable* to their own legislative majority *for the conduct of the government.* Such a relationship prompts close cooperation between the executive and legislative branches. The legislative majority of the cabinet forms a party team which as such can readily be held responsible for its policies. This governmental system is built around the parties, which play the key role in it (p. 35).

The committee stopped short of endorsing a move to cabinet government, however, on grounds that it was "not a practicable way of getting more effective parties." The committee has not been alone in this appraisal. Odegard (1956, p. 71) called such basic constitutional changes "unlikely and probably undesirable," and Arthur Schlesinger (1974, p. 461) has even gone so far as to proclaim that "the call for the conversion of the United States to parliamentary government must be accounted an exercise in political fantasy."

Stopping short of calling for such drastic change, however, many (including the APSA 1950, p. 75; Koenig 1981, p. 72; Neustadt 1976, p. 254) have proposed changing the terms for members of the House of Representatives or both houses of Congress (as suggested by Koenig and Neustadt) to four years, to coincide with the president's term of office. The APSA Committee argued that "if the elections for these offices coincide, recurrent emphasis upon national issues would promote legislative-executive party solidarity," and Koenig stated that "an election so conducted might produce a president and two houses of Congress in better harmony on party and policy outlook than the present fragmented elections permit." Again, though, however meritorious this proposal may seem for generating closer president-congressional party ties, it is not likely to be implemented. Amendments require congressional initiative, and as Neustadt lamented, "lacking popular demand, the natural conservatism of established institutions will keep Congress and the party organizations quite resistant to reforms that could give *him* clear advantage over *them*"

(1976, p. 254). The requisite popular demand is certainly not in evidence today, and the persistent popularity of separation of powers (which concurrent terms would partially circumvent) as a check on the presidency will undoubtedly keep the demand from developing.

More popular have been various proposals to create greater reliance of the president and/or members of Congress on their party organizations. For presidents and Congress alike, motivation to take the party seriously seems to be directly proportional to the resources the party has to offer — either uniquely or with some advantage over other political institutions. Hence, the proposals are directed at strengthening the party organizations so as to enhance the relevant resources. Though many of these proposals would require changes in statutes or party rules and procedures, none would require constitutional revision. Such proposals include:

- channeling public campaign funding through the party organizations, rather than providing it directly to candidates' own committees
- extending party-controlled public financing to congressional campaigns as well as to the presidential campaigns
- returning more control over presidential candidate selection to the party organization by mandating that more delegates be selected by nonprimary means
- returning more control over congressional candidate selection to any of several means, possibly including preprimary party endorsement of candidates
- the parties' holding regular midterm conventions (as the Democrats have already been doing since 1974) to "invigorate the organization, consider policy questions, and hold officials elected under the party label accountable for the actions on party platform positions" (Committee on Party Renewal 1980)
- changing congressional organization and rules in ways that would promote stronger party discipline
- the parties' promoting *national* policy discussions at the local level, including the use of local party "clubs" to "build a grass roots organizational base of continuing support" for the president (Reagan 1963, p. 86)
- the parties' making better use of television to promote national issues and the parties themselves.[2]

(Some sources where these and other proposals made or discussed: Committee on Party Renewal 1980; APSA 1950; Koenig 1981, pp. 150-52; Cronin 1980b, pp. 186-88; Reagan 1963, pp. 86-87; Rose 1980, p. 317.)

While political scientists have generally assessed proposals such as these to be more reasonable than constitutional change, there is no reason to expect that they would be given a warm reception by the institutions that they are intended to bind to party.

A president can hardly be expected to enthusiastically endorse proposals intended to constrain his independence by making him more reliant on party, when in the present arrangement "no party mechanisms constrain him in the exercise of his constitutional powers or political influence" (Pious 1979, p. 121). At the very least, many of the above proposals would make it more difficult for the president to dominate the party for his own purposes. Members of Congress can hardly be expected to support legislation or procedural reforms that are obviously intended to constrain their political behavior. Therein lies a major hindrance to stronger parties and a stronger president-party relationship in the future.

The change that is necessary to make the other proposals feasible, and that in some ways could make them unnecessary, would be the most difficult of all to achieve. What is required is nothing short of a wholesale change in attitudes toward party — attitudes of voters and of congressmen, and perhaps, most importantly, attitudes of presidents! If presidents should decide to take parties more seriously, their words and actions could go far in leading the others to follow suit.

In an age when parties are finding it increasingly difficult to address the new issues of postindustrial America and thereby to regenerate a solid base of popular support, enthusiastic and creative leadership is essential to guide the thorough rebuilding process that would be necessary to restore the parties to a place of prominence in national politics. Yet, at a time when party leadership seems so critically needed, presidents have turned their creativity toward finding ways of conforming to (and in fact helping to shape) a new type of politics that is largely devoid of party influence.[3] To the extent that they succeed in doing so — or at least to the extent that they continue to see the aparty politics as being less costly than party politics — presidents are not likely to commit to their parties the kinds of resources that could make a difference.

Hope for stronger president-party relations, then, would have to rest on the slim possibility that future presidents might take a more altruistic approach toward parties. However, it would require an individual who is indeed unique — a president who would judge the benefits of strong parties for the *system* to be more important than the costs involved for himself, *and* who would be willing to pay the price. Few who would be president are likely to embrace proposals to limit their own flexibility and that of their office in order to serve the cause of party.

So the record of recent president-party relations has primarily been one of neglect mixed with dominance, though the relationship has not been totally devoid of party leadership, a fact that has certainly been documented in the pages of this book. Since it is very unlikely that presidential attitudes—or, for that matter, the attitudes of the rest of Americans—will change dramatically in favor of stronger parties, the most likely prognosis for the future of president-party relations is for more of the same.

Even with all that has been said here, it is still a valid question whether presidents *should* play a larger role in party leadership and, more generally, whether Americans *should* want stronger parties. Those who propose changes to encourage rejuvenated parties and more active presidential involvement in them almost always assume three basic premises: that parties are (still) essential to stable and effective government and responsible politics in the United States, that strong central party leadership is to be valued both for party and systemic reasons, and that presidents are the proper ones (or at least the only ones with the capability) to provide such leadership. Yet each of these premises has been questioned in the past, and each is deserving of renewed, thoughtful discussion today.

Are parties really essential to effective democratic government, especially with the new developments in mass political communication, campaign techniques, and interest organizations that have seemed to make political parties (at least as we have known them in the past) less necessary? Can parties be reoriented to address the very complex problems and issues of postindustrial America? Should the role of president as party leader be strengthened, even if such a move would challenge the independence of Congress and of the state and local party organizations? Are presidents really the only (or the best) possible leaders for their parties, especially when the greatest strides in rejuvenating party organization recently have taken place without presidents to lead (that is, under the leadership of William Brock for the Republicans, and now Charles Manatt for the Democrats)? And has all of the emphasis on presidential party leadership diverted attention from attempting to deal with the potentially more critical absence of effective *policy* leadership for the opposition party? It is not within the scope of this book to attempt answers to all of these questions, but we would be terribly remiss not to suggest that it is nagging questions such as these that lie squarely in the path of attempts to strengthen the parties or president-party relations.

Questions concerning the role of parties in America are not new. What is new is the context within which such questions are asked today. Attention was drawn to the place of parties in the politics of earlier decades by the 1950 APSA Committee's "Responsible Parties" report, but there have been important changes in government, and especially in the nature of American politics, since the 1960s. What is needed today is a complete reassessment of the proper role of political parties *in the government and politics of the 1980s.*

Whether they like it or not, party and presidency have become too interrelated over the years to allow either to totally dismiss the other. The future of the parties—and, to a lesser extent, the future effectiveness of the presidency—will be affected by the nature of their relationship. Hence, any thorough reappraisal of the role of parties must include an equally thorough reconsideration of president-party relations—what they have been and what they should be.

Given the low level of citizen interest in parties today, it would seem to fall to scholars and practitioners of both the presidency and the parties to initiate such an examination. My colleagues in this book—and the others whose works have been cited here—have laid a firm foundation upon which future investigation may rest.

NOTES

1. For a discussion of the alternatives to parties, see Harmel and Janda (1982, Chapter 8). For a discussion of the changed American politics "after the reign of parties," see Sorauf (1980, pp. 408-09).

2. Other proposals are directed toward *resisting* attempts to reduce reliance on party even further. Cronin (1980b, p. 190), for instance, argues against direct election of the president, a national primary election, a six-year renewable presidential term.

3. Just as presidents seem to be conforming to an apartisan presidency, the parties may be refocusing on nonpresidential politics. For evidence that at least the Republican National Committee may be increasingly turning its attention to state and local politics, see Bibby (1980) and Cotter and Bibby (1980).

REFERENCES

American Political Science Association. 1950. "Toward a More Responsible Two-Party System; A Report of the Committee on Political Parties, American Political Science Association." *American Political Science Review* 44 (September), supplement.

Bass, Harold F., Jr. 1977. "Presidential Responsibility for National Party Atrophy." Paper delivered at the Annual Meeting of the American Political Science Association, Washington, D.C.

———. 1978. "Presidential Responsibility for National Party Organization, 1945-1974." Ph.D. diss., Vanderbilt University.

Bibby, John F. 1980. "Party Renewal in the National Republican Party." In *Party Renewal in America*, ed. Gerald M. Pomper, pp. 102-15. New York: Praeger.

Broder, David. 1972. *The Party's Over: The Failure of Politics in America.* New York: Harper and Row.

Brown, Roger G. 1980. "Party Leadership in the Contemporary Presidency: A Counter Assessment." Paper delivered at the Annual Meeting of the Southern Political Science Association, Atlanta.

_____ , and David M. Welborn. 1982. "Presidents and their Parties: Performance and Prospects." *Presidential Studies Quarterly* 12 (Summer): 302-16.

Carter, Jimmy. 1982. *Keeping Faith: Memoirs of a President.* New York: Bantam.

Committee on Party Renewal. 1980. "Strengthening the Political Parties: A National Position Paper of the Committee on Party Renewal, June 1980." Printed in "Party Line," an informal occasional newsletter of the Committee on Party Renewal, Eagleton Institute, Rutgers University.

Cotter, Cornelius P., and John F. Bibby. 1980. "Institutional Development of Parties and the Thesis of Party Decline." Political Science Quarterly 95 (Spring): 1-27.

Cronin, Thomas E. 1980a. "A Resurgent Congress and the Imperial Presidency." *Political Science Quarterly* 95 (Summer): 209-37.

_____ . 1980b. "The Presidency and the Parties." In *Party Renewal in America*, ed. Gerald M. Pomper, pp. 176-93. New York: Praeger.

Crotty, William J., and Gary C. Jacobson. 1980. *American Parties in Decline.* Boston: Little, Brown.

Harmel, Robert, and Kenneth Janda. 1982. *Parties and their Environments: Limits to Reform?* New York: Longman.

Hodgson, Godfrey. 1980. *All Things to All Men: The False Promise of the Modern American Presidency.* New York: Simon and Schuster.

Koenig, Louis W. 1981. *The Chief Executive.* New York: Harcourt Brace Jovanovich.

Ladd, C. Everett, and Charles D. Hadley. 1978. *Transformation of the American Party System*, 2d ed. New York: Norton.

Milkis, Sidney M. 1981. "Party Leadership and the Creation of the Modern Presidency." Paper delivered at the Annual Meeting of the Midwest Political Science Association, Cincinnati, April.

_____ . 1982. "Franklin D. Roosevelt and the Decline of Political Parties." Paper delivered at the Annual Meeting of the Midwest Political Science Association, Milwaukee, April.

Neustadt, Richard E. 1960, 1976. *Presidential Power: The Politics of Leadership.* (1st ed., 1960). New York: John Wiley.

Odegard, Peter H. 1956. "Presidential Leadership and Party Responsibility." *Annals of the American Academy of Political and Social Science* 307 (September): 66-81.

Pious, Richard M. 1979. *The American Presidency*. New York: Basic Books.

Reagan, Michael. 1963. "Toward Improving National Policy Planning." *Public Administration Review* 23 (March): 10-19.

Roberts, Steven V. 1983. "The GOP: A Party in Search of Itself." New York *Times Magazine*, March 6, pp. 31-80.

Robinson, Donald A. 1974. "Presidents and Party Leadership: An Analysis of Relations between Presidents, Presidential Candidates, and their Parties' National Committee Headquarters since 1952." Paper delivered at the Annual Meeting of the American Political Science Association, Chicago, September.

Rose, Richard. 1980. "Government against Sub-Governments: A European Perspective on Washington." In *Presidents and Prime Ministers*, ed. Richard Rose and Ezra Suleiman, pp. 284-347. Washington, D.C.: American Enterprise Institute.

Schlesinger, Arthur M., Jr. 1974. *The Imperial Presidency*. New York: Popular Library.

Seligman, Lester. 1978. "The Presidential Office and the President as Party Leader (with a Postscript on the Kennedy-Nixon Era)." In *Parties and Elections in an Anti-Party Age*, ed. Jeff Fishel, pp. 295-302. Bloomington: Indiana University Press.

Sorauf, Frank J. 1980. *Party Politics in America*. 4th ed. Boston: Little, Brown.

Additional Sources

Cunningham, Noble E., Jr. 1981. "Presidential Leadership, Political Parties, and the Congressional Caucus, 1800-1824." In *The American Constitutional System Under Strong and Weak Parties*, ed. Patricia Bonomi, James MacGregor Burns, and Austin Ranney, pp. 1-20. New York: Praeger.

Egger, Rowland. 1972. *The President of the United States*. New York: McGraw-Hill.

Goldman, Ralph M. 1969. "Titular Leadership of the Presidential Parties." In *The Presidency*, ed. Aaron Wildavsky, pp. 384-410. Boston: Little, Brown.

Greenstein, Fred I. 1979. "Eisenhower as an Activist President: A Look at New Evidence." *Political Science Quarterly* 94 (Winter 1979-80): 575-99.

INDEX

Cook, Rhodes, 80
Coolidge, Calvin, 24, 48
Cortelyou, George B., 47
Cotter, Cornelius, 60, 70, 77, 82, 83, 140
Crisp, Mary D., 221
Criswell, John, 106
Croly, Herbert, 170
Cronin, Thomas E., 6, 9, 11n, 12, 13, 82, 241, 250, 251, 252, 256, 257, 259
Cronkite, Walter, 219
Crotty, William J., 3, 65, 82, 97, 254
Crouse, Timothy, 100
Cuban missile crisis, 136
Cummings, Homer, 159, 169
Cummings, Milton C., 129
Curtis, Kenneth, 75, 77, 104, 107
cycles of presidential partisanship, 28; Barnum-Hanna, 44-48; Chandler, 41-44; Farley, 48-51; Madison, 30-35; Reagan, 51; Van Buren, 36-41

Daley, Richard, 106
Danforth, John, 137
Dauer, Manning, 31
David, Paul T., 23, 60, 61, 64, 79, 101, 109, 217
Davis, James W., 65
Dawson, Donald, 69
Deaver, Michael, 68, 92
Delano, Frederick, 158
delegate selection procedures, 11n, 79, 97, 104, 115 (see also convention)
Democratic National Committee, 71-72, 140, 141
Democratic Party, 5, 22, 26, 37
Dennis, Jack, 13
Dent, Harry, 69
Destler, I. M., 187
Dewey, Thomas, 23, 49
DeLoach, Cartha, 114
direct primary, 97, 162-63
Dirksen, Everett, 205, 207
Doig, Jameson W., 70

Dole, Robert, 75, 77, 106, 107
Donovan, Robert J., 75, 187, 198
Douglas, Stephen A., 40
Drew, Elizabeth, 102, 107, 108, 111, 113, 114
Dutton, Frederick, 109

Edwards, George C. III, 16, 129, 186, 187, 191, 193, 194, 201, 236, 252
Edwards, James, 107
Ehrlichman, John, 68, 109, 188-89, 205
Eisenhower, Dwight D., 23, 24, 49, 52, 64, 68, 69, 75, 79, 81, 99, 100, 101, 105, 108-09, 114, 138, 186, 187, 198, 203, 204, 205, 207, 249
Elder, Shirley, 190
Electoral College, 36
Epstein, Leon, 11n, 13
"Era of Good Feeling," 33-34
Eubank, Robert, 129
Evans, Rowland, 71-72, 76, 81, 100, 106, 109, 112, 132, 199

factional behavior, typology based on, 20-21
Fahrenkopf, Frank, 76, 78
Farley, James A., 23, 26, 29, 48-49, 61, 62, 158, 160, 161, 167-68
Farney, Dennis, 193
Federal Election Commission, 143
Federalist Papers, 33
Federalist Party, 22, 31
Fenno, Richard, 67, 68
Ferrell, Robert H., 75
Fillmore, Millard, 22, 40
Finney, Tom, 106, 112
Fishel, Jeff, 16, 232
Fleming, Thomas J., 81
Flynn, Edward, 162
Foley, Michael, 190
Foley, Thomas, 189, 204
Ford, Gerald, 24, 50, 69, 73, 98, 99, 101, 102, 106, 107, 110-14, 138, 141, 185, 186, 189, 204, 205, 209, 219, 242, 249

Lofton, John, 79
Lord, Donald C., 170
Lugar, Richard, 140
Lyon, Peter, 101

Mackenzie, G. Calvin, 69
MacNeil, Neil, 207
Madison, James, 20, 25, 29, 32, 33, 34
Magruder, Jeb S., 100, 106, 107
Malbin, Michael J., 80, 102, 112, 220, 221, 224
Manatt, Charles, 261
Manatos, Andrew, 190
Manatos, Mike, 190
Manley, John F., 236
Mann, Dean E., 70
Mann, Thomas E., 200
Mansfield, Mike, 187, 207
Marcy, William L., 39
Markus, Greg, 223
Martin, John B., 65
Martin, Joseph, 49, 187
Mason, John Y., 39
mass media, 12, 13, 26, 29-30, 52, 97, 257
Matthews, Donald R., 65, 185
Maverick, Maury, 158
May, Ernest R., 100
Mayhew, David, 129
McCarthy, Eugene, 108
McCarthy, Joseph, 207
McCloskey, Paul, 107
McDonald, John, 113
McGough, Kent, 113
McGovern-Fraser Commission, 97, 116
McGrath, J. Howard, 73, 77
McGrory, Mary, 140
McIntyre, Thomas, 133
McKinley, William, 23, 26, 45, 46
Meagher, John, 110
Meese, Edwin, 68
Meier, William H., 162

Meir, A. L., 158
Merriam, Robert, 109
Merry, Robert W., 194
Michel, Robert, 92
midterm convention, 42, 80, 103-04, 107, 114
midterm election campaign: campaign strategy, 251; determinants of results, 129-30; effects of presidential role, 126-29; organizational environment in, 139-44; partisanship as factor in president's role, 137-38; political environment in, 131-39; president requested to stay away, 133-34, 253; presidential role in, 90, 125-48, 198-201, 250-51; recommendations to strengthen president's role, 146-47; role of nonincumbent presidential candidate in, 144-46; success of president's party in, 199-201
Milkis, Sidney M., 16, 127, 251
Mitchell, Stephen, 62, 81
Mondale, Walter, 133, 134, 145, 146
Monroe, James, 25, 33-35
Moore, Jonathan, 102
Moos, Malcolm, 109, 129
Morgan, Robert J., 38
Morse, Anson, 31
Morton, Rogers, 73, 77
Morton, Thruston, 64, 81
motivations and resources for leading/following, 9, 12, 14, 146, 250-51, 259
Mowry, George E., 155
Moyers, Bill, 109, 114
Moynihan, Daniel P., 111, 199
Muchmore, Lynn, 11n
Mueller, John E., 132
Mullen, Arthur, 127
Mullen, William F., 208
Murphy, Charles, 110

274

ABOUT THE EDITOR
AND CONTRIBUTORS

ROBERT HARMEL is Associate Professor of Political Science at Texas A&M University, coauthor of *Parties and their Environments: Limits to Reform?*, and author or coauthor of several articles on political parties and legislative behavior.

HAROLD F. BASS, Jr., is Associated Professor of Political Science at Ouachita Baptist University and author of a Ph.D. dissertation and several professional papers on the topic of presidents and parties.

ROGER G. BROWN is Assistant Professor of Political Science at Iowa State University and author or coauthor of several articles and professional papers on the presidency and parties.

GEORGE C. EDWARDS III is Professor of Political Science at Texas A&M University and author of several books and numerous articles on the presidency, including *Presidential Influence in Congress* and *The Public Presidency*.

JEFF FISHEL is Professor of Government and Public Administration and Co-Director of the Center for Congressional and Presidential Studies at The American University and author of *Party and Opposition*, the forthcoming *Presidents and Promises*, and numerous articles.

RALPH M. GOLDMAN is Professor of Political Science at San Francisco State University, author of seven books, including *Search for Consensus: The Story of the Democratic Party*, the forthcoming *Transnational Parties: Organizing the World's Precincts*, and author of many articles in scholarly journals, encyclopedias, and collected works.

SIDNEY M. MILKIS is Assistant Professor of Political Science at DePauw University and author of a Ph.D. dissertation and numerous professional papers on the topic of Franklin D. Roosevelt and his relationship to the Democratic Party.

HOWARD L. REITER is Associate Professor of Political Science at the University of Connecticut, author of numerous articles on political parties and nominating procedures, and author of a book-length study of recent changes in presidential nomination.